T0335727

Discovery and Fusion of Uncertain Knowledge in Data

East China Normal University Scientific Reports
Subseries on Data Science and Engineering

ISSN: 2382-5715

Chief Editor
Weian Zheng
Changjiang Chair Professor
School of Finance and Statistics
East China Normal University, China
Email: financialmaths@gmail.com

Associate Chief Editor
Shanping Wang
Senior Editor
Journal of East China Normal University (Natural Sciences), China
Email: spwang@library.ecnu.edu.cn

This book series reports valuable research results and progress in scientific and related areas. Mainly contributed by the distinguished professors of the East China Normal University, it will cover a number of research areas in pure mathematics, financial mathematics, applied physics, computer science, environmental science, geography, estuarine and coastal science, education information technology, etc.

Published

Vol. 6 *Discovery and Fusion of Uncertain Knowledge in Data*
Kun Yue (Yunnan University, China), Weiyi Liu
(Yunnan University, China), Hao Wu (Yunnan University, China),
Dapeng Tao (Yunnan University, China) and
Ming Gao (East China Normal University, China)

Vol. 5 *Review Comment Analysis for E-commerce*
by Rong Zhang (East China Normal University, China),
Aoying Zhou (East China Normal University, China),
Wenzhe Yu (East China Normal University, China),
Yifan Gao (East China Normal University, China) and
Pingfu Chao (East China Normal University, China)

Vol. 4 *Opinion Analysis for Online Reviews*
by Yuming Lin (Guilin University of Electronic Technology, China),
Xiaoling Wang (East China Normal University, China) and
Aoying Zhou (East China Normal University, China)

More information on this series can also be found at http://www.worldscientific.com/series/ecnusr

(Continued at end of book)

East China Normal University Scientific Reports–Vol. 6

Discovery and Fusion of Uncertain Knowledge in Data

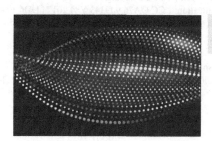

Kun Yue
Yunnan University, China

Weiyi Liu
Yunnan University, China

Hao Wu
Yunnan University, China

Dapeng Tao
Yunnan University, China

Ming Gao
East China Normal University, China

World Scientific

NEW JERSEY · LONDON · SINGAPORE · BEIJING · SHANGHAI · HONG KONG · TAIPEI · CHENNAI · TOKYO

Published by

World Scientific Publishing Co. Pte. Ltd.

5 Toh Tuck Link, Singapore 596224

USA office: 27 Warren Street, Suite 401-402, Hackensack, NJ 07601

UK office: 57 Shelton Street, Covent Garden, London WC2H 9HE

Library of Congress Cataloging-in-Publication Data

Names: Yue, Kun, author.

Title: Discovery and fusion of uncertain knowledge in data / by
    Kun Yue (Yunnan University, China), Weiyi Liu (Yunnan University, China),
    Hao Wu (Yunnan University, China), Dapeng Tao (Yunnan University, China),
    Ming Gao (East China Normal University, China).

Description: [Hackensack] New Jersey : World Scientific, 2017. | Series:
    East China Normal University scientific reports ; 6 | Includes bibliographical references.

Identifiers: LCCN 2017030350| ISBN 9789813227125 (hc : alk. paper) |
    ISBN 9789813227132 (pbk : alk. paper)

Subjects: LCSH: Data mining.

Classification: LCC QA76.9.D343 Y84 2017 | DDC 006.3/12--dc23

LC record available at https://lccn.loc.gov/2017030350

British Library Cataloguing-in-Publication Data

A catalogue record for this book is available from the British Library.

Desk Editor: Herbert Moses

Typeset by Stallion Press
Email: enquiries@stallionpress.com

Printed in Singapore

*My deepest gratitude goes first and foremost to my family,
including my father, my mother, my wife Kailin and
my daughter Yuxin, for their endless love, constant support,
and the joy they have brought to my life.*

Kun Yue

Preface

In recent years, with the rapid development of data acquisition and IT infrastructures, as well as the popularity of social networks and Web2.0 applications, more and more massive, heterogeneous, uncertain and dynamically changing data are generated and stored in distributed systems. Discovering implied knowledge from data is always the topic with great attention for data understanding, data utilization and information services. Generally, data analysis is the most important task in big data research due to the indispensable data-centered applications and corresponding decision support requirements, prompting DaaS (Data as a Service) and AaaS (Analysis as a Service). In view of inherent characteristics of massive, distributed, uncertain and dynamically changing data, uncertainty is ubiquitous with respect to the implied knowledge. Thus, from the perspective of big data and knowledge engineering, acquisition, representation, inference and fusion of uncertain knowledge implied in data are the critical problems, exactly the focus of this book.

As one of the popular and important probabilistic graphical models, Bayesian network (BN) is the effective framework for representing and inferring uncertain knowledge by means of qualitative and quantitative manners. In this book, adopting BN as the framework of knowledge representation and inferences, we consider the following issues:

- **Learning BN from massive data using MapReduce.** We propose a parallel and incremental approach for data-intensive learning of BN from massive, distributed and dynamically changing data by using MapReduce to extend the classic scoring & search algorithm. First, we give a two-pass MapReduce-based algorithm to evaluate the scoring metric of minimum description length and extend the classic hill-climbing algorithm to obtain the optimal model. Then, we give the concept of influence degree to measure the coincidence between the current BN and new data, followed by the corresponding two-pass MapReduce-based algorithm for BN's incremental learning.

- **Inferences of large-scale BN using MapReduce.** We propose a parallel approach for inferring uncertain knowledge using MapReduce with respect to large-scale BNs that may be learned from massive data or constructed for complex applications. First, we give the idea for storing a BN into a distributed file system, while regarding the large-scale BN itself as massive data stored by a distributed manner. Then, we give the parallel algorithm using MapReduce to retrieve probability parameters in the distributed file system and ultimately compute the joint probability distribution in terms of the chain rule in probability theory. Further, we give a case study to discover user similarities in social media by the proposed algorithm for data-intensive probabilistic inferences.
- **BN-based lineage representation and analysis over uncertain data.** We propose an approach for representing and analyzing lineages over uncertain data by adopting BN as the framework of uncertain knowledge in lineage expressions and corresponding uncertain data. First, we give the algorithm for transforming the Boolean-formulae lineage expression into directed acyclic graphs (DAGs) equivalently to guarantee the theoretic correctness of the constructed probabilistic graphical model, as a certain mechanism for fusing logical and probabilistic knowledge. Then, we give the algorithm for lineage inference query processing over uncertain data by incorporating BN's probabilistic inferences as the underlying technique.
- **Lineage-driven and BN-based error detection in uncertain data.** We propose a method for tracing errors in uncertain databases by adopting BN as the framework for representing and inferring correlations among data. We first give the algorithm to construct a BN for an anomalous query to represent correlations among input, intermediate and output data specified by lineages. Then, we define a notion of blame for ranking candidate errors, and give the algorithm for computing the degree of blame for each candidate error based on BN's probabilistic inferences.

- **Fusion of uncertain knowledge in dynamic data.** We propose a method for achieving the global uncertain knowledge during a period of time by fussing the uncertainties of multiple time slices efficiently. First, we give the method for representing the uncertain knowledge in each time slice by extending the qualitative probabilistic network (EQPN), as the qualitative abstraction of BN. Then, we give the semantics-preserving method for fusing the graphical structures of time-series EQPNs based on the concept of Markov equivalence, and a superposition method for fusing parameters of time-series EQPNs.

Kun Yue
Kunming, China
August, 2017

About the Authors

Kun Yue, born in 1979, is a professor of computer science, the vice dean of School of Information Science and Engineering at Yunnan University. He received his M.S. degree in computer science from Fudan University in 2004, and received his Ph.D. degree in computer science from Yunnan University in 2009. His research interests include massive data analysis, artificial intelligence, and knowledge engineering. He has been in charge of more than 20 research grants including the Natural National Science Foundation of China, Foundation for Key Program of Ministry of Education of China, Key Program of Natural Science Foundation of Yunnan Province, etc. He has published more than 80 papers in academic journals including *IEEE Transactions on Cybernetics, Information Sciences, Knowledge-Based Systems, Applied Soft Computing, Neurocomputing, and Applied Intelligence* and presented at many conferences including DASFAA, CIKM, BigData, etc. He has published three monographs on data management and analysis in the Science Press and Tsinghua University Press, and has been granted four China invention patents on knowledge discovery. He received the first prize in Yunnan Province's Nature Science Award in 2009 and the Science & Technology Award for Young Talents of Yunnan Province in 2015. He was awarded as the young academic and technical leader of Yunnan Province in 2016. He is the director of Chinese Association for Artificial Intelligence (CAAI), a member of CAAI Uncertainty in Artificial Intelligence Society, and a member of CCF Database Society.

Weiyi Liu, born in 1950, is a professor of computer science at the School of Information Science and Engineering at Yunnan University. He graduated from Huazhong University of Science and Technology in 1976. His research interests mainly include artificial intelligence and data and knowledge engineering. He has been in charge of 15 research grants including the Natural National Science Foundation of China and Natural Science Foundation of Yunnan Province. He has published more than 100 papers in academic journals including *IEEE Transactions on Systems, Man and Cybernetics (Part B), Information Sciences, Fuzzy Sets and Systems, Applied Soft Computing, The Computer Journal*, and *Journal of Computer Science and Technology*. He has published two monographs on data modeling and analysis in the Science Press. He received the first prize in Yunnan Province's Nature Science Award in 2001 and 2009.

Hao Wu, born in 1979, is an associate professor and a postdoctoral fellow of School of Information Science and Engineering at Yunnan University. He received his Ph.D. degree in computer science from Huazhong University of Science and Technology in 2007. His research interests include knowledge discovery, information retrieval and recommendation system. He has been in charge of more than 10 research grants including the Natural National Science Foundation of China, China Postdoctoral Science Foundation Natural Science Foundation of Yunnan Province, etc. He has published more than 70 papers in academic journals including *Knowledge-Based Systems, Personal and Ubiquitous Computing, Scientometrics*, and *Journal of the American Society for Information Science and Technology*, and presented at many conferences including DASFAA, CIKM and SAC, etc. He served as an editorial member for the *International Journal on Advances in Software*.

Dapeng Tao, born in 1977, is a professor of pattern recognition and intelligent information processing of the School of Information Science and Engineering at Yunnan University. He received his B.E degree from Northwestern Polytechnical University in 1999 and his Ph.D. degree from South China University of Technology in 2014. Over the past years, his research interests have included machine learning, computer vision, and robotics. He has authored and co-authored more than 40 papers in

IEEE Transactions on Neural Networks and Learning Systems, IEEE Transactions on Cybernetics, IEEE Transactions on Multimedia, IEEE Transactions on Circuits and Systems for Video Technology, IEEE Signal Processing letters, Information Sciences, etc.

Ming Gao, born in 1980, is an associate professor in School of Data Science and Engineering at East China Normal University (ECNU). He received his Ph.D. degree in computer science from Fudan University in 2011. Prior to joining ECNU, he worked as a postdoctoral fellow at Social Network Mining Research Group in School of Information System, Singapore Management University. His main research interests include distributed database monitoring, database consistency, user profiling, social mining (community detection on social networks and understanding topological structure of networks), and uncertain data management. He has published more than 50 papers in academic journals including *IEEE Intelligent Systems, Data Mining and Knowledge Discovery, and The Computer Journal*, and has presented at many conferences including ICDE, DASFAA, and SIGIR, etc. He served as a reviewer for *ACM Transactions on Management Information Systems, Social Network Analysis and Mining Journal*, WWW 2014, KDD 2014, and VLDB 2014.

Acknowledgments

This research was supported by the National Science Foundation of China (Nos. 61472345, 61562090, 61562091 and 61462056), the Key Program of Applied Basic Research Foundation of Yunnan Province (Nos. 2014FA023 and 2014FA028), the Program for the second batch of Yunling Scholar of Yunnan Province (No. C6153001), the Program for Excellent Young Talents of Yunnan University (No. WX173602), and the Program for Innovative Research Team in Yunnan University (No. XT412011).

We thank all friends, Profs. Aoying Zhou, Xuejie Zhang, Xiaodong Fu, Cheqing Jin, Xiaoling Wang, Dr. Liang Duan, Zidu Yin, Jin Li and Binbin Zhang, without whom the technical contributions of this book cannot be worked out.

We would like to express our sincere thanks and appreciation to the people at World Scientific Publishing, for their generous help throughout the publication preparation process.

Acknowledgment

This research was supported by the National Science Foundation of China No. (73213393, 61342030 of 502307 and 5713... ...), the grants ... ...

Contents

Chapter 1

Introduction

1.1 Background and Motivation

To discover knowledge from data is always the subject of great interest and importance in data mining, machine learning and artificial intelligence paradigms. Knowledge discovered from data can be integrated with that specified by experts, and provides the basis for prediction and decision making. With the development of data acquisition, socialization and IT infrastructures, more and more heterogeneous data are generated dynamically and stored in distributed systems. For example, the scale of Web data is increased rapidly in information services based on Web2.0 and cloud computing, such as e-commerce, on-line advertising, micro-blogging, etc. [5, 15]; the applications of sensor data analysis, RFID networks, multimedia databases, location-based services, object identification and data integration make real-world data often exhibit uncertainty and impreciseness [42, 128, 142, 177].

Actually, a large number of applications has been transformed into data-centered ones, while big data analysis and knowledge discovery have attracted much attention both in academic and industry paradigms due to the indispensable requirements of data understanding, data utilization and information services [79, 92, 167, 177, 178]. Further from the perspective of knowledge engineering, acquisition, representation, inference and fusion are critical problems and techniques in real world applications of intelligent systems. To obtain implicit conclusions from the described knowledge is knowledge inference problem, which is one of the important tasks in knowledge discovery. To combine various knowledge frameworks with various theoretic foundations or corresponding to various databases is knowledge fusion problem, which is more and more important in big data background [134, 167]. Basic ideas and classic mechanisms in knowledge engineering make big data analysis strengthened, while the constantly emerging characteristics of data make knowledge engineering confronted with novel significance and challenges simultaneously.

Thus, it is desirable to develop appropriate methods for knowledge discovery and fusion in view of inherent characteristics of massive, distributed, uncertain and dynamically changing data. Various methods have been proposed by researchers from various perspectives or by various underlying theories and techniques. In particular, uncertainty is ubiquitous in real applications and uncertain knowledge is ubiquitously implied in data. For example, *Cancer* holds with the probability of 64% if both *Smoking* and *X-ray* hold; *Cancer* is caused by *Smoking* with the probability of 32%. Generally, uncertainty in artificial intelligence is the new development of artificial intelligence in big data era [31, 142, 177].

Upon the above interpretation, we are to establish the connection between massive/uncertain/dynamic data management and knowledge engineering, and specifically exploit the methods for acquisition, representation, inference and fusion of uncertain knowledge implied in data. As one of the important probabilistic graphical models, Bayesian network (BN) is the effective framework for representing and inferring uncertain knowledge [128]. BN is a directed acyclic graph (DAG) of random variables as nodes, each of which has a conditional probability table (CPT) to describe the dependencies among the variables. BN has been widely used in realistic applications of data analysis, prediction and decision making, since it provides a graphical and concise mechanism for describing dependencies and simplifying joint probability distributions.

By adopting BN as the framework of knowledge representation and inferences, in this book we present our research findings of uncertain knowledge discovery and fusion by incorporating the massive, distributed, uncertain and dynamically changing characteristics concerned in data analysis applications. For this purpose, it is necessary to consider the following two fundamental problems: *model construction* and *knowledge inference*, which is in line with the basic roadmap of uncertain knowledge research [44, 142, 167].

For the first problem, constructing the DAG of a BN is the most important and challenging step, upon which CPTs can be obtained easily. We consider the following two kinds of roadmaps:

(1) DAG can be learned from data by measuring the likelihood-based coincidence between candidate model and sample data, and thus the hill-climbing induced optimal one is exactly the required model. From this model-learning point of view, the massive, distributed and dynamic changing characteristics make it necessary to develop a parallel, incremental and efficient approach.

(2) DAG can be transformed directly from specific tasks of data processing (e.g., query processing) or domain knowledge (e.g., knowledge graph). Specifically, the DAG can be achieved by a transformation from another kind of knowledge framework (e.g., first-order predicate logical lineage expression). As well, the DAG can be also achieved by fusing relevant knowledge frameworks with various theoretic foundations or corresponding to various databases. From this model-transformation point of view, the semantics preservation or equivalence makes it necessary to develop theoretically sound algorithms.

For the second problem, we consider the following two aspects of concerns.

(1) Large-scale BNs learned from massive data or constructed for complex applications make corresponding inferences by classic algorithms infeasible due to the exponential complexity with respect to large amounts of nodes and probability parameters. This makes it necessary to develop data-intensive inference algorithms by regarding BN itself as a massive dataset.

(2) Probabilistic inference is the fundamental step for knowledge-based applications (e.g., probabilities of query results or probabilities of inputs inducing errors over uncertain data), which makes it necessary to develop effective inference algorithms oriented to specific applications.

Surrounding the above two fundamental problems, we use MapReduce [48, 49] as the programming model for data-intensive computing to implement aggregation computations upon massive data. Simultaneously, we incorporate the inherent relationship among first-order predicate logic, logical implication and DAGs into the construction of BNs. We incorporate the concepts of Markov equivalence [161], blame [35] and evidence fusion [150] into the semantics description and induction of uncertain knowledge. Generally, the contents of this book are summarized as follows:

(1) By extending the classic algorithm for learning BN from data, we give a parallel and incremental method for learning BN from distributed, massive and changing data using MapReduce [62, 184, 185].

(2) By extending the classic algorithm for inferring uncertain knowledge with a BN, we give a parallel inference method for computing joint probability distributions with large-scale BNs using MapReduce, as well as the case study of user similarity discovery by the proposed inference algorithm [170, 178].

(3) By taking lineage analysis over uncertain data as the representative paradigm, we give a method for transforming lineage expressions (i.e., logical knowledge) into BN (i.e., probabilistic knowledge), and then give the algorithms for lineage processing based on probabilistic inferences [182, 187].

(4) By taking BN as the framework of uncertain knowledge representation and inferences, we further give an algorithm for detecting errors in query processing over uncertain data [57, 58].

(5) By adopting qualitative probabilistic network (QPN) [163], the qualitative abstraction of classic BN, as the knowledge framework, we give a semantics-preserving method for fusing uncertain knowledge in time-series data [183, 186].

1.2   Challenges, Research Issues and Basic Ideas

1.2.1   *Learning and inferring uncertain knowledge in massive and changing data using MapReduce*

Classic algorithms for learning and inferring BN cannot suit practical applications of big data analysis. BN learning should be consistent with the physically distributed dataset, and is much more critical and challenging than that in classic situations since there is no universally theoretical and practical roadmap but explicit application-driven nature and pervasively implied uncertainties.

The first challenge and most important step for BN learning and consequent inferences is to construct the DAG from distributed massive data. We extend the scoring & search algorithm [37] for model evaluation and incorporate the hill-climbing search [76, 158] for model selection, where specific scoring metrics (e.g., minimal description length (MDL) [141, 153]) are adopted. For this purpose, we use MapReduce for data-intensive processing of aggregation queries with respect to marginal probabilities in MDL and compute the MDL score for a given model and massive dataset, since the computation cost is expensive in terms of large scale of datasets.

Second, to keep the coincidence between the model and dynamically changing data is highlighted but challenging, which needs incremental revision of the learned model in response to the distributed new data. We focus on incremental revision of DAG instead of just CPTs, where the former is more challenging than the latter addressed in the state-of-the-art achievements of BN's incremental learning. For this purpose, we define the concept of influence degree based on likelihood to measure the coincidence between the current BN and new data. Then, we compute the influence degree of each node by using MapReduce to determine the nodes, centered on which the model should be revised.

Third, to fulfill probabilistic references efficiently with large-scale BNs is challenging, since the execution time is exponential to the number of nodes in a BN when computing joint probabilities according to the chain rule. From data-intensive computing point of view, we regard a large-scale BN as a massive dataset and make it stored as ⟨key, value⟩ pairs into a distributed file system (DFS). Then, we transform the operations concerned in probabilistic inferences as those on the DFS, and consequently fulfill probabilistic inferences using MapReduce. Further, we give a case study to discover user similarities in social media by the proposed algorithm for data-intensive probabilistic inferences.

1.2.2 *Representing and inferring uncertain knowledge for lineage processing over uncertain data*

With respect to the uncertain characteristics of data, lineages (a.k.a provenance) over uncertain data facilitate the correlation and coordination of uncertainty in query results with uncertainty in the input data, and lineage processing consists in tracing the origin of uncertainties based on the process of data production and evolution [12, 67].

First, probabilistic inference is the most challenging issue in the paradigm of uncertain data management [43], which is based upon the representation of uncertain knowledge reflected in the process of query processing. Thus, we consider adopting BN-based representation of lineages to describe the complex correlations among data objects and corresponding uncertainties, which cannot be well represented by the classic Boolean formulae of lineage expressions [52]. For this purpose, we transform the logical Boolean formulae into DAGs equivalently with respect to logical semantics and derive CPTs by defining function-based parameters in terms of logical constraints in the lineage expression. Finally, we construct BNs to represent lineages, called lineage BN, satisfying the properties of a probabilistic graphical model and guaranteeing the correctness of corresponding inferences theoretically.

Second, lineage inference query processing is to obtain the marginal probabilities on given uncertain data objects or posterior conditional probabilities conditioned on result tuples. This is more challenging than to obtain the probabilities of query results from input tuples, since the marginal or posterior probabilities cannot be derived directly from the Boolean lineage expressions. Thus, by incorporating the specialties of lineage analysis, we answer the lineage inference queries effectively by probabilistic inferences with the constructed lineage BN.

1.2.3 *Representing and inferring uncertain knowledge for tracing errors in uncertain data*

Data in uncertain databases may not be absolutely correct, and worse, may be erroneous. To clean the uncertain databases, such as tracing errors to detect erroneous probabilities of result tuples or find the input tuples contributed to incorrect output, is challenging due to complex correlations among data.

First, inference of input tuples contributed to incorrect output is more challenging than detection of erroneous probabilities of result tuples. Aiming at the former task of uncertain database cleaning, it is critical to describe the correlations among input, intermediate and output data in query execution to effectively support inferences of implied uncertain knowledge. For this purpose, we consider adopting BN as the framework of uncertain knowledge and construct BN according to the execution process of relational queries over uncertain databases.

Second, to find and rank candidate errors, we give the concept of blame inspired by that in causal model [35]. Then, we compute the degree of blame for each candidate error based on probabilistic inferences with the constructed BN by incorporating the mechanisms of possible world [12, 42] and reject sampling [142].

1.2.4 *Fusing uncertain knowledge in dynamic data*

Confronted with the dynamic changing data and BN-based knowledge framework, it is necessary to achieve the global uncertain knowledge during a period of time for decision making by fusing or combining participating BNs of multiple time slices consistently while satisfying the demands of high efficiency and instantaneousness. It is impractical to reconstruct the desired global BN from the integrated time-series databases, or combine the time-series BNs directly, since the original time-series databases may not be available, the efficiency cannot be guaranteed as well, and the combination of CPTs is not straightforward and inefficient.

First, it is not realistic to obtain the ultimate BN as exact as those to be combined, and too strict quantitative mechanisms are inappropriately precise for the applications of fusing uncertain knowledge. To this end, we consider adopting QPN as the underlying framework for modeling and fusing time-series uncertain knowledge by taking as input time-series BNs, where a QPN has the same DAG as the corresponding BN and use qualitative influences to substitute CPTs [163].

Second, to preserve the maximal equivalent-independency information commonly implied in participating time-series QPNs is critical for fusing DAGs. For this purpose, we first enhance general QPNs by augmenting interval-valued weights derived from corresponding BNs, and then fuse the DAGs based on the concept of Markov equivalence and relevant properties.

Third, to avoid conflicts of qualitative parameters in terms of the specialties of time series is critical for fusing parameters. For this purpose, we fuse the participating qualitative parameters by differentiating the influences with interval-valued weights and obtain ultimate results by incorporating the basic principle of evidence combination [150].

1.3 Organization

The remainder of this book is organized as follows:

In Chapter 2, we give the parallel algorithms for learning uncertain knowledge from massive, distributed and dynamically changing data using MapReduce.

In Chapter 3, we give the parallel algorithms for inferring uncertain knowledge of large-scale BNs.

In Chapter 4, we give the method for uncertain knowledge representation and inferences for lineage processing over uncertain data.

In Chapter 5, we give the method for uncertain knowledge representation and inferences for detecting errors in uncertain data.

In Chapter 6, we give the method for fusing time-series uncertain knowledge.

Finally in Chapter 7, we give summary and discuss future work.

Chapter 2

Data-Intensive Learning of Uncertain Knowledge

In this chapter, we propose a parallel and incremental approach for data-intensive learning of BN from massive, distributed and dynamically changing data by extending the classic scoring & search algorithm and using MapReduce. First, we adopt the minimum description length (MDL) as the scoring metric and give a two-pass MapReduce-based algorithm for computing required marginal probabilities and scoring candidate graphical models upon sample data. Then, we give the corresponding strategy for extending the classic hill-climbing algorithm to obtain the optimal structure, as well as that for storing a Bayesian Network (BN) by ⟨key, value⟩ pairs. Further in view of the dynamic characteristics of changing data, we give the concept of influence degree to measure the coincidence of current BN with new data, and then propose a two-pass MapReduce-based algorithm for BN's incremental learning. Experimental results show the efficiency, scalability and effectiveness of our methods.

2.1 Motivation and Basic Idea

By adopting Bayesian Network (BN) as the framework, discovering uncertain knowledge from the massive, distributed and dynamically changing data can be looked upon as the learning of BN with respect to these inherent characteristics of the sample data.

In recent years, learning BN from data is always one of the important methods for modeling uncertain knowledge, the basis of uncertainty inferences and corresponding applications. Without loss of generality, the methods for learning BN include the following three categories:

generic dependency-analysis-based and scoring & search-based algorithms [17, 18, 23, 25, 31, 32, 37, 76, 153, 158], parallel learning algorithms [168, 176] and incremental learning algorithms [93, 145, 151, 155, 174]. When confronted with big data analysis, learning BN is much more critical and challenging than before since there is no universally theoretical and practical roadmap but explicit application-driven nature and pervasively implied uncertainties. First, different from the classical learning algorithms run on centralized single-node architectures, learning BN from the massive, distributed and dynamically changing data should be consistent with the physically distributed sample dataset. Second, different from the parallel learning algorithms that focus on simultaneous execution of the computation steps for datasets that do not fit even on a single disk, the desired learning algorithm should be further adapted to the massive data for efficient and data-intensive processing of aggregation queries. The existing learning algorithms are impractical for datasets spanning Terabytes and Petabytes. Third, different from most of the current incremental learning algorithms that focus on conditional probability table's (CPTs') incremental modification, the desired learning algorithm should make the incremental learning of BN structures emphasized with respect to the distributed new data. Thus, it is necessary to develop a novel parallel and incremental approach for data-intensive learning of BNs while focusing on BN's structure learning and incremental revision.

It is well known that the programming models like MapReduce [48, 49] run on Hadoop [165] were proposed as the high-level abstraction for designing and implementing efficient and provably correct parallel algorithms upon massive data. It dramatically simplifies the design and implementation of a restricted class of parallel algorithms and has been adopted as the de-facto model for distributed computation on a massive scale where input is partitioned across a set of machines in a cluster. Generally, MapReduce can provide a programming model for both parallel and data-intensive processing highlighted in BN learning from data, which is adopted as the rationale of parallel algorithms in our method.

As the representative and preliminary learning algorithm, we adopt the scoring & search method and further make corresponding extensions based on MapReduce, which can be actually borrowed to paralyze the dependency-analysis-based methods. With respect to a scoring & search algorithm and the specialties of the massive, distributed and dynamically changing data, we will have to fulfill the following two data-intensive tasks:

- Parallel evaluation of the scoring function to measure whether a candidate graphical model is coincident with the sample data. Thus, the optimal model among candidate ones can be selected accordingly to obtain the ultimate BN structure.
- Definition and parallel evaluation of the influence of new data on the current BN. Thus, the subgraphs that should be incrementally revised can be determined.

For the first task, we adopt the well-accepted minimum description length (MDL) [141, 153] as the scoring metric and discuss the corresponding extension with data-intensive computations, where we focus on the marginal probabilities of various subsets of random variables in the sample data. We know that the joint probability distribution (JPD) under each assignment of the random variables can be transformed into multiplications of conditional probability factors given a BN structure, which can be obtained by statistics (i.e., aggregation queries) on sample data. To evaluate the MDL scoring function is mainly to compute the required conditional probability factors upon the current BN structure, which can be further reduced to relevant marginal probabilities. Meanwhile, we note that marginal probabilities for each subset of the random variables can be computed independently, so we propose the two-pass parallel algorithm based on MapReduce. In the first pass, we use map functions to count the number of each subset of variables in the required marginal probabilities appearing in each sample, and reduce functions to count the number of each subset of variables appearing in the whole sample set. ⟨key, value⟩ pairs are adopted to describe the input data and the results of MapReduce functions. Then, we can obtain all the required marginal probabilities by an algorithm executed on the local machine. By the same way in the second pass, we use map functions to obtain the JDP for each sample and use reduce functions to ultimately obtain the MDL score of the current candidate BN structure. By extending the well-accepted hill-climbing algorithm [158], we can search the optimal BN structure iteratively according to the scores. To further support the BN's incremental learning, we give the ⟨key, value⟩ pair representation and storage strategy of a BN.

For the second task, we propose the concept of influence degree to describe the influence of the variation of BN nodes' probability parameters on the coincidence between the current BN structure and the new data. Similar to the above parallel computation for evaluating the MDL scoring function, we also use two-pass MapReduce algorithms to preprocess the input data and ultimately fulfill the influence degree evaluation for each node in the BN.

Then, the nodes influenced by new data can be identified, which consequently determines the centers of subgraphs that need to be revised incrementally. In particular, we can easily obtain the node whose influence degree is larger than a given threshold. For these nodes in the current BN also as variables in the new data, we learn the subgraph again from the new data using the same data-intensive method of MDL-based scoring & search as the method for learning the current BN. For the relevant variables not in the current BN (but in the new data), we obtain the optimal subgraph centered on these variables and then add the edges into the current BN.

It is worth noting that the above algorithms for learning BNs from distributed, massive and changing data actually provide a platform-independent and general idea centered on data-intensive computing, since MapReduce is typically an intuitively described methodology and preliminary roadmap for parallel computing on a massive scale. Generally speaking, the main advantages of our methods in this chapter can be summarized as follows:

- Effective extension of the classical scoring & search algorithm for learning BNs to a broader range by eliminating the efficiency bottleneck to a great extent oriented to massive, physically distributed, and dynamically changing, both structured and unstructured sample sets universally generated in data-intensive computing situations and realistic data-centered applications.
- Generic ideas for scalable and incremental learning of uncertain knowledge by incorporating MapReduce-based parallel and data-intensive computing techniques.

2.2 Related Work

BN has become an established framework for representing and inferring uncertain knowledge [128, 142]. It has been widely used in many different aspects of intelligent applications. The construction of a BN involves structure learning and CPT learning. In these years, many algorithms have been proposed to induct BN structures from various perspectives or based on various underlying techniques. For example, Cheng *et al.* [31] and Cheng [32] gave the classical dependency analysis algorithms based on the information theory. Cooper and Herskovits [37] gave the CH scoring metric and greedy search algorithm. Heckerman *et al.* [76] gave the hill-climbing search algorithm for model selection, and Tsamardinos *et al.* [158] gave the max–min hill-climbing algorithm by introducing some strategies of structure-based optimization and elimination of redundant computations. By adopting the MDL metric [141] for sending the sample data through the BN structure, Suzuki [153] gave the branch and bound technique. Recently, focusing on structure learning as well, Brenner and Sontag [18] gave a new scoring function that is computationally easier to maximize as the amount of data increases. Cano *et al.* [25] gave the method of integrating expert knowledge when learning BN from data. Campos and Ji [23] gave a branch and bound algorithm for structure learning by integrating structural constraints with data in a way to guarantee global optimality. These algorithms focus more on the algorithmic techniques, such as conditional independence tests, scoring functions and optimal model selection, than the nature of sample data actually desired to be extended with respect to the explosively increased data in recent years.

Confronted with massive datasets, three categories of algorithms for BN learning were proposed: computation reduction, parallel computing and data-intensive computing. As for the first class, Bouhamed *et al.* [17] gave a heuristic for BN structure learning based on data clusters, and Friedman *et al.* [65] gave the learning method for reducing search space by restricting the parents of each variable to belong to a small subset of candidates. Run on centralized single-node architectures, these methods are not well suited for the situations with massive and distributed data. For the second class, Lam and Segre [94] proposed the scalable algorithm that exploited both properties and MDL-based scoring metric and a distributed, asynchronous and adaptive search technique. Xiang and Chu [168] and Yu *et al.* [176] proposed the parallel algorithm for BN learning. Focusing on parallel execution of the learning process, these methods concern few aspects of data-intensive aggregations and statistics on massive data, and the data-intensive mechanisms on massive data are still desirable.

As for the third class, BN's structure and parameters can be learned by paralyzing the classical learning algorithms based on MapReduce. Wolfe *et al.* [166] gave the distributed expectation maximization (EM) algorithm upon the MapReduce topology, where the dataset is divided into several splits and each node makes computations for one split. Chen *et al.* [29] extended the classical three-phase dependency analysis method to learn a BN from large-scale unstructured Web data by using MapReduce. Basak *et al.* [11] gave the method for accelerating BN parameter learning using Hadoop and MapReduce. Compared with data-intensive learning of parameters, the data-intensive learning of structures is more critical and challenging.

Generally, scoring & search-based algorithms are widely used and studied, since the algorithms themselves can be executed straightforwardly and the orientations can be fulfilled easily, which makes it necessary to develop the data-intensive scoring & search algorithms while reflecting the massive, distributed and dynamically changing nature.

Recently, MapReduce abstraction has been successfully applied to a broad range of data analysis. Bahmani *et al.* [9] gave the method for discovering the densest subgraph from large-scale graphs by using the streaming and MapReduce models. Nandi *et al.* [120] discussed data cube materialization and mining over MapReduce. Pande *et al.* [126] gave the parallel learning algorithm of tree ensembles with MapReduce. Li *et al.* [97] improved MapReduce based on quantitative analysis of Hadoop I/O and proposed a platform for incremental and one-pass analysis of massive data. Aiming at machine learning and data mining of massive data in the cloud, Low *et al.* [106] proposed the distributed GraphLab to provide a mechanism of asynchronized iterative computations and make the algorithm design easier than that directly using MapReduce. In this chapter, we adopt MapReduce as the programming model to fulfill the required data-intensive tasks. Metwally *et al.* [112] gave the MapReduce framework for all-pair similarity joins of multisets and vectors.

Incremental learning is naturally applied in data analysis or knowledge discovery and always paid much attention [78]. In the BN community, incremental learning methods have been followed with great attention as well. For example, Friedman and Goldszmidt [63] investigated the sequential update of BN structures without repeated data inspection by considering the tradeoff between the quality of the learned networks and the amount of information that is maintained about past observation. Lam [93] gave an approach to refining BN structures from new data based on the MDL principle. Shi and Tan [151] gave a polynomial-time- and constraint-based technique for incremental learning of BN structures by hill-climbing search on candidate parent sets. Tian *et al.* [155] gave the method for incremental learning of BNs with hidden variables. Yasin and Leray [174] gave the method for incremental learning of BN structures for high-dimensional data stream analysis by discovering local skeletons. Specifically in the privacy-preserving paradigm, Samet *et al.* [145] gave a new version of sufficient statistics based on the K2 algorithm with respect to newly coming sensitive data. However, these incremental learning algorithms cannot be suitable for the situations with distributed massive data, where efficient data processing is indispensable and previously seen data will not be preserved.

Therefore, in this chapter, we concentrate on parallel and incremental learning of BNs from massive, distributed and dynamically changing data from the original idea of the scoring & search algorithm and MDL evaluation. By using data-intensive computing techniques based on MapReduce, we are to augment the parallel and incremental ideas into the general BN learning and BN incremental learning algorithms.

2.3 Preliminaries

To provide a technical context for later discussions, we introduce preliminaries on the classical scoring & search algorithm for learning BN structures from data, starting from the definition of a general BN, and the MapReduce model.

2.3.1 Scoring & search for learning BN structures

Definition 2.1. A BN is a directed acyclic graph (DAG) $G = (V, E)$, in which the following holds [26, 28]: (1) V is the set of random variables which makes up the nodes of the network. (2) E is the set of directed edges connecting pairs of nodes. An arrow from node X to node Y means that X has a direct influence on Y ($X, Y \in V$ and $X \neq Y$). Each node X is independent of its non-descendants given its parents. (3) Each node has a CPT that quantifies the effects that the parents have on the node. The parents of node X are all those that have arrows pointing to X.

A BN represents the JPD in products, and every entry in the JPD can be computed from the information in the BN by the chain rule $P(V_1, \ldots, V_n) = \prod_{i=1}^{n} P(V_i \mid Parents(V_i))$.

Before introducing the scoring & search algorithm [37, 76, 158], we first present the original MDL scoring metric [141, 153] to measure the coincidence of a DAG with the given sample data. To send the sample dataset D through a BN G by describing D as the message of bits, the best BN is that achieving the minimal length of messages F, defined as follows:

$$F(G|D) = \sum_{i=1}^{m} \log_2 P(t_i) + |G|\frac{\log_2 m}{2}, \quad t_i \in D. \qquad (2.1)$$

In this scoring function, G is supposed as a BN with binary variables, D is the sample dataset, m is the total number of samples and t_i is a sample in D (a row in the sample dataset). $|G|$ is the number of parameters required in G and $|G| = \sum_{j=1}^{n} 2^{|Parents(V_j)|}$, where $|Parents(V_j)|$ is the number of parents of V_j. Thus, the BN G with the minimal value of F is the desired one, and the smaller the value of F, the larger the coincidence between G and the sample dataset.

It is straightforward that the basic and most frequent computation task in Eq. (2.1) is to compute the marginal probability values of various subsets of the random variables with respect to each sample (i.e., row). This is illustrated by the following:

Example 2.1. The DAG G and dataset D with 100 samples are shown in Figure 2.1 and Table 2.1, respectively, where *Count* denotes the number of the same sample.

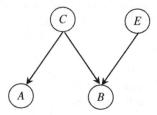

Figure 2.1 DAG of a BN.

Table 2.1 Sample data.

A	B	C	E	Count
1	1	1	1	54
1	1	1	0	1
1	0	1	1	7
1	0	1	0	27
0	1	1	1	3
0	1	1	0	2
0	0	0	1	4
0	0	0	0	2

We can compute $|G|^{\frac{\log_2 m}{2}}$ easily, since $|G| = 8$ and $m = 100$. From Table 2.1, we know there are eight different samples all together, and the JPD for each sample upon the DAG in Figure 2.1 can be computed respectively. For example, we have

$$P(t_1 = (1, 1, 1, 1)) = P(A = 1, B = 1, C = 1, E = 1)$$
$$= P(C = 1)P(E = 1)P(B = 1 \mid C = 1, E = 1)P(A = 1 \mid C = 1)$$
$$= P(C = 1)P(E = 1)\frac{P(B = 1, C = 1, E = 1)}{P(C = 1, E = 1)}\frac{P(A = 1, C = 1)}{P(C = 1)}$$
$$= 0.94 \times 0.68 \times 0.9 \times 0.95 = 0.569.$$

Then, we have $-\log_2 P(t_1) = 0.814$. Similarly, we can obtain the joint probabilities of other samples and compute $F(G \mid D)$.

Algorithm 2.1 LearnBN_HC

Input:

V: the set of random variables

D: the sample dataset on V

F: the MDL scoring function given in Eq. (1)

G_0: the initial BN structure without edges

Output: BN's DAG

Steps:

1: $G \leftarrow G_0$; *oldScore* $\leftarrow F(G_0|D)$ // Score of G_0 with respect to D

2: While true Do

3:    $G^* \leftarrow$ null; *newScore* $\leftarrow +\infty$

4:    For each G' obtained by adding, deleting or reversing an edge on G Do

5:       *tempScore* $\leftarrow F(G'|D)$

6:       If *tempScore* < *newScore* Then

7:          $G^* \leftarrow G'$; *newScore* $\leftarrow$ *tempScore*

8:       End If

9:    End For

10:   If *newScore* < *oldScore* Then

11:      $G \leftarrow G^*$; *oldScore* $\leftarrow$ *newScore*

12:   Else

13:      Return G

14:   End If

15: End While

By incorporating MDL and hill-climbing, the scoring & search algorithm starts from a graph without edges and generates a series of candidate models by adding, deleting or reversing an edge to modify the current model locally. The model with the minimal score will be adopted as the basis for the next time of search, which will be made iteratively until the score will not be decreased. The above ideas are summarized in Algorithm 2.1. Upon the returned DAG, the corresponding CPTs can be computed easily.

Example 2.2. Suppose there are three candidate models, G_1, G_2, G_3, with respect to the current node A in the first pass of the hill-climbing search, shown in Figure 2.2(a). If G_1 is optimal according to the MDL scores, then the candidate models can be generated by adding $C \rightarrow A$ and $E \rightarrow A$ respectively, on G_1, shown in Figure 2.2(b).

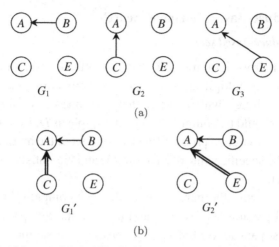

Figure 2.2 Candidate models in hill-climbing search. (a) Candidate models in the first pass. (b) Candidate models in the second pass.

2.3.2 *MapReduce model*

The MapReduce programming model simply includes two functions: the map function transforms input data into ⟨key, value⟩ pairs, and the reduce function is applied to each list of values that correspond to the same key. MapReduce attracts away complex distributed system issues, thereby providing users with rapid utilization of computing resources [48, 49].

To achieve parallelism, the MapReduce system essentially implements "group data by key, then apply the reduce function to each group". This computation model, referred to as MapReduce group-by, permits parallelism because the extraction of ⟨key, value⟩ pairs and the application of the reduce function to each group can be performed in parallel on many nodes. The system code of MapReduce implements this computation model and other functionalities such as scheduling, load balancing and fault tolerance. The MapReduce program of an analytical query includes both the map and reduce functions generated from the query and the system code.

As the most popular open-source implementation of MapReduce, Hadoop [165] uses block-level scheduling and a sort-merge technique to implement the group-by functionality for parallel processing. The Hadoop distributed file system (HDFS) handles the reading of job input data and writing of job output data. In this chapter, we implement our MapReduce-based algorithms on HDFS and then conduct all required experiments.

2.4   MapReduce-Based Scoring & Search

2.4.1   *MapReduce-based scoring*

It can be seen from Example 2.1 that the JPD of each sample can be transformed into a multiplication of conditional probability factors and then marginal probabilities, which will be the most time-consuming operation, since the JDP should be computed for each sample in D. Further, the value of each required marginal probability is dependent of the model's graphical structure G, the specific value of each sample and the statistics of the whole sample dataset.

Now, we discuss the parallel algorithm for computing the marginal probabilities by using MapReduce and propose the two-pass algorithms, where the first-pass algorithm is to preprocess the sample data and the second-pass algorithm is to compute the marginal probabilities.

(1) The first-pass algorithm

As for the certain candidate model, we use map functions to obtain ⟨key, value⟩ pairs from each sample, where key is the subset of variables (with specific values respectively) required for evaluating the MDL score, and value is 1. We use reduce functions to obtain the ultimate number of each subset appearing in the whole sample dataset, which we then store in the file M consisting of ⟨key, value⟩ pairs. The above ideas are given as follows:

Algorithm 2.2 Count_For_MarginalProb

Map (*key*: file name of D, *value*: samples in D)
  For each row r in D Do
    Emit (*subset*, "1")
    //*subset* consists of variables and the specific values in the required marginal
      probability parameters w.r.t. G
  End For
Reduce (*key*: variable subset, *values*: counter list)
  $c \leftarrow 0$
  For each *subset*'s value v in *values* Do
    $c \leftarrow c + \text{ParseInt}(v)$
  End For
  Emit (*subset*, AsString (c))

---

key = subset	value
$A = 1$	1
$B = 1$	1
$A = 1, B = 1$	1
$C = 1$	1
$E = 1$	1

(a)

key = subset	value
$A = 1$	1
$B = 1$	1
$A = 1, B = 1$	1
$C = 1$	1
$E = 0$	1

(b)

key = subset	value
$A = 1$	89
$A = 0$	11
$B = 1$	60
$B = 0$	40
$A = 1, B = 1$	55
$A = 1, B = 0$	34
$A = 0, B = 0$	6
$C = 1$	94
$C = 0$	6
$E = 1$	68
$E = 0$	32

(c)

Figure 2.3 Results of Algorithm 2.2. (a) Result of map functions in Algorithm 2.2 for the first 54 samples. (b) Result of map functions in Algorithm 2.2 for the 55th sample. (c) Results of reduce functions in Algorithm 2.2.

Example 2.3. For the candidate structure G_1 in Figure 2.2(a) and sample data in Table 2.1, the required conditional probability factors are $P(A)$, $P(B)$, $P(A \mid B)$, $P(C)$ and $P(E)$, and thus we need to compute the marginal probabilities on the subsets of A, B, AB, C and E. By executing the map functions in Algorithm 2.2, we can obtain the $\langle$key, value$\rangle$ pairs for each sample in Table 2.1. For the first 54 samples with ($A = 1$, $B = 1$, $C = 1$, $E = 1$), we can obtain the $\langle$key, value$\rangle$ pairs as Figure 2.3(a) for 54 times. For the 55th sample with ($A = 1$, $B = 1$, $C = 1$, $E = 0$), we can obtain the $\langle$key, value$\rangle$ pairs as shown in Figure 2.3(b). By executing the reduce functions in Algorithm 2.2 by summing the values for each key, we can obtain the number of each key in the whole sample dataset shown in Figure 2.3(c).

Then, we use Algorithm 2.3 to derive all required marginal probabilities from M in the local machine without communication cost, taking as input $\langle$key, value$\rangle$ pairs (i.e., the file M) obtained by the reduce function of Algorithm 2.2. We also store the result of Algorithm 2.3 in the file M' consisting of $\langle$key, value$\rangle$ pairs.

(2) The second-pass algorithm

According to the required marginal probabilities in the multiplication, we can obtain the JDP for each row in D by using map functions. Then

---
Algorithm 2.3 Compute_MarginalProb

Input: M // $\langle key, value \rangle$ pairs, the result of Algorithm 2.2
Output: Marginal probabilities of concerned subsets
Steps:
　For each row in M Do
　　MarginalProb(key) $\leftarrow$ $value/m$
　　//key is the subset, $value$ is the appearing times of the subset, and m is
　　　the total number of the given samples
　　Emit (key, AsString (MarginalProb(key)))
　End For

Algorithm 2.4 Compute_Score

Map (key: file name of D, $value$: samples in D)
　$P(r) \leftarrow 1$
　For each row r in D Do
　Obtain MarginalProb(key) from M' according to key for computing the JDP
　　of r
　　$P(r) \leftarrow P(r)$*MarginalProb(key)
　　// not differentiating multiplication or division
　Emit (r, $P(r)$)
　End For
Reduce (key: r, $values$: probability list)
　$s \leftarrow 0$
　For each probability p in $values$ Do
　　$s \leftarrow s + \log_2 p$
　End For
　Emit (G, AsString ($s + |G| \log_2 m/2$))
　// G is the current candidate graphical structure and m is the total number
　　of the given samples

---

according to Eq. (2.1), we can further obtain the MDL score of G with respect to D by using reduce functions. The above ideas are given as follows:

Example 2.4. We revisit the sample data in Table 2.1 and the result of Algorithm 2.2.

(1) By Algorithm 2.3, the marginal probabilities, $P(A = 1)$ and $P(B = 1)$, will be 0.89 and 0.60, respectively based on the pairs $\langle A = 1, 89 \rangle$ and

$\langle B = 1, 60 \rangle$ in Figure 2.3(c). In the same way, we can obtain all the marginal probabilities for the subsets in M.

(2) By the map functions in Algorithm 2.2.4 and the marginal probabilities in M', the JDPs for each sample can be obtained in parallel, such as the JDP of the first sample from $P(C = 1)$, $P(E = 1)$, $P(B = 1, C = 1, E = 1)$, $P(C = 1, E = 1)$ and $P(A = 1, C = 1)$.

For each candidate graphical structure, we can obtain the MDL score based on Algorithms 2.2–2.4, where we focus on the JPD computation for each sample, the most time-consuming step. By using the MapReduce model, the classical scoring approach is extended to suit the situations with massive data and consequently develop the parallel algorithms. Actually, if the given sample dataset includes a small set of variables corresponding to small candidate graphical structures, we can preprocess the sample dataset and compute all possible marginal probabilities that may be concerned in all possible candidate graphical structures, while the marginal probabilities can also be computed by Algorithms 2.2 and 2.3 as well.

2.4.2 Optimal structure search and BN storage

Scoring more than one candidate graphical structure can be fulfilled independently by Algorithm 2.4, and then the optimal structure can be selected easily by the hill-climbing search. The cost of generating a candidate structure is generally much less than that of scoring this structure, which means that the cost of scoring all candidate structures dominates the total cost of the algorithm. Thus, we can just replace Step 5 in Algorithm 2.1 by "*tempScore*←Compute_Score(G', D)" using Algorithm 2.4 to fulfill the MDL-based scoring & search. For the situations with a large number of candidate structures that need to be generated and scored in parallel, the algorithm can be achieved easily.

Then, the CPTs can be calculated easily based on the constructed DAG structure, while Algorithms 2.2 and 2.3 can also be adopted for statistics from the given massive sample dataset. Thus, the BN can be learned from the given dataset that may be a certain snapshot or slice in a dynamically changing environment. To this end, we will have to store the initial BN persistently and then make incremental revision as mentioned in Section 2.1. Moreover, once the BN is learned as the compact representation of the original sample data, probabilistic inference queries in realistic applications can be answered by searching the BN, which also makes it indispensable to store the BN using disk persistently instead of main memory transiently.

In line with the MapReduce-based parallel processing, Hadoop-like platforms and the specialties of BN, we store the DAG and corresponding CPTs into a file consisting of logical rows represented as ⟨key, value⟩ pairs. To reflect the dependence relationships between child and parent nodes qualitatively and quantitatively, we define key and value as $(X = x_i,$ $Pa(X) = v_j)$ and $P(X = x_i|Pa(X) = v_j)$, respectively, where

- x_i is the value of X,
- $Pa(X)$ is the parent(s) of X, and the value of $Pa(X)$ is v_j,
- $P(X = x_i|Pa(X) = v_j)$ is the conditional probability as one item in the CPT of X.

Example 2.5. The BN in Figure 2.4(a) can be represented and stored as ⟨key, value⟩ pairs in Figure 2.4(b), where each variable is assumed to be binary (i.e., valued 1 or 0).

It is clear that the ⟨key, value⟩ pair representation like Figure 2.4(b) can be easily stored into a file or flat table, and then loaded into the data management or analysis platforms for data-intensive computing.

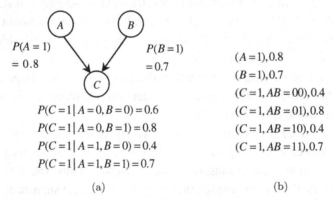

(a)   (b)

Figure 2.4 BN and its ⟨key, value⟩ pair representation. (a) A simple BN. (b) ⟨key, value⟩ pairs of the BN.

2.5 MapReduce-Based Incremental Learning

To reflect the dynamically changing property of the real-world massive data, it is necessary to revise the initially learned BN in an incremental manner. In this section, we first discuss the method for measuring the influence degree of the new data on the current BN to determine the nodes that should be revised, which is the most challenging and important step for BN's incremental learning. Then, we give the strategy of incremental revision of the current BN in response to new data.

2.5.1 *Influence degree of BN nodes*

Intuitively, the representation of the current BN (denoted G_o) may be inconsistent with the new data (denoted D_n). Given the graphical structure of the current BN, a new set of CPTs can be easily obtained corresponding to the new data. To define the influence degree, we suppose a new BN, denoted G_n, consisting of the same graphical structure with that of G_o and the new CPTs, can be obtained. The variation of parameters in the CPT is dependent on the distribution of D_n and influences the coincidence between D_n and G_o. From the perspective of variation, we discuss the influence degree of BN nodes in response to D_n. For each node, we obtain the proportion of the variation of probability parameters from the CPTs of G_o and G_n.

Definition 2.2. The proportion of node X's probability parameters with variations is called the variation degree of the parameters of X, denoted as $\Delta(P(X|\mathrm{Pa}(X)))$, and

$$\Delta(P(X|\mathrm{Pa}(X))) = \sum_{u_{ij} \in U} |u_{ij}^o - u_{ij}^n|/k, \qquad (2.2)$$

where

- U is the set of probability parameters of X in G_o and G_n, $U = U_o \cup U_n = \{u_{ij} \in U_o \text{ or } u_{ij} \in U_n\}$, and U_o and U_n is the set of probability parameters of X in G_o and G_n, respectively.
- $u_{ij} \in U$ denotes the conditional probability that X will take on the value $X = x_i$ given its parents $\mathrm{Pa}(X)$ that takes on the value $\mathrm{Pa}(X) = v_j$.
- k is the number of probability parameters in U, and $k = |U|$.
- $u_{ij}^o = 0$ if $u_{ij} \notin U_o$, and $u_{ij}^n = 0$ if $u_{ij} \notin U_n$.

Table 2.2   Probability parameters.

(a) U_o of node C

$P(C|AB)$	$v_1 = a_1b_1$	$v_2 = a_1b_2$	$v_3 = a_2b_1$	$v_4 = a_2b_2$
$C = c_1$	$u^o_{11} = 0.9$	$u^o_{12} = 0.8$	$u^o_{13} = 0.7$	$u^o_{14} = 0.6$
$C = c_2$	$u^o_{21} = 0.9$	$u^o_{22} = 0.2$	$u^o_{23} = 0.3$	$u^o_{24} = 0.4$

(b) U_n of node C

$P(C|AB)$	$v_1 = a_1b_1$	$v_2 = a_1b_2$	$v_3 = a_2b_1$	$v_4 = a_2b_2$	$v_5 = a_3b_1$	$v_6 = a_3b_2$
$C = c_1$	$u^n_{11} = 0.6$	$u^n_{12} = 0.5$	$u^n_{13} = 0.4$	$u^n_{14} = 0.3$	$u^n_{15} = 0.2$	$u^n_{16} = 0.1$
$C = c_2$	$u^n_{21} = 0.4$	$u^n_{22} = 0.5$	$u^n_{23} = 0.6$	$u^n_{24} = 0.7$	$u^n_{25} = 0.8$	$u^n_{26} = 0.9$

Example 2.6. Suppose U_o and U_n on node C of the same BN structure in Figure 2.4(a) is shown in Tables 2.2(a) and 2.2(b), respectively. According to Definition 2, $|U| = 12$, and $\Delta(P(C|AB)) = (0.3 + 0.3 + 0.3 + 0.3 + 0.3 + 0.3 + 0.3 + 0.3 + 0.2 + 0.8 + 0.1 + 0.9)/12 = 0.37$.

It is worth noting that G_o and D_n may still be coincident even if there is great variation of probability parameters. Thus, we further discuss the influence of parameter variations on the coincidence between G_o and D_n, which we represent by the probability of observing D_n upon g_o, denoted $P(D_n|g_o)$, where we use g_o to denote the DAG structure of G_o. Intuitively, the larger the value of $P(D_n|g_o)$, the better the coincidence between D_n and g_o will be. The total influence of the new data on g_o consists of all the variation of $P(D_n|g_o)$ with respect to all the variations of u_{ij}. This means that the expression $\int_{u^o_{ij}}^{u^n_{ij}} \frac{\partial P(D_n|g_o)}{\partial u_{ij}} du_{ij}$ describes the influence of u_{ij}'s variation on $P(D_n|g_o)$. Thus, for each node X, we use the average influence of all X's parameter variations on $P(D_n|g_o)$ to describe the influence of parameter variations of X on $P(D_n|g_o)$.

Definition 2.3. $\frac{1}{k}\sum_{u_{ij} \in U} \int_{u^o_{ij}}^{u^n_{ij}} \frac{\partial P(D_n|g_o)}{\partial u_{ij}} du_{ij}$, denoted $\mathrm{ID}(X)$, is called the influence degree of parameter variations of X on $P(D_n|g_o)$.

It can be seen from Definition 2.3 that the computation of the influence degree concerns many difficult integral calculations. Thus, we give a linear approximate expression based on the variation degree in Eq. (2.2) to make the influence degree of node X be computed efficiently. We replace $P(D_n|g_o)$ with the log likelihood, $\ln P(D_n|g_o)$, since the increase in the log likelihood is proportional to that in the likelihood. Russell and Norvig [142] showed that each of these derivatives can be calculated as

$$\frac{\partial \ln P(D_n|g_o)}{\partial u_{ij}} = \sum_{r \in D_n} \frac{P(x_i v_j|r)}{u_{ij}}, \tag{2.3}$$

where r is a sample (i.e., row) in D_n.

So, we have the following linear approximation expression

$$\int_{u_{ij}^o}^{u_{ij}^n} \frac{\partial \ln P(D_n|g_o)}{\partial u_{ij}} du_{ij} \approx \frac{\sum_{r \in D_n} P(x_i v_j|r)}{u_{ij}^o} |u_{ij}^o - u_{ij}^n|. \tag{2.4}$$

Note that $\sum_{r \in D_n} P(x_i v_j|r) = m_{ij}$, where m_{ij} is the number of samples in D_n satisfying $X = x_i$ and $\mathrm{Pa}(X) = v_j$. Then, we have

$$\frac{1}{k} \sum_{u_{ij} \in U} \int_{u_{ij}^o}^{u_{ij}^n} \frac{\partial P(x_i v_j|r)}{\partial u_{ij}} du_{ij} = \frac{1}{k} \sum_{u_{ij} \in U} \frac{m_{ij}}{u_{ij}^o} |u_{ij}^o - u_{ij}^n|. \tag{2.5}$$

This means that $\frac{1}{k} \sum_{u_{ij} \in U} \int_{u_{ij}^o}^{u_{ij}^n} \frac{\partial P(D_n|g_o)}{\partial u_{ij}} du_{ij}$ can be approximately represented as

$$\frac{1}{k} \sum_{u_{ij} \in U} \frac{m_{ij}}{u_{ij}^o} |u_{ij}^o - u_{ij}^n|. \tag{2.6}$$

Based on the influence degree given in Eq. (2.6), the nodes influenced by the new data can be identified. By the decreasing order of the influence degrees, we can consider revising the current BN centered on the node with the currently largest influence degree, similar to the node selection strategy adopted in Algorithm 2.1. By giving a threshold of the influence degree, we can consider revising the current BN concerted on the nodes whose influence degree is larger than the threshold.

2.5.2 *MapReduce-based measurement of the influence degree*

We note that it is necessary to compute m_{ij} for each u_{ij} with respect to G_o and D_n, but different m_{ij} can be computed independently. This motivates us to consider computing all required m_{ij} values by executing a parallel MapReduce algorithm once. Then, we note that G_n can be stored in one file storing G_o according to the strategy given in Section 2.4.2, and thus u_{ij}^o and u_{ij}^n can be obtained in parallel for evaluating Eq. (2.6). For the above two kinds of tasks, we are also to develop two-pass MapReduce algorithms to measure the influence degree of X in line with the inherent properties of D_n.

(1) The first-pass algorithm

For each $x_i v_j$ ($X = x_i$, $Pa(X) = v_j$) of node X in g_o and the values in D_n, we use map functions to obtain the $\langle$key, value$\rangle$ pairs from each sample (row) in D_n, where key is $x_i v_j$ and value is 1. We use reduce functions to obtain the ultimate number of samples in D_n satisfying $X = x_i$ and $Pa(X) = v_j$. The above ideas are given as follows:

Algorithm 2.5 Count_mij

Map (*key*: file name of D_n, *value*: samples in D_n)

  For each row r in D_n Do

    Emit $(x_i v_j,$ "1")

  End For

Reduce (*key*: $x_i v_j$, *values*: counter list)

  result $\leftarrow 0$

  For each $x_i v_j$'s value v in *values* Do

    result $\leftarrow$ *result*+ParseInt(v)

  End For

  Emit $(x_i v_j,$ AsString (*result*))

---

(2) The second-pass algorithm

According to the BN's storage strategy, we assume that G_o and G_n are stored in a file F consisting of $\langle$key, value$\rangle$ pairs. Two rows with the same key $x_i v_j$ (i.e., ($X = x_i$, $Pa(X) = v_j$))) in F means that one derives from D and the other derives from D_n. Thus, taking as input F, we use map functions to obtain and group the probabilities for each $x_i v_j$. Then, we use reduce function to obtain $\frac{m_{ij}}{u_{ij}^o}|u_{ij}^o - u_{ij}^n|$ relevant to $x_i v_j$, whose results are also stored into a file, denoted F', consisting of $\langle$key value$\rangle$ pairs, where key is the number of parameters relevant to $x_i v_j$ and value is $\frac{m_{ij}}{u_{ij}^o} |u_{ij}^o - u_{ij}^n|$. Finally, we give a local algorithm to aggregate the results of the above reduce functions without communication costs taking as input F'. The above ideas are given as follows:

Algorithm 2.6 Count_each_uij

Map (*key*: file name of F, *value*: rows in F)
    //G_o and G_n are stored in F
    For each row r in F Do
        Emit $(x_i v_j, p_{ij})$ //p_{ij} means $P(X = x_i | \mathrm{Pa}(X) = v_j)$
    End For
Reduce (*key*: $x_i v_j$, *values*: probability list)
    $s \leftarrow 1$
    For each $x_i v_j$'s value p_{ij} in *values* Do
    //Two $\langle x_i v_j, p_{ij} \rangle$ pairs, one derives from D and the other derives from D_n
    $t_s \leftarrow p_{ij}; s \leftarrow s + 1$
    End For
    $d_s \leftarrow |t_1 - t_2|$
    Emit $\left(s, \text{AsString} \left(\frac{m_{ij}}{t_1} * d_s \right) \right)$

Algorithm 2.7 Count_ID

Input: F' // $\langle key, value \rangle$ pairs, the result of Algorithm 6
Output: Influence degree of node X
Steps:
    $k \leftarrow 0; ID_{ij} \leftarrow 0$
    For each row in T Do
        $k \leftarrow k + key; ID_{ij} \leftarrow ID_{ij} + value$
        //*key* is number of parameters relevant to $x_i v_j$, *value* is $\frac{m_{ij}}{u_{ij}^o} |u_{ij}^o - u_{ij}^n|$
    End For
    Return ID_{ij} / k

2.5.3 *Incremental learning strategies*

To reflect the new data with respect to the current BN G_o, we focus on the necessary revisions of the subgraphs centered on the nodes in G_o and D_n, and appropriate augmentation of the subgraphs centered on the nodes not in G_o but just in D_n. In this section, we mainly discuss the strategy of the incremental revision of the BN's DAG structure for these two cases.

Case 1. Let A_o be the set of variables in D_n also appearing as nodes in G_o, and $A_o = \{X | X \in D_n, X \in G_o\}$. To make incremental revisions on G_o, we will determine the subgraph required to be revised, that is, the nodes with great influence degrees and the "radius" as the range of revision propagation. The incremental revision can be fulfilled by the following steps:

Step 1. We obtain the influence degree $ID(X)$ of node X in A_o by Algorithms 2.5–2.7 given in Section 2.5.2. If $ID(X) > \varepsilon$, then the subgraph centered on X should be revised, where ε is a given threshold of the influence degree.

Step 2. We select the Markov blanket of X as the radius to revise the subgraph, since the Markov blanket [128] of node X, denoted $MB(X)$, in a BN includes X's direct parents, X's direct successors and the other direct parents of X's direct successors, by which we can obtain the directly-dependent nodes of X.

Step 3. We learn the subgraphs centered on X and those in $MB(X)$ again from D_n by the data-intensive algorithm given in Section 2.4. In this process, candidate graphical substructures are generated according to the topological order of the nodes in G_o to preserve the parent–child relationships and avoid cycles in the ultimate graphical structure.

Case 2. Let A_n be the set of variables in D_n but not in G_o, and $A_n = \{Y | Y \in D_n, Y \notin G_o\}$. To augment the variables in A_n into G_o, for each Y in A_n, we learn the subgraph from D_n centered on Y by the data-intensive algorithm given in Section 2.4 and then add the edges into G_o if no cycles are generated.

Finally, all the CPTs can be revised according to the ultimate DAG by the statistical computation analogous to Algorithms 2.2 and 2.3 taking as input the new data.

2.6 Experimental Results

In this section, we show experimental results and performance studies to test the efficiency, correctness and effectiveness of the methods presented in this chapter.

2.6.1 *Experimental setup*

The experiment platform was established on Hadoop including six machines with Pentium(R) Dual-Core CPU E5700 @ 3.00 GHz @ 3.01 GHz and 2 GB main memory. In the HDFS cluster, there are one NameNode and six DataNodes, on each of which the versions of Hadoop, Linux and Java are 0.20.2, Ubuntu 10.04 and JDK 1.6, respectively. All the codes were written in Java.

Chest-clinic network (a.k.a. Asia network) [32] is a belief network for a hypothetical medical domain about whether a patient has *tuberculosis, lung cancer* or *bronchitis*, related to their *X-ray, dyspnea*, Visit To Asia and *smoking status*. The general structure of this network is shown in Figure 2.5 and contains 8 nodes and 8 arcs. Each node has only two possible values (i.e., True or False) described by 1 or 0, respectively. In the experiments, we adopted the chest-clinic network and the corresponding sample data [32] as the benchmark BN and preliminary test data, respectively. Upon the initial 1000 rows, we generated various-sized sample datasets (0.2 GB, 1 GB, 2 GB, 4 GB, 6 GB, 8 GB, 10 GB and 12 GB) randomly according to the values appearing in the initial set, where about every one million rows of data amount to the size of 15.26 MB.

HepaerII network [125] is a belief network for diagnosis of liver disorders with 70 nodes. In the same way, we generated various-sized sample dataset randomly according to the values appearing in the initial

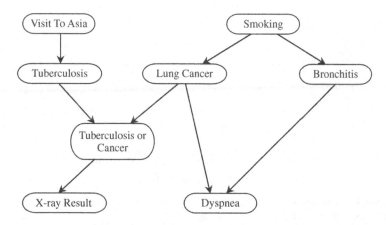

Figure 2.5 The Chest-clinic network structure.

dataset. We adopted HepaerII network as the BN with large number of nodes in scalability test.

We implemented our algorithms of MapReduce-based learning and incremental revision of BNs. We tested the execution time, speedup and efficiency of the MapReduce-based parallel algorithms for BN learning. Then, we tested the correctness and effectiveness of the incremental revision and the efficiency improvement of BN incremental learning. In the experiments, the number of map tasks (MTs) is identical to that of CPUs on each machine by default, and the number of reduce task (RT) is set to one. The execution time of map and RTs, as well as the algorithm's total execution time, is obtained directly from the records of JobTrackers.

2.6.2 *Performance of the MapReduce-based learning algorithm*

(1) Execution time

- *Total time*

  The total time (TT) of learning the chest-clinic BN includes that of executing the MTs, RT and HDFS start-up. First, we tested the total time upon various numbers of DataNodes with the increase of sample data, shown in Figure 2.6. It can be seen that the TT for the same

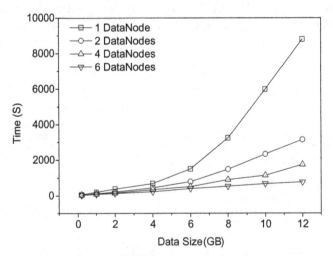

Figure 2.6 TT of learning the chest-clinic BN parallelly based on MapReduce upon various DataNodes with the increase of sample data.

sized sample data is decreased with the increase of DataNodes. As the special case of parallel execution, the situation with just one DataNode can be looked upon as that of the sequential manner, in which the TT is sharply increased with the increase of sample data size, especially for the situations with larger than 6 GB sample data in our experiment environments. Under the HDFS with more than 2 DataNodes, the TT is basically linear to the sample data size. There is not much TT difference when the size is less than 1 GB. With the increase of sample data, the TT is increased gradually as more and more DataNodes are included in the HDFS. This is consistent with the inherence of the MapReduce-based parallel algorithms, and the larger the sample dataset, the more significantly of the advantage of our learning method will be exhibited.

Further, we tested the TT upon various numbers of DataNodes with the increase of sample data with respect to the HepaerII network that is larger than chest-clinic, shown in Figure 2.7. It can be easily seen that the tendency of execution time increase is basically consistent with that in Figure 2.6. For each size of the sample data upon the same number of DataNodes, the execution time with respect to HepaerII is larger than

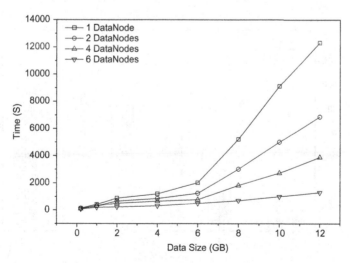

Figure 2.7   TT of learning the HepaerII BN parallelly based on MapReduce upon various DataNodes with the increase of sample data.

that with chest-clinic due to the more random variables as nodes when learning the network, but the TT increase is not sensitive to the number of nodes in the network. Thus, we conclude that our data-intensive learning algorithm is scalable to the size of sample data and that of the BN nodes.

- **Total time vs. algorithm time**

We call the time of executing the map and RTs as algorithm time (AT). We compared the TT and the AT upon the HDFS with six DataNodes when learning the chest-clinic BN from various-sized sample datasets, as shown in Figure 2.8. The proportions of the start-up time in the TT are 4.64%, 4.56%, 3.1% and 5.57%, respectively, for the situations upon 1, 2, 4, and 6 DataNodes, respectively. Meanwhile, we compared the TT and AT when learning the BN from 6 GB sample data with the increase of DataNodes, as shown in Figure 2.9. In the TT, the proportions of start-up time are 8.33%, 6.9%, 5.26%, 5.69%, 3.12%, 2.63% and 1.97%, respectively, for the situations with 1 GB, 2 GB, 4 GB, 6 GB, 8 GB, 10 GB and 12 GB sample data.

It can be seen that the start-up will basically spend a fixed time under the situations with various-sized sample data or upon various numbers of DataNodes. With the increase of DataNodes, the proportion of the

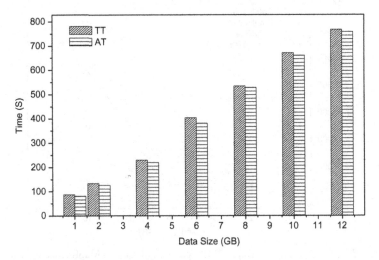

Figure 2.8 TT vs. AT with various sample data sizes.

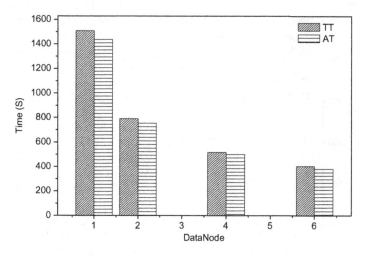

Figure 2.9 TT vs. AT with various DataNodes.

start-up is slightly increased for communication, and the larger the sample data, the less the proportion. This means that the efficiency of the whole system execution is mainly dependent on that of the MTs and RTs, which makes the conclusion derived from the TT tests in Figure 2.6 also appropriate for the AT tests.

Further, we tested the influence of HDFS block size as the representative factor on the algorithm performance. Upon 6 DataNodes, we recorded the execution time of MTs and that of RTs, as well as the AT when the HDFS block size is 32 MB, 64 MB, 128 MB, 256 MB and 512 MB, respectively. The results on the 2 GB and 4 GB sample data are shown in Figures 2.10(a) and 2.10(b), respectively. AT is decreased when the block size is increased from 32 MB to 128 MB on 2 GB sample data, while AT is decreased when the block size is increased from 32 MB to 256 MB on 4 GB sample data due to the decreased cost of communication.

It can be seen that MT is increased and RT is decreased with the increase of HDFS block sizes. Under the given experimental configuration, when the block size is increased to a certain value, the execution time will be decreased due to the increased cost of a MT. The larger the sample data size, the larger the block size that will not make AT decreased. This is consistent with the general characteristics of

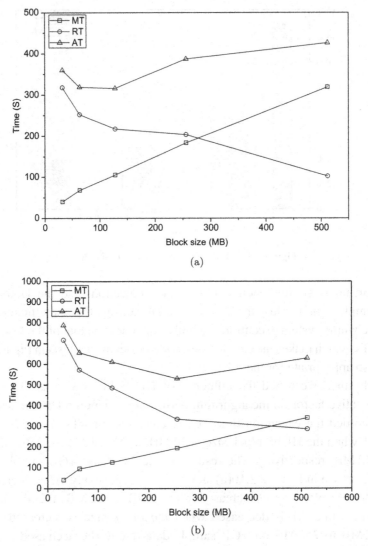

Figure 2.10   Influence of HDFS block sizes on algorithm's execution time. (a) MT, RT and AT on 2 GB sample data. (b) MT, RT and AT on 4 GB sample data.

MapReduce run on HDFS. In view of the trade-off between computation granularity and communications, this makes us be able to configure the HDFS block size according to the scale of sample data to improve the efficiency adaptively.

(2) Speedup and parallel efficiency

The speedup of a parallel algorithm is defined as the ratio of the parallel execution time and the sequential time. We tested the speedup of the MapReduce-based parallel algorithm for learning the chest-clinic BN upon various numbers of DataNodes with the increase of sample data, shown in Figure 2.11. It can be seen that the more the DataNodes or the larger the sample dataset, the larger the speedup, which is consistent with the general conclusion of parallel algorithms. Specifically, the speedup is increased from 1.61 to 10.5 when the sample data is increased from 0.2 GB to 12 GB upon six DataNodes, and the speedup is increased from 2.99 to 10.5 when the DataNodes are increased from 2 to 6 for 12 GB sample data. In both situations, the achieved speedup is 10.5, which approaches the ideal value (i.e., speedup is 12 for six dual core DataNodes), that is, our proposed learning algorithm is 10.5 times faster than the sequential algorithm. This means that the influence of sample data size on speedup is more than that of the DataNode number, that is, the larger the sample data the more dramatic efficiency improvement will be achieved.

The efficiency of a parallel algorithm is defined as the ratio of the speedup and the number of processors from the system. We tested the

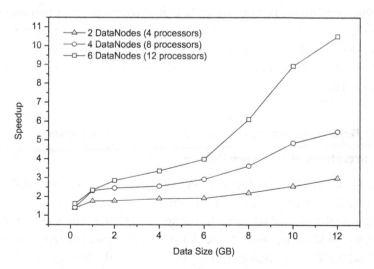

Figure 2.11 Speedup of learning the chest-clinic BN.

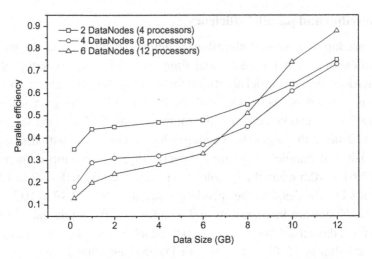

Figure 2.12   Parallel efficiency of learning the chest-clinic BN.

efficiency of our proposed parallel learning algorithm upon various numbers of DataNodes with the increase of sample data, shown in Figure 2.12. It can be seen that when the sample data is less than 6 GB, the parallel efficiency is decreased with the increase of DataNodes and the processors' utilization ratio is lowered. When the sample data is larger than 8 GB, the efficiency upon six DataNodes is higher than that upon two and four DataNodes, which means that the parallel efficiency depends on the trade-off among sample data size, DataNode number and the required communication. From this point of view, our proposed algorithm is scalable for massive data.

2.6.3 *Performance of the MapReduce-based incremental learning*

(1) Correctness of Influence Degree

From the chest-clinic sample dataset with 6000 rows, we learned the BN by PowerConstructor [32]. For simplicity, we ignored the CPTs when illustrating the learned BN, which is denoted as G and shown in Figure 2.5. Then, we divided the whole dataset into two parts with 5000 rows (denoted D_o) and 1000 rows (denoted D_n), respectively. By the algorithm given in Section 2.5.2, we learned a BN from D_o, denoted G_o and shown in

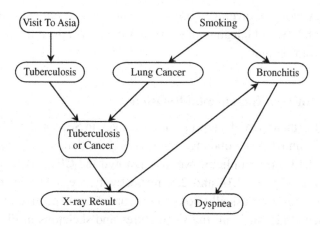

Figure 2.13 Current BN, G_o, learned from 5000 row data.

Table 2.3 Influence degree and the G_o's revision.

Node	ID	Rev
Visit To Asia	0.593	NO
Tuberculosis	12.525	NO
Smoking	25.51	NO
Lung Cancer	47.667	YES
Tuberculosis or Cancer	60.242	YES
X-ray Result	17.172	YES
Bronchitis	101.208	YES
Dyspnea	101.208	YES

Figure 2.13. In this experiment, G was looked upon as the standard network that should have been learned incrementally from G_o and D_n.

We obtained the influence degree from D_n given G_o by Eq. (2.6) in Section 2.5.1. To test the correctness of the influence degree, we considered whether the influence degrees are consistent with the expected revisions from G_o to G. We first gave the influence degree (ID) and the results of whether the revision has been done for each node (Rev), shown in Table 2.3. For node X, "YES" means that the edges connected to X are revised, and "NO" otherwise. It can be seen that the larger the influence degree, the more the probability the node has been revised during the incremental revision, except the revision on "X-ray Result". Thus, from the perspective of node revision, the average correctness ratio of the influence degree is $1 - 1/8 = 87.5\%$, which guarantees the correctness of the influence degree metric to some extent.

(2) Correctness of Incremental Revision

Based on the incremental learning strategy given in Section 2.5.3 by taking as input G_o and D_n, we obtained the revised BN, denoted G_n and shown in Figure 2.14. For simplicity, we also ignored the CPTs. By comparing G_n and G in Figures 2.14 and 2.5, respectively, we note that these two BNs' structures are basically consistent from the perspective of Markov equivalence [142], since all the v-structures and skeletons in Figure 2.14 are equivalent to those in Figure 2.5, except the v-structure on Dyspnea. From the actual inherence point of view, the newly added edge from "X-ray Result" to "Dyspnea" in G_o is also reasonable.

It is the slight difference of the structures between G_n and G that makes us further test G_n's effectiveness by comparing the inference results on G_n and those on G and G_o for the same inference task. We defined the error of G_n's inference as the absolute value of the difference between the inference result on G_n and that on G. We regarded that the inference result was improved by incremental revision if the result on G_n is much closer than that on G_o with respect to that on G. We chose some representative inferences and presented their inference results on G, G_n and G_o (denoted

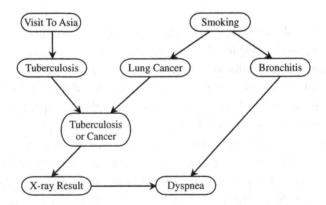

Figure 2.14   BN, G_n, by incremental revision on G_o.

Table 2.4 Errors and improvement of G_n's inferences.

Probabilistic reasoning	R (%)	R_n (%)	R_o (%)	Error (%)	Improved
P (Lung Cancer $= 1 \mid$ Smoking $= 1$)	9.86	9.85	9.86	0.01	NO
P (Tuberculosis or Cancer $= 1 \mid$ Smoking $= 1$)	10.4	10.4	10.3	0	NO
P (X-ray Result $= 0 \mid$ Smoking $= 1$)	15.5	15.8	15.1	0.3	YES
P (Bronchitis $= 1 \mid$ Smoking $= 1$)	58.7	59.5	59.7	0.8	YES
P (Dyspnea $= 1 \mid$ Smoking $= 1$)	52.9	53.4	53.5	0.5	YES
P (Smoking $= 1 \mid$ Lung Cancer $= 1$)	82.8	83.1	82.3	0.3	YES
P (X-ray Result $= 0 \mid$ Lung Cancer $= 1$)	98.4	95.5	94.8	2.9	YES
P (Bronchitis $= 1 \mid$ Lung Cancer $= 1$)	53.7	54.1	54.2	0.4	YES
P (Dyspnea $= 1 \mid$ Lung Cancer $= 1$)	82.5	65.6	64.4	16.9	YES
P (Smoking $= 1 \mid$ Bronchitis $= 1$)	65.2	66.7	66.7	1.5	NO
P (Lung Cancer $= 1 \mid$ Bronchitis $= 1$)	7.11	7.18	7.2	0.07	YES
P (Tuberculosis or Cancer $= 1 \mid$ Bronchitis $= 1$)	7.66	7.78	7.8	0.12	YES
P (X-ray Result $= 0 \mid$ Bronchitis $= 1$)	13.3	13.1	13	0.2	YES
P (Dyspnea $= 1 \mid$ Bronchitis $= 1$)	78.3	79.5	76.5	1.2	YES

R, R_n and R_o, respectively), the corresponding error and whether they improved, respectively, as shown in Table 2.4. It can be seen that the errors of G_n's inference are less than 3% except that of the 9th inference task. The maximal, minimal and average errors are 16.9%, 0% and 1.8%, respectively, which verifies that high precisions of the inferences can be achieved with the revised BN. It can also be seen that 78.6% results are improved by incremental revision, and even the results without improvement are still quite close to those on G. Thus, we conclude that the incrementally revised BN can be reliably applied for probabilistic inferences.

(3) Execution Time

- **Execution time of influence degree evaluation**

  As illustrated by Figures 2.8 and 2.9, the execution time of the whole algorithm mainly depends on that of the MTs and RTs. Thus, we first tested the TT of influence degree evaluation (for all the nodes in G_o) upon various numbers of DataNodes with the increase of new sample data, shown in Figure 2.15. The execution time is linearly increased with

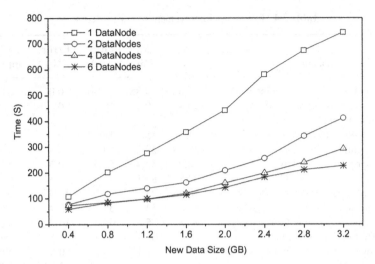

Figure 2.15 Execution time of evaluating the influence degree based on MapReduce upon various DataNodes with the increase of new data.

the increase of the new sample data, and the more the DataNodes, the less the execution time. This means that the influence degree can be evaluated in a reasonable period of time, and this result is similar to that shown in Figure 2.6 except that the new sample data is always much less than those used to learn G_o.

- **Benefit vs. cost on execution time**
  To test the effectiveness of the incremental learning, we compared the complete relearning time from the whole sample dataset (i.e., $D_o \cup D_n$) (denoted CT), the influence degree evaluation time (denoted IT) and the subgraph revision time (denoted RT) upon six DataNodes with the increase of D_o (denoted $|D_o|$). In this experiment, we divided each of the initially generated 4 GB, 6 GB, 8 GB, 10 GB and 12 GB sample datasets into two parts including a fixed 1 GB new data and 3 GB, 5 GB, 7 GB, 9 GB and 11 GB original data, respectively. Further, for the 1 GB new data, we replaced each original value by its opposite one of 1, 2, 3 and 4 variables, respectively, corresponding to nodes that will be revised. The comparisons of CT, IT and RT when revising 1, 2, 3 and 4 nodes are shown in Figures 2.16(a)–2.16(d), respectively.

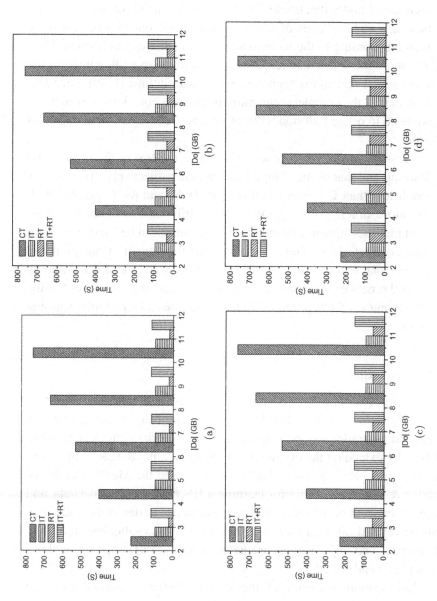

Figure 2.16 Comparisons of CT, IT, RT and IT + RT. (a) 1 node revised. (b) 2 nodes revised. (c) 3 nodes revised. (d) 4 nodes revised.

IT basically keeps a fixed value for all cases in Figure 2.16, since it just depends on the new data size. RT is slightly increased with the increase of nodes that need revision, since it depends on the size of the new data and the times of executing the MapReduce-based scoring & search according to the incremental learning strategy in Section 2.5.3. The more the nodes that need revision, the more execution time for the incremental revision is spent, but the execution time is still much less than that of the complete relearning from the whole dataset even when we need to revise four nodes out of the chest-clinic BN including eight nodes.

(IT + RT) and CT can be looked upon as the cost of the incremental learning and that of the complete relearning respectively. (IT + RT) is much less than CT even when $|D_o|$ is 3 GB, and the larger the $|D_o|$, the more dramatic the execution time difference will be. It can be seen that the efficiency of incremental learning can be 4–6 times faster than complete relearning, which presents the benefit of our proposed incremental revision strategy. Thus, the execution time is decreased by several orders of magnitude by incremental learning, which verifies the effectiveness of our proposed MapReduce-based incremental learning strategy.

2.7 Conclusions

To construct the framework for representing and inferring uncertain knowledge from massive, distributed and dynamically changing data, we presented a parallel and incremental approach for data-intensive learning of BNs by extending the original MDL-based scoring & search algorithm and using MapReduce. Specifically, we presented the MapReduce-based scoring & search algorithm for learning a BN from the massive data, and gave the concept of influence degree of BN nodes to detect the nodes that will be revised, as well as the MapReduce-based evaluation algorithm. Theoretical and experimental results showed that our proposed methods are scalable and effective.

Optimization strategies of the scoring metric evaluation can also be incorporated into our method for further improvement. Study of MapReduce-based parallel and incremental acquisition of uncertain knowledge provides some inspiration for knowledge discovery and management supporting data-intensive computing. As the initial exploration of data-intensive learning of BNs, the presented methods in this chapter also establish some basis for probabilistic inferences of large-scale BN and the association or casual analysis highlighted in realistic big data environments.

Chapter 3

Data-Intensive Inferences of Large-Scale Bayesian Networks

In this chapter, we are to develop the method for data-intensive probabilistic inferences of uncertain knowledge represented by large-scale Bayesian Networks (BNs), which could be learned by the method presented in Chapter 2 from massive data or given corresponding to complex applications. Efficiency highlighted in real applications based on BN inferences makes it challenging due to the exponential complexity with respect to the scale of nodes in directed acyclic graph (DAG) and parameters in conditional probability tables (CPTs). Thus, we give a parallel inference method for computing joint probability distributions with large-scale BNs using MapReduce by extending the classic algorithm for BN's exact inferences. In the method, we adopt the large-scale BN as a massive dataset stored in distributed systems, and consequently transform the concerned steps in BN inferences into data-intensive operations upon the distributed file storage. Then, we give a case study to discover user similarities in social media by the proposed algorithm for data-intensive probabilistic inferences. Experimental results show the efficiency and effectiveness of the proposed method.

3.1 Motivation and Basic Idea

Highlighted in big data analysis, inferences and associations could be addressed by means of Bayesian Network (BN)-based uncertain knowledge representation and inferences from some certain extent. Meanwhile, probabilistic inference is the fundamental task for BN-centered data analysis, intelligent processing, and decision support for complex applications [75, 128, 142]. For example, we can use a BN to represent the dependencies

47

among users in a social network, where nodes and edges stand for users and their similarity relationships respectively. Then, indirect similarities among users could be discovered by means of BN's probabilistic inferences, since the uncertain dependence inductions can be well expressed as conditional or posterior probability computations. Thus, both qualitative user similarities and corresponding quantitative similarity degrees can be achieved.

It is known that BN's exact probabilistic inferences will be fulfilled in exponential time [36, 128], which makes efficient inferences be challenging and paid much attention. To this end, variable elimination was proposed to optimize the exact probabilistic inference algorithm [142], and some approximate algorithms for BN inferences were proposed as well [129]. From the perspective of parallel execution of inference steps, many distributed or parallel algorithms were proposed in recent years. For example, Yang *et al.* [172] gave the distributed algorithm for multi-hop recommendation by BN inferences, and Ma *et al.* [107] proposed the parallel method for evidence propagation in junction trees and BN' exact inferences on multicore using MapReduce. These methods focus on the operations in BN inferences regardless of the scale of BN itself, so will not make sense when confronted to BNs with large-scale nodes and conditional probability tables (CPTs). Thus, these algorithms naturally cannot suit such real world situations as aforementioned similarity discovery in social media.

As mentioned in Chapter 1, large-scale uncertain knowledge repre-sented by BNs is indispensable in the background of big data and group decision for complex applications, which makes it necessary to guarantee the scalability of large-scale BN inferences. For example, massive social media always concern a good many of users that lead to a large-scale BN with a good many of nodes. Thus, it is desirable to develop the scalable mechanism for probabilistic inferences of large-scale BNs to bridge the gap between indispensable requirements of BN-based analysis and incapability of state-of-the-art BN's inference algorithms.

From one hand, to compute joint probability distributions (JPDs) according to the chain rule is the underlying technique of BN's exact inferences, where summation and multiplication of probabilities are two preliminary operations. From the data-intensive computing point of view, we regard a large-scale BN as a massive dataset and make it stored as ⟨key, value⟩ pairs into a distributed file system (DFS). Then, we transform the operations concerned in probabilistic inferences into those on the DFS, and consequently fulfill probabilistic inferences using MapReduce, since summation and multiplication are actually parallelizable aggregation operations upon the distributed storage of BNs [185].

With respect to the BN-based discovery of similarities in social media, we make a case study as well as the application of our proposed inference method into realistic social data analysis. Based on the idea of BN's exact probabilistic inferences, we give the MapReduce-based parallel algorithm for BN inferences to achieve the uncertainty of dependence relationships among users contributed to the degree of user similarity. By considering both BN's graphical properties and probabilistic inferences, we ultimately obtain the indirect similarity degrees between users.

To test the feasibility of our method, we implement the algorithms presented in this chapter and make experiments by adopting the DBLP [47] and Sina Weibo social media datasets upon the Hadoop based platform. Experimental results show the efficiency and effectiveness of our method.

3.2 Parallel Inferences of BN using MapReduce

We first revisit the idea for storing BN in a distributed file system, given in Section 2.4.2. The DAG and corresponding CPTs are stored into a file, denoted as T_{BN}, consisting of logical rows represented as ⟨key, value⟩ pairs in line with the MapReduce-based data-intensive computation, Hadoop like platforms and the specialties of a BN. To reflect the dependence relationships between child and parent nodes, key and value is $(A_i, Pa(A_i))$ and $P(A_i|Pa(A_i))$ respectively, where

- $Pa(A_i)$ denotes the set of parent node(s) of A_i,
- $P(A_i|Pa(A_i))$ denotes the conditional probability of A_i given $Pa(A_i)$.

Example 3.1. Table 3.1 shows the T_{BN} fragment of the BN in Figure 3.1.

Without loss of generality, we use $P(A = 1|X = 1)$ to represent the conditional or posterior probability of $A = 1$ given $X = 1$. For convenience of expression, we call A as target variable and X as evidence variable.

Table 3.1 T_{BN} fragment of the BN in Figure 3.1.

key $= (A_i, Pa(A_i))$	value $= P(A_i|Pa(A_i))$
$A_1 = 1$	0.71
$A_1 = 0$	0.29
$A_2, A_1 = 1, 1$	0.8
$A_2, A_1 = 0, 1$	0.2
$A_2, A_1 = 1, 0$	0.3
$A_2, A_1 = 0, 0$	0.7
$A_4, (A_2 A_3) = 1, (11)$	0.5
$A_4, (A_2 A_3) = 0, (11)$	0.5
$A_4, (A_2 A_3) = 1, (10)$	0.67
$A_4, (A_2 A_3) = 0, (10)$	0.33
$\cdots$	$\cdots$

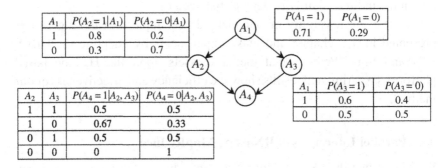

Figure 3.1 A simple BN.

According to the principle of BN's probabilistic inferences, the probability of A conditioned on X is denoted as follows:

$$P(A = 1|X = 1) = \frac{P(A = 1, \quad X = 1)}{P(X = 1)}. \tag{3.1}$$

This means that the computation of $P(A = 1|X = 1)$ can be transformed into that of two marginal probabilities, $P(A = 1, X = 1)$ and $P(X = 1)$, where $P(A = 1, X = 1)$ can be computed by the sum of the JPDs of all possible values of the combination of latent variables in U except A and X. According to the conditional independence relationships described in BN, each JPD can be transformed as the multiplication of a series of conditional probability distributions, which can be obtained by retrieving T_{BN}. $P(X = 1)$ can be obtained analogously. All the required possible values of marginal probabilities will be computed and stored in a distributed file system, denoted as T_{JPD}.

As is pointed out that Markov blanket (MB) of a certain node A, denoted $MB(A)$, in a BN consists of the direct parents, direct children, and the other parents of the direct children [128]. $MB(A)$ describes the "relatives" nodes of A, and it has been proved semantically that the nodes in $MB(A)$ are conditionally independent of other nodes with respect to A. For simplification of probability computation, we use $MB(A)$ to decrease the concerned latent variables while preserving the conditional independence semantics. For example, to compute $P(A_1 = 1|A_2 = 1)$ upon the BN in Figure 3.1, we just consider the latent variable A_3 since $MB(A_1) = \{A_2, A_3\}$, and thus $(A_1 = 1, A_2 = 1, A_3 = 1)$ and $(A_1 = 1, A_2 = 1, A_3 = 0)$ are included in T_{JPD}.

We give the method in Algorithm 3.1 based on MapReduce for probabilistic inferences of large-scale BNs to derive the uncertainty of the dependence relationship between a pair of users. In the algorithm, the map functions are used to find the entries in T_{BN} concerned in the current probabilistic inference task; reduce1 functions are used to obtain the JPD for each possible value of the combination of concerned variables, and reduce2 functions are used to obtain the required marginal probabilities by adding the concerned JPDs.

Example 3.2. Upon the BN in Figure 3.1 and T_{BN} fragment in Table 3.1, we show the probabilistic inference process of $P(A_1 = 1|A_2 = 1)$ by Algorithm 3.1.

(1) According to Eq. (3.1), we know

$$P(A_1 = 1|A_2 = 1) = \frac{P(A_1 = 1, A_2 = 1)}{P(A_2 = 1)}.$$

Meanwhile, $(A_1 = 1, A_2 = 1, A_3 = 1)$ and $(A_1 = 1, A_2 = 1, A_3 = 0)$ are included in T_{JPD}, since $MB(A_1) = \{A_2, A_3\}$.

(2) Taking $P(A_1 = 1, A_2 = 1)$ as example, we compare the records in T_{BN} with those in T_{JPD} respectively. As for $A_1 = 1$, there are two rows in T_{JPD} including $A_1 = 1$. Thus, we can obtain $\langle(A_1 = 1, A_2 = 1, A_3 = 1), 0.71\rangle$ and $\langle(A_1 = 1, A_2 = 1, A_3 = 0), 0.71\rangle$

Algorithm 3.1 Probabilistic inferences of large-scale BNs

Map(*key, value*)
String *key*: File name of T_{BN}
String *value*: Records (i.e., entries) of CPTs in T_{BN}
For each record r in T_{BN} Do
  If *r.key* (i.e., $A_iPa(A_i)$) is in $T_{JPD}.row$ Then
    //Each *row* in T_{JPD} corresponds to a possible value of the combination of
    concerned variables with respect to the MB of the target user node
    Emit $\langle row, P(A_iPa(A_i))\rangle$ //Stored in T_{JPD}
  End If
End For
Reduce1(*key, values*)
String *key*: row in T_{JPD}
Iterator *values*: current list
result ← 1
For each value v in *values* Do
  result ← *result* × *ParseDouble*(v)
End For
Emit $\langle row, result\rangle$
Reduce2(*key, values*)
String *key*: row in T_{JPD}
Iterator *values*: current list
result ← 0
For each value v in *values* Do
  result ← *result*+*ParseDouble*(v)
End For
Emit ⟨row, result⟩

---

by the Map functions in Algorithm 3.1. Analogously, we can obtain $\langle(A_1 = 1, A_2 = 1, A_3 = 1), 0.8\rangle$ and $\langle(A_1 = 1, A_2 = 1, A_3 = 0), 0.8\rangle$ for $(A_2 = 1, A_1 = 1)$, as well as $\langle(A_1 = 1, A_2 = 1, A_3 = 1), 0.6\rangle$ and $\langle(A_1 = 1, A_2 = 1, A_3 = 0), 0.5\rangle$ for $(A_3 = 1, A_1 = 1)$.

(3) By the Reduce1 functions in Algorithm 3.1, we can obtain

$$P(A_1 = 1, A_2 = 1, A_3 = 1) = 0.71 \times 0.8 \times 0.6 = 0.341,$$

$$P(A_1 = 1, A_2 = 1, A_3 = 0) = 0.71 \times 0.8 \times 0.5 = 0.284.$$

(4) By the Reduce2 functions in Algorithm 3.1, we can obtain $P(A_1 = 1,$ $A_2 = 1) = P(A_1 = 1, A_2 = 1, A_3 = 1) + P(A_1 = 1,$ $A_2 = 1, A_3 = 0) = 0.625$. Analogously, we can obtain $P(A_2 = 1)$ and $P(A_1 = 1 | A_2 = 1)$.

3.3 Discovering Similar Users in Social Media Based on BN Inferences

In this section, we make a case study of user similarity discovery in social media using BN's graphical properties and probabilistic inferences given in Algorithm 3.2.

3.3.1 *Problem statement*

User-generated data include social behavioral interactions (e.g., "follow" or "comment" behaviors w.r.t. user blogs or ratings), which reflects user preference, mutual relationship understanding or evolution [19, 71, 131, 135], support product recommendation, link prediction or profitable advertising [85, 112, 147, 160].

In recent years, as one of the important issues of social media analysis, user similarity discovery has been paid much attention and various research findings have been achieved oriented to the applications of user targeting, personalized services, etc. For example, Anderson *et al.* [8] measured the similarity between two users based on that of interests by a distance metric and that of social ties by using a measure of overlap in the evaluated people. Bhattacharyya *et al.* [14] defined the similarity measure between a pair of users by the frequency and relative location of user keywords by combining both network and profile similarities. Crandall *et al.* [39] regarded that users were similar due to their association to the same communities. Kleinberg [89] defined the graph-model based user similarity. Nakatsuji *et al.* [119] defined a user similarity measure based on users' assessments and classes of products. Liu *et al.* [104] decided user similarities by local context and global preference of user behaviors from quantitative ratings. Akcora *et al.* [6] proposed a user similarity measure for online social networks by combining network and profile similarities. Nisgav *et al.* [124] considered similar users if their answers to some queries are mostly identical. Schelter *et al.* [148] gave the scalable similarity-based neighborhood method with MapReduce. Xu *et al.* [171] investigated the potential friendship among users from users' link with friends and their checkins at various positions in mobile social networks, and thus achieved well performance with aggregated features of user similarities. Nillius *et al.* [123] defined a similarity measure between isolated tracks based on BN and associated the identities of isolated tracks by graph constraints and similarity measures. As for specific domains, Ying *et al.* [175] gave the similarity measure in the paradigm of location based services.

In the above methods, user similarities were measured from the results of user behavior execution, by which the users with behavioral similarities can be found. The similarities between two users can be measured locally, but the similarities between them may be actually influenced by several other ones. This means that it is hard to achieve the similarities between any pair of users efficiently.

It is quite intuitive that whether two users in social media are similar or not is generally uncertain instead of either exactly similar or dissimilar, which is more obvious when confronted to large-scale social networks or social behavioral interactions [70]. Actually, user similarities should be represented not only by the assertion that A is similar to B but also the uncertain dependence degree that how much A is similar to B in the universe of all concerned users. More importantly, it is desirable to find indirect similarities between a pair of users without physical connections in social networks.

Social behavioral interactions (e.g., "follow" or "comment" behaviors with respect to user blogs or ratings) directly associated among users, as a special kind of behavioral records, can reflect user similarities straightforwardly. Thus, in this case study, we incorporate BN's mechanisms of uncertainty representation and inferences into the problem of user similarity discovery by adopting BN as the framework for social user modeling and the basis for user similarity discovery. With respect to large-scale social networks, we suppose that a large-scale BN, called user BN and abbreviated as UBN, has been established to represent similarities among users globally, where nodes and directed edges stand for users and corresponding direct similarities, respectively.

Then, we are to induce direct or indirect similarities with similarity degrees between any pair of users to answer the *ad hoc* similarity queries by a unified computing mechanism. In particular, to induce the indirectly similar users to a certain user X, we consider the structural properties of the BN subgraph centered on X, as well as the uncertain dependence degree of possibly similar users to X by the proposed data-intensive algorithm for inferences large-scale BNs in Section 3.2. Then, we combine the two indirect similarity degrees obtained from these two perspectives to obtain the ultimate similarity degree.

3.3.2 *Discovering indirect similar users*

Definition 3.1. A UBN is a pair $G = (G_U, S)$, where

(1) $G_U = (U, E)$ is the DAG of the UBN, and U is the set of nodes (i.e., users) in G_u. Each node in U stands for a user, denoted as A_i and valued 1 or 0, where 1 indicates that A_i is concerned in T, and 0 otherwise. E is the set of directed edges connecting pairs of nodes, which reflect direct similarity relationships among them.

(2) $S = \{P(A_i|Pa(A_i))\}$ is the set of conditional probabilities and consists of the CPT of A_i in G_U, where $Pa(A_i)$ is the set of parent nodes of A_i.

Akcora *et al.* [6] gave the method for measuring user similarities within two-hop distance from the perspective of the graphical structure. Inspired by this idea and the specialties of UBN as a probabilistic graphical model, we consider the range of possible similar users based on the concept of Markov blanket [128]. For user A, we are to determine the user(s) in $MB(A)$ to which A is similar indirectly. Thus, the range of A's similar user is defined by $MB(A)$ like the two-hop distance to reflect both structural and probabilistic semantics.

Let $X \in MB(A)$ be possible similar users to A, we first measure the closeness of the connections between A and X (i.e., the density of the common subgraph affiliated with these two nodes in the UBN $G = (G_U = (U, E), S)$) as the indirect similarity degree from the perspective of UBN's graphical structural properties.

Definition 3.2. The mutually similar subgraph of A and X, abbreviated as $MSG(A, X)$, is $G_M(A, X) = (U_M(A, X), E_M(A, X))$, where

$U_M(A, X) = \mathrm{MB}(A) \cap \mathrm{MB}(X)$, and $E_M(A, X) = \{(x, y)|x, y \in U_M, x, y) \in E\}$.

Analogously, we use $G_S = (\mathrm{MB}(A) \cup \{A\}, E_S(A))$ to denote the subgraph consisted of the nodes in $\mathrm{MB}(A) \cup \{A\}$, where $E_S(A)$ is the set of edges consisted of the nodes in $\mathrm{MB}(A) \cup \{A\}$. Then, the closeness of the connections between A and X is defined by the ratio of the size of $\mathrm{MSG}(A, X)$ to that of G_S as follows:

$$\mathrm{Sim}_S(A, X) = \frac{\log |EM_S(A, X)|}{\log |E_S(A)|}, \quad 0 \le \mathrm{Sim}_S(A, X) \le 1, \quad (3.2)$$

where the size of a subgraph is defined as the number of edges, denoted as $|E_M(A, X)|$ and $|E_S(A)|$ for $\mathrm{MSG}(A, X)$ and $G_S(A)$ respectively, and the logarithm scale is adopted to decrease the possible dramatic difference between $|E_M(A, X)|$ and $|E_S(A)|$.

Intuitively, Eq. (3.2) reflects that the denser the subgraph affiliated with A and X, the closer the relationship of X to A, and thus X is more likely to be similar to A. Following, we give an example to illustrate the above idea.

Example 3.3. We consider a UBN ignoring CPTs, shown in Figure 3.2. First, we can obtain $\mathrm{MB}(A) = \{B, C, D, E, X_1, X_2\}$, $\mathrm{MB}(X_1) = \{A, B, C, F\}$ and $\mathrm{MB}(X_2) = \{A, D, E\}$.

(1) By Definition 3.2, we can obtain $U_M(A, X_1) = \{A, B, C\}$, $E_M(A, X_1) = \{(A, B), (C, B), (A, C)\}$, and $E_S(A) = \{(A, B), (C, B), (A, C), (X_1, B), (C, X_1), (A, D), (A, E), (D, X_2), (X_2, E)\}$. Then, we have $\mathrm{Sim}_S(A, X_1) = \frac{\log |E_M(A, X_1)|}{\log |E_S(A)|} = \frac{\log 3}{\log 9} = 0.5$.

(2) Analogously, we can obtain $E_M(A, X_2) = \{(A, D), (A, E)\}$ and $\mathrm{Sim}_S(A, X_2) = \frac{\log 2}{\log 9} = 0.32$.

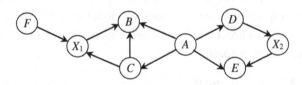

Figure 3.2 An example of UBN.

Thus, X_1 is more similar to A than X_2, which is consistent with people's intuition that the subgraph affiliated to A and X_1 is denser than that to A and X_2.

To obtain $E_M(A, X)$ and $E_S(A)$, we could retrieve the key in T_{UBN} (as T_{BN} in Section 3.2) as follows. If $X \in Pa(A)$, then A is the parent node of X, and thus both the value of $|E_M(A, X)|$ and that of $|E_S(A)|$ will be increased by one. If $X = A$, then each node in $Pa(A)$ is the parent node of A, and thus $|E_M(A, X)|$ and $|E_S(A)|$ will be increased by one. Upon the distributed storage of the UBN, as given in Section 3.2, the above computations for $E_M(A, X)$ and $E_S(A)$ can be fulfilled by map functions, and the number of edges relevant to X can be aggregated by reduce functions.

Then, we use $\text{Sim}_Q(A, X)$ to denote the dependency degree of user X on A. By Algorithm 3.1, $\text{Sim}_Q(A, X)$ could be implemented by UBN's probabilistic inference as follows:

$$\text{Sim}_Q(A, X) = \frac{P(A = 1, X = 1)}{P(X = 1)}, \quad 0 \le \text{Sim}_Q(A, X) \le 1, \quad (3.3)$$

where A is called as target user.

Finally, to achieve the ultimate indirect similarity degree of user X to A, we simply combine the UBN's graphical structure based and probabilistic inference based indirect similarity degrees as follows.

$$\text{Sim}(A, X) = \alpha \text{Sim}_S(A, X) + \beta \text{Sim}_Q(A, X), \quad 0 \le \alpha, \ \beta \le 1, \quad (3.4)$$

where α is the weight of the structure-based indirect similarity and β is that of the probabilistic-inference based indirect similarity.

Following, we mainly discuss the theoretic properties of $\text{Sim}(A, X)$ in Eq. (3.4) to guarantee its effectiveness and applicability as a similarity measure between users. It can be seen that $\text{Sim}_S(A, B)$ may not equal $\text{Sim}_S(B, A)$, and $\text{Sim}_Q(A, B)$ may not equal $\text{Sim}_Q(B, A)$ as well. More importantly, the similarity measure in Eq. (3.4) can provide a comparable basis for finding similar users, since the similarity degree is order-preserving and the specific sequence of similar users can be obtained regardless of the order of users in U. This also verifies the effectiveness of our proposed algorithm for data-intensive probabilistic inferences of large-scale BNs. The above conclusion is given in Theorem 3.1 as follows.

Theorem 3.1. *For any three uses (say A, B, C) in U, we suppose B, $C \in \text{MB}(A)$. If $\text{Sim}(A, B) > \text{Sim}(A, C)$ under $U_1 = \{A, B, C\}$, then $\text{Sim}(A, B) > \text{Sim}(A, C)$ still holds under $U_2 = \{A, C, B\}$.*

Proof. According to Eq. (3.4), we have

$$\text{Sim}(A, B) = \alpha \cdot \text{Sim}_S(A, B) + \beta \cdot \text{Sim}_Q(A, B),$$

$$\text{Sim}(A, C) = \alpha \cdot \text{Sim}_S(A, C) + \beta \cdot \text{Sim}_Q(A, C).$$

According to Eqs. (3.2) and (3.3), we have

$$\text{Sim}(A, B) = \alpha \cdot \frac{\log |E_M(A, B)|}{\log |E_S(A)|} + \beta \cdot P(A = 1|B = 1),$$

$$\text{Sim}(A, C) = \alpha \cdot \frac{\log |E_M(A, C)|}{\log |E_S(A)|} + \beta \cdot P(A = 1|C = 1).$$

B lies before C in U_1, and thus B is a parent or ancestor node of C in the U_{BN}, which means that there exists the substructure $B \to C$ or $B \to \cdots \to C$. If B is a parent of C, then $C \in \text{MB}(B)$ and $B \in \text{MB}(C)$. Analogously, C lies before B in U_2, and thus C is a parent or ancestor node of B in the U_{BN}, which means that there exists the substructure $C \to B$ or $C \to \cdots \to B$. If C is a parent of B, then $B \in \text{MB}(C)$ and $C \in \text{MB}(B)$. This means that $\text{MB}(B)$ and $\text{MB}(C)$ are identical either under U_1 or U_2, and thus $|E_M(A, B)|$ is identical to $|E_M(A, C)|$.

Thus, to prove that $\text{Sim}(A, B) > \text{Sim}(A, C)$ holds under U_1, and then it also holds under U_2, is to prove that $P(A = 1|B = 1) > P(A = 1|C = 1)$ holds under U_1, and then it also holds under U_2. For simplification of discussion and without loss of generality, we consider B as a parent of C under U_1 and C as a parent of B under U_2.

By Eq. (3.1) and under U_1, we have

$$P(A = 1|B = 1) = P(A = 1)P(B = 1|A = 1)P(C = 0|A = 1, B = 1)$$

$$+ P(A = 1)P(B = 1|A = 1)P(C = 1|A = 1, B = 1),$$

$$P(A = 1|C = 1) = P(A = 1)P(B = 0|A = 1)P(C = 1|A = 1, B = 0)$$

$$+ P(A = 1)P(B = 1|A = 1)P(C = 1|A = 1, B = 1).$$

Since $P(A = 1|B = 1) > P(A = 1|C = 1)$, we have

$$P(A = 1)P(B = 1|A = 1)P(C = 0|A = 1, B = 1)$$
$$> P(A = 1)P(B = 0|A = 1)P(C = 1|A = 1, B = 1).$$

That is

$$P(C = 0, A = 1, B = 1)P(A = 1) > P(C = 1, A = 1, B = 1)P(A = 1).$$

Thus, we have

$$P(C = 0, B = 0|A = 1) > P(C = 1, B = 0|A = 1).$$

By Eq. (3.1) and under U_2, we know

$$P(A = 1|B = 1) = P(A = 1)P(B = 1|A = 1, C = 1)P(C = 1|A = 1)$$
$$+ P(A = 1)P(B = 1|A = 1, C = 0)P(C = 0|A = 1),$$

$$P(A = 1|C = 1) = P(A = 1)P(B = 1|A = 1, C = 1)P(C = 1|A = 1)$$
$$+ P(A = 1)P(B = 0|A = 1, C = 0)P(C = 1|A = 1).$$

We know

$$P(B = 1|A = 1, C = 0)P(C = 0|A = 1)$$
$$= \frac{P(B = 1, A = 1, C = 0)}{P(A = 1, C = 0)} \frac{P(C = 0, A = 1)}{P(A = 1)}$$
$$= P(B = 1, C = 0|A = 1).$$

Analogously, we know $P(B = 1|A = 1, C = 1)P(C = 1|A = 1) = P(B = 0, C = 1|A = 1)$. $P(A = 1|B = 1) > P(A = 1|C = 1)$ holds as well under U_2, since $P(C = 0, B = 0|A = 1) > P(C = 1, B = 0|A = 1)$ holds.

Thus, we can conclude that $\text{Sim}(A, B) > \text{Sim}(A, C)$ holds under U_2. $\qquad \square$

3.4 Experimental Results

3.4.1 *Experiment setup*

The experiment platform was established upon Hadoop [165] including six machines with Pentium(R) Dual-Core CPU E5700 @3.00 GHz @3.01 GHz and 2 GB main memory. The HDFS cluster includes one NameNode and six DataNodes, on each of which the version of Hadoop, Linux and Java is 0.20.2, Ubuntu 10.04, and JDK 1.6, respectively. All the codes were written in JAVA. We generated our test data from DBLP datasets [47] that provide bibliographic information related to computer science journals and proceedings in the areas like database, network and machine learning. We carried out experiments on the extracted DBLP dataset containing 1552402 authors with 1.3 GB size to test the efficiency and effectiveness of data-intensive probabilistic inferences of large-scale BNs, as well as the effectiveness of the UBN-based user similarity discovery.[a] Further, we tested the effectiveness of the UBN-based user similarities upon the Sina Weibo social media dataset. In our experiments, the number of map tasks is identical to that of CPUs on each machine by default, and the number of reduce tasks is set to one. The execution time of 16 map and reduce tasks, as well as the algorithm's total execution time is obtained directly from the records of JobTrackers.

3.4.2 *Efficiency of data-intensive inferences of large-scale BNs*

In the experiments, the total execution time of map tasks, reduce tasks and HDFS start-up is called *total time* and abbreviated as TT. The execution time of map tasks and reduce tasks (except that of the HDFS start-up) is called *algorithm time* and abbreviated as AT.

From one hand, the efficiency of Algorithm 3.1 is mainly dependent of the execution of Map and Reduce functions (i.e., AT). From another hand, it is known that the efficiency of BN inferences mainly dependent of the number of nodes in the BN. Thus, to test the efficiency of Algorithm 3.1 for MapReduce-based BN inferences, we recorded AT of the algorithm under various numbers of DataNodes with the increase of BN nodes, shown

---

[a]BN can be constructed from the records of co-author relationships as social behavioral interactions by the methods in [105].

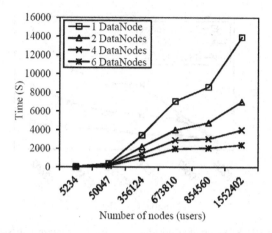

Figure 3.3　AT of Algorithm 3.1 with the increase of BN nodes.

in Figure 3.3. It is straightforward that AT is increased slowly with the increase of BN nodes under various numbers of DataNodes, and the more the DataNodes, the more slowly the increase of AT.

Speedup is defined as the ratio of the time of parallel execution and that of sequential execution, and it is used to measure the times by which the parallel algorithm improves the corresponding sequential algorithm. Parallel efficiency is defined as the ratio of the speedup and the number of processors in the system (referred to as DataNodes in our experiments). Then, under various numbers of DataNodes in the HDFS, we tested the speedup and parallel efficiency of Algorithm 3.1 with the increase of BN nodes, shown in Figures 3.4 and 3.5, respectively. It can be seen that the tendency of the increase of speedup and parallel efficiency of Algorithm 3.1 are similar to those of Algorithm 3.1 with the increase of BN nodes. Under the situation with the same number of DataNodes, the more the nodes, the closer the speedup will be to the ideal situation. When the number of nodes is increased from 5234 to 1552401, the speedup of Algorithm 3.1 is increased from 1.441 to 5.521, close to 6 as the ideal value under six DataNodes. Meanwhile, with the same number of UBN nodes, the more the DataNodes, the larger the speedup, and the speedup is increased from 1.961 to 5.521 when the DataNodes are increased from 2 to 6 with 1552402 BN nodes.

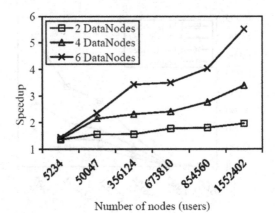

Figure 3.4 Speedup of Algorithm 3.1 with the increase of BN nodes.

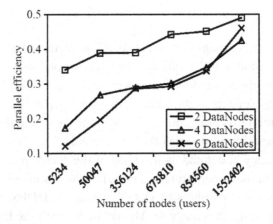

Figure 3.5 Parallel efficiency of Algorithm 3.1 with the increase of BN nodes.

This means that the MapReduce algorithm can be well suitable for the probabilistic inferences of large-scale BNs. Thus, we can conclude that Algorithm 3.1 can be efficiently used for discovering the similarities (similarity search executed for several times) between users upon the constructed BN (BN construction executed just once).

3.4.3 *Effectiveness of data-intensive inferences of large-scale BNs*

To test the effectiveness of Algorithm 3.1 for BN inferences, we compared the results of the user similarities discovered by Algorithm 3.1 and the general BN's inference algorithm [128, 142] with the same BN, as well as the straightforward statistics upon the corresponding social behavioral interactions. By the method given in Chapter 2, we constructed a BN with 100 nodes, and then we randomly chose 10 pairs of nodes to compute the conditional probabilities as described by Eq. (3.1). We obtained the inference result by Algorithm 3.1 and that by Netica [121] (a well-adopted BN inference tool), denoted as I_A and I_N respectively. Meanwhile, we computed the probability from the behavioral interactions by straightforward statistics, denoted as I_{STA}. We used $Error_{A-N}$ and $Error_{A-STA}$ to denote the difference (i.e., absolute of the minus value) between I_A and I_N and that between I_A and I_{STA} respectively. The comparisons are shown in Table 3.2. It can be seen that the maximal, minimal and average value of $Error_{A-N}$ is 1%, 0 and 0.5% respectively. The difference between I_A and I_N derives from the introduction of Markov blanket in Algorithm 3.1 for BN inferences. Meanwhile, the maximal, minimal and average value of $Error_{A-STA}$ is 2%, 0 and 1.2% respectively.

The above results show that the inference results obtained by Algorithm 3.1 are both basically equal to those obtained by the general BN's inference algorithm and quite close to those obtained by straightforward statistics from behavioral interactions. Thus, the algorithms for BN inferences given in this chapter can be effectively used to represent and infer the dependence relationships as well as the corresponding uncertainties,

Table 3.2 Inference results obtained by Algorithm 3.1, general BN's inference algorithm and straightforward statistics.

No. of node pairs	I_A	I_N	I_{STA}	$Error_{A-N}$	$Error_{A-STA}$
#1	0.64	0.64	0.66	0	0.02
#2	0.38	0.384	0.391	0.004	0.011
#3	0.55	0.548	0.53	0.002	0.02
#4	0.91	0.909	0.913	0.001	0.003
#5	0.88	0.861	0.88	0.019	0
#6	0.73	0.728	0.72	0.002	0.01
#7	0.92	0.93	0.895	0.01	0.025
#8	0.81	0.817	0.819	0.007	0.009
#9	0.66	0.66	0.648	0	0.012
#10	0.85	0.855	0.86	0.005	0.01

and finally establish the basic framework for discovering user similarities between social users.

3.4.4 Effectiveness of UBN-based user similarities

To test the effectiveness of the discovered user similarities, we compared the results obtained by our method and those by the known $L1$-Norm [50] and Cosine metrics [143] respectively, defined as follows:

$$L1(A, X) = \frac{|S_A \cap S_X|}{|S_A| \cdot |S_X|}, \quad Cos(A, X) = \frac{|S_A \cap S_X|}{\sqrt{|S_A| \cdot |S_X|}},$$

where S_A and S_X is the set of users directly connected to A and X respectively in the UBN.

Upon the UBN constructed from the DBLP test data by the method in Chapter 2, we randomly chose a target user and 10 possible similar users, denoted as A and $X_1, X_2, \ldots, X_{10}$ respectively, and then computed the similarity degrees of these 10 users to the target user. For each pair of users, we obtained the similarity degrees by Eq. (3.3), those by the above $L1$-Norm and Cosine metrics respectively, shown in Table 3.3.

It is clear in Table 3.3 that the comparable tendency of the similarity degrees of the 10 pairs of users by the 3 metrics is consistent, which means that our UBN-based method is effective from the perspective of discovering user similarities. Furthermore, it can be seen that both $Sim(A, X_7)$ and

Table 3.3 Similarity degrees by UBN-based, $L1$-Norm and Cosine metrics upon DBLP dataset.

	UBN-based	$L1$-Norm	Cosine
$Sim(A, X_1)$	0.686	0.074	0.805
$Sim(A, X_2)$	0.541	0.063	0.626
$Sim(A, X_3)$	0.501	0.062	0.592
$Sim(A, X_4)$	0.474	0.039	0.28
$Sim(A, X_5)$	0.334	0.041	0.263
$Sim(A, X_6)$	0.257	0.039	0.276
$Sim(A, X_7)$	0.128	0.039	0.243
$Sim(A, X_8)$	0.114	0.039	0.243
$Sim(A, X_9)$	0.113	0.031	0.223
$Sim(A, X_{10})$	0.101	0.029	0.171

Table 3.4 Similarity degrees by UBN-based, $L1$-Norm and Cosine metrics upon Sina Weibo dataset.

	UBN-based	$L1$-Norm	Cosine
$\text{Sim}(A, X_1)$	0.534	0.055	0.716
$\text{Sim}(A, X_2)$	0.502	0.052	0.704
$\text{Sim}(A, X_3)$	0.403	0.041	0.625
$\text{Sim}(A, X_4)$	0.338	0.041	0.603
$\text{Sim}(A, X_5)$	0.305	0.036	0.598
$\text{Sim}(A, X_6)$	0.213	0.034	0.483
$\text{Sim}(A, X_7)$	0.211	0.034	0.482
$\text{Sim}(A, X_8)$	0.105	0.021	0.357
$\text{Sim}(A, X_9)$	0.102	0.019	0.357
$\text{Sim}(A, X_{10})$	0.009	0.018	0.231

$\text{Sim}(A, X_8)$ are equal to 0.039 by the $L1$-Norm metric and 0.234 by the Cosine metric, but $\text{Sim}(A, X_7)$ and $\text{Sim}(A, X_8)$ are comparable with different similarity degrees (0.128 and 0.114 respectively) by our method. From this point of view, our method can provide a finer granularity than the $L1$-Norm and Cosine metrics, since the results can also be comparably differentiated by our method even for the equal results by the $L1$-Norm and Cosine metrics.

Further, we constructed the UBN from the 80% Sina Weibo dataset by the method given in Chapter 2. Analogously, we randomly chose a target user and 10 possible similar users, and the similarity degrees obtained by Eq. (3.3), those by $L1$-Norm and Cosine metrics are shown in Table 3.4. The above conclusion on DBLP dataset also holds for discovering similar users in real Sina Weibo social media, which means that our method can be used to discover and rank similar users effectively.

Then, we chose the users (i.e., nodes in the UBN) whose behavioral interactions exist in the left 20% Sina Weibo dataset, and obtained the similar users for each one by straightforward search if there is direct forward/comment/like relationship, denoted as *CS* and called 1-order similarity. At the same time, we obtained the similar users for each one by UBN, $L1$-Norm and Cosine respectively, upon which we tested the recall (the ratio of discovered similar users to those in *CS*) respectively under various numbers of UBN nodes, shown in Figure 3.6. It can be seen

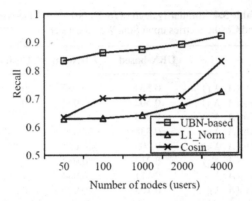

Figure 3.6 Recall by UBN-based, L1-Norm and Cosine metrics under various number of UBN nodes (users).

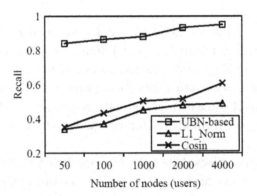

Figure 3.7 2-order recall by UBN-based, L1-Norm and Cosine metrics under various number of UBN nodes (users).

that the recall of our UBN-based method is higher than that by L1-Norm and Cosine metrics, and the more the UBN nodes the higher the recall.

Following, we tested the effectiveness of our method for discovering indirect user similarities by considering recall with respect to the 1-order, 2-order and 3-order similarities. The 2-order *CS* of user A consists of the directly similar users of A(denoted as S_A) and those directly similar to the users in S_A, and the 3-order *CS* can be obtained analogously. We tested the recall of 2-order similarities by UBN, L1-Norm and Cosine, respectively, under various numbers of UBN nodes, shown in Figure 3.7. As well, we tested the recall of 1-order, 2-order and 3-order similarities by

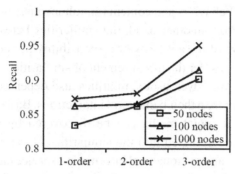

Figure 3.8 1-order, 2-order and 3-order recall by UBN-based metric under various number of UBN nodes (users).

our UBN-based method under various numbers of UBN nodes, shown in Figure 3.8. It can be seen that the 2-order recall of our UBN-based method is much higher than that by $L1$-Norm and Cosine metrics. The larger the order, the larger the difference between the recall of our method and the other 2 metrics. Meanwhile, the larger the order, the larger the recall of our UBN-based method, and this tendency is clearer and clearer with the increase of UBN nodes. This means that our method can make the indirectly similar users discovered effectively, especially for large-scale UBNs.

3.5 Conclusions

To make probabilistic inferences with large-scale BNs, learned from massive data or constructed for complex applications, we presented the data-intensive inference algorithm by adopting the BN as a massive dataset and using MapReduce. As the typical case in real applications, we presented the idea for discovering user similarities in social media based on BN's graphical properties and probabilistic inferences. Theoretic and empirical analysis showed the efficiency and effectiveness of the data-intensive method in this chapter. By our method, user similarities as well as the corresponding uncertainties can be discovered by a finer granularity than the classic methods.

From one hand, the similarities between social users not only depend on the social behavioral interactions but also the contents involved in the interactions (e.g., blogs, comments and paper titles), which makes us consider the user behaviors and contents simultaneously upon the proposal in this chapter. From another hand, the similarities between social users are also dependent of the authority or responsibility of one user on others, which makes us consider the measurement of similarities by incorporating user importance. Moreover, user similarities also depend on users' profile or preference other than their behavioral interactions. Based on our method, user preference in social media can be discovered by a data-intensive mechanism and incorporated into the similarities between relevant users. Then, the accurate and personalized information service can be carried out, such as user targeting, product/advertisement recommendation, and so on.

Chapter 4

Uncertain Knowledge Representation and Inference for Lineage Processing over Uncertain Data

In this chapter, we focus on the representation and processing of lineages over uncertain data, where we adopt Bayesian Network (BN) as the framework of uncertainty representation and inferences. Starting from the lineage expressed as Boolean formulae for Selection–Projection–Join (SPJ) queries over uncertain data, we give a method to transform the lineage expression into directed acyclic graphs (DAGs) equivalently. Specifically, we discuss the corresponding probabilistic semantics and properties to guarantee the correctness of probabilistic inferences theoretically. Then, we propose the function-based method to compute the conditional probability table (CPT) for each node in the DAG. The BN for representing lineage expressions over uncertain data, called lineage BN and abbreviated as LBN, is constructed while generally suitable for both safe and unsafe query plans. Therefore, we give the variable-elimination-based algorithm for LBN's exact inferences to obtain the probabilities of query results, called LBN-based query processing. Then, we focus on obtaining the probabilities of inputs or intermediate tuples conditioned on query results, called LBN-based inference query processing, and give the Gibbs-sampling-based algorithm for LBN's approximate inferences. Experimental results show the efficiency and effectiveness of our methods.

4.1 Motivation and Basic Idea

Real-world data often exhibit uncertainty and impreciseness due to the imperfect nature of data-acquiring devices in many applications, such as sensor data analysis, RFID networks, multimedia databases, location-based services, object identification, data integration, and so on. Uncertain data management is the subject of great interest, concerning modeling, analysis and optimization [2, 3, 43, 190]. In recent years, integration [4], query evaluation [69, 84, 169], analysis and knowledge discovery [41, 88] of uncertain data were widely studied. It is pointed out that [43] probabilistic inference is the most challenging issue in the paradigm of uncertain data management.

Lineage (a.k.a provenance) processing over uncertain data consists in tracing the origin of uncertainties based on the process of data production and evolution. It is an important research issue in the paradigm of uncertain data, and useful for cleansing and quality management, query processing, optimization, integration, assessment and recovery [12, 67, 87]. From the database query point of view, lineages can help users understand where data come from and how they are derived [10, 159]. In particular, lineages over uncertain data can be used to selectively compute confidence values for tuples of query results of interest [41].

Lineages in uncertain data facilitate the correlation and coordination of uncertainty in query results with uncertainty in the input data [12]. The probabilities (i.e., confidence values) of the query results can be computed upon lineage expressions. For example, the confidence of tuple 31 in Example 1 can be easily obtained by its lineage $\lambda(31) = 11 \wedge 21$ and the probabilities of the input tuple 11 and 21.

Example 4.1. Figure 4.1 shows an example of uncertain data and lineages [146], where *prob* represents tuple t's probability under the assumption of tuple independence, and $\lambda(t)$ represents the lineage expression of t.

Attends

ID	Person	Day	Prob
11	Garcia-Molina	Monday	0.8
12	Garcia-Molina	Wednesday	0.7
13	Ullman	Wednesday	0.6

Events

ID	Day	Event	Prob
21	Monday	Reception	0.8
22	Tuesday	Museum	1.0
23	Wednesday	Banquet	0.9

EventRoster = $\pi_{person, event}$ (Attends⋈Events)

ID	Person	Event	Prob	Lineage
31	Garcia-Molina	Reception	0.64	$\lambda(31) = 11 \wedge 21$
32	Garcia-Molina	Banquet	0.63	$\lambda(32) = 12 \wedge 23$
33	Ullman	Banquet	0.54	$\lambda(33) = 13 \wedge 23$

EventAttendees = π_{person}(EventRoster)

ID	Person	Prob	Lineage
41	Garcia-Molina	0.8668	$\lambda(41) = (11 \wedge 21) \vee (12 \wedge 23)$
42	Ullman	0.54	$\lambda(42) = 13 \wedge 23$

Figure 4.1 An example of uncertain data and lineages.

In the methods of lineage processing [136] based on uncertainty-lineage database (ULDB) [146], Boolean formulae were adopted to represent lineages, such as $\lambda(31) = 11 \wedge 21$ in Example 4.1, as the basis for computing desired probabilities. However, Boolean formulae, as the logical representation of knowledge, cannot be used to well describe the complex correlations among data objects and the corresponding uncertainties. Furthermore, the logical inferences on Boolean formulae are always not equivalent to probabilistic inferences [52] that are really critical for lineage processing over uncertain data. Accordingly, the probabilities of query results were derived from the Boolean lineage expressions directly, but the correctness cannot be guaranteed theoretically.

Moreover, lineage-based inference queries, such as $P(11, 12, 23)$ and $P(11|\ 41)$ in Example 4.1, for obtaining the marginal probabilities on given uncertain data objects or posterior conditional probabilities conditioned on the result tuples cannot be answered, since the lineage expressions represented by Boolean formulae cannot provide a general mechanism for probabilistic inferences. Seemingly for the inference queries of conditional probability computation like $P(11|\ 41)$, Koch and Olteanu [90] proposed the method to compute exact confidences and evaluate Boolean condition queries on probabilistic databases by looking upon some prior knowledge (e.g., functional dependencies) as constraints and introducing some heuristics. But the conditional probabilities are computed depending on prior knowledge, and the constraints are actually different from lineages. This makes the inference query like $P(11|\ 41)$ still not solved, since the conditions are specific results of data evolution instead of predefined constraints. This means that the lineage-based inference queries still cannot be answered effectively based on the method in [90]. Therefore, it is desirable to establish an underlying model to support equivalently probabilistic representation of Boolean lineage expressions for SPJ queries over uncertain data and effective probabilistic inferences. Correspondingly, it is also necessary to develop an efficient and general method for lineage processing concerted on probabilistic inferences, especially for the lineage-based inference queries. These two are exactly the problems that we will address in this chapter.

To represent the complex correlations among uncertain objects glob-ally, graphical models were naturally adopted for uncertain data manage-ment and mining [27, 52, 189]. Further focusing on uncertainty other than the representation of qualitative correlations, a special graphical model, called probabilistic graphical model (PGM) can provide a framework for both correlation representation and uncertainty inferences. As one of the popular and important PGMs, Bayesian Network (BN) is the effective and widely used framework for uncertainty representation and inferences by means of qualitative and quantitative manners [128, 132, 142]. BN is a directed acyclic graph (DAG) of random variables as nodes, each of which has a conditional probability table (CPT) to describe the quantitative dependencies among the variables. BN has solid theoretical basis on the probability theory and there have been many effective algorithms for prob-abilistic inferences with BNs. Actually, lineages describe the causalities between input and output [26], which exactly can be represented by a BN. This establishes an effective mechanism for probabilistic inferences and lineage processing intuitively, and exactly the basis of our work in this chapter.

Recently, BN has been adopted in uncertain data management to describe the correlations among uncertain data objects [64, 98, 99, 149, 162]. Meanwhile, the graphical model has also been applied to the man-agement of lineages of workflow and uncertain data [69, 83, 88, 128, 137]. But in these methods on BN-based query evaluation [98, 99, 149] and lineage processing [26, 83, 88, 137], correlations among uncertain data objects or lineage expressions are described or modeled by BNs, and probability computations are simplified by the conditional independencies and implemented by BN's inference algorithms. On the other hand, Pearl [128] has concluded that a DAG can be regarded as a PGM for uncertainty inferences only if this DAG is also a probability model that satisfies the necessary conditions that a graphical model can be looked upon as a probabilistic model. This means that the above methods focus on the BN-based correlation representation and probability computation over uncertain data, but the probabilistic-model-satisfied BN construction and its corresponding probabilistic semantics have not been addressed, that is, the theoretical equivalence between the correlations among uncertain objects concerned in Boolean lineage expressions and those in the corresponding

BN cannot be guaranteed. Then, the effectiveness of probabilistic inferences and the correctness of inference query processing results cannot be guaranteed as well.

Consequently, we [182] previously explored the PGM-based representation of lineages in uncertain data focusing on safe relational SPJ queries. However, the PGM-based representation of lineage expressions of unsafe query plans has not been addressed. From the perspective of lineage representation, it is necessary to extend this method to develop a general PGM-based representation of lineages without regard for the safety of the corresponding SPJ queries. BN's probabilistic inferences were mentioned (e.g., the methods in [128]), but the effective and general algorithm for lineage-based probability computation of SPJ query results or the evaluation of inference queries has not been developed. Therefore, it is also desirable to develop general probabilistic inference algorithms by incorporating the characteristics of lineages in uncertain data.

The above discussions motivate our study on effective and general BN-based lineage representation for both safe and unsafe SPJ query plans, while basically focusing on the DAG's semantic equivalence with the Boolean lineage expressions and its correctness as a probabilistic model theoretically. Meanwhile, the above discussions also motivate our study on efficient and general lineage processing centered on probabilistic inferences. Targeting these two aspects, we will have to address the following two problems:

(1) How to construct a probabilistic-model-satisfied graphical model and ultimately obtain the BN from the given Boolean lineage expressions for SPJ queries over uncertain data?
(2) How to process inference queries of lineages over uncertain data generally and efficiently?

For the problem (1) as the basis of this chapter, we also consider the relational SPJ queries over the given uncertain data as the representative of lineages that will be discussed later. To construct a BN, a DAG and the corresponding CPT for each node will be achieved respectively, for which our ideas are given as follows: To obtain the DAG as the desired BN's graphical structure, we consider transforming the given lineage expressions into the DAG by preserving the conditional independencies implied in the Boolean formulae. This is challenging since the knowledge representation in logical scenario is always not equivalent to that in probabilistic one [128]. The integration of logical and probabilistic knowledge was discussed in [82, 96, 103] generally, but the equivalent transformation from relational operations on databases into PGM still cannot be made effectively from both theoretical and technical perspectives.

It is well known that in mathematical logic, a Horn clause is a disjunction of literals with at most one positive literal. The unique conclusion can be obtained in the Horn-clause-based logical inferences, and Horn clauses can be transformed into equivalent logical implications conveniently [132, 142]. For example, the Horn clause $\overline{11} \vee \overline{21} \vee 31$ is equivalent to the implication $11 \wedge 21 \rightarrow 31$. In line with this basic idea and the equivalent logical transformations of Horn clauses, we are inspired by the proposal in [102], and mainly give the algorithm for transforming the equivalent Horn clauses of the Boolean lineage expression into a DAG as the dependency model, called lineage graph (LG). LG is constructed generally for the lineages corresponding to both safe and unsafe SPJ query plans. Further, we discuss the properties of conditional independency of an LG, and prove that LG satisfies the necessary conditions that a graphical dependency model can be looked upon as a probabilistic model. Therefore, the correlations among uncertain tuples concerned in the lineage expression for either a safe or unsafe SPJ query plan can be described by a PGM, and thus the feasibility of probabilistic inferences in processing lineages can be guaranteed theoretically.

To obtain the CPT for each node in an LG, we consider the idea of function parameters [149, 182], LG's inherent properties and the characteristics of BN's probabilistic inferences. For the nodes without parents, we obtain the CPTs from given uncertain data directly. For those with parents, we define functions that satisfy the Boolean formulae of lineage expressions based on the graphical characteristics and conditional independencies implied in an LG. Accordingly, the BN, called lineage BN (LBN) can be constructed to represent the lineage expressions over the given uncertain data.

For the problem (2), we are to generalize the current methods for both computing the probabilities of query results based on the lineage expressions (case 1), and answering inference queries for computing the marginal probabilities on given uncertain data objects or posterior conditional probabilities conditioned on the result tuple (case 2).

It is known that to compute the probabilities of the query results is frequently #P hard [41, 146]. From the BN-based probabilistic inference point of view, case 1 is the special situation of the case 2. Actually, the execution time of BN's exact inferences is exponential to BN's size (i.e., number of nodes in the BN or that of concerned tuples in the lineage expression) [128, 142]. This motivates us to develop an approximate algorithm of LBN inferences for processing lineages efficiently. Fortunately, Markov Chain Monte Carlo (MCMC) is an effective idea for Bayes computation widely used in recent years, among which Gibbs sampling is a Monte Carlo probabilistic algorithm as the simplest and the most widely used [77, 128, 129]. By this algorithm, sampling is conducted while satisfying a certain conditional probability distribution, and the samples that come from posterior or marginal distributions can be obtained when the iteration times are large enough. Therefore, based on the basic idea of Gibbs sampling and the specialties of lineage processing over uncertain data, we give an algorithm for approximate inferences of the LBN.

To test and verify the methods given in this chapter, we made experiments on benchmark and manual data. Experimental results show the efficiency and effectiveness of our methods.

4.2 Related Work

Gao *et al.* [67] surveyed the underlying techniques of lineage management in database paradigm and pointed out the rationale and challenges of lineage processing over uncertain data. As the basis of many research findings on lineage processing over uncertain data, ULDB (Uncertainty-Lineage Database) [12] is the uncertain database model oriented to lineage processing with respect to relational queries, and forms the basis of the Trio system. Consequently based on ULDB, various methods have been proposed from various perspectives [136, 146]. For example, aiming at large-scaled lineages, Ré and Suciu [136] proposed approximate lineage and the corresponding technique for query processing. Sarma *et al.* [146] proposed the method for computing the probabilities of ULDB query results based on lineage expressions. In these methods, Boolean formulae, a kind of logical description, were used to represent lineages over uncertain data, which are not always equivalent to a probabilistic description highlighted in lineage processing over uncertain data.

It has been pointed out that PGM can be used to describe the correlations or dependencies among data objects. Koller and Friedman [91] introduced the concepts, methods and techniques of PGM. Deshpande and Sarawagi [51] pointed out the important role of PGM in database research. Recently, BN has been adopted in uncertain data management to describe the correlations among uncertain data objects. Friedman *et al.* [64] proposed the method for learning probabilistic relational models (PRM). Wang *et al.* [162] extended the PRM and gave the methods for processing relational queries over probabilistic databases, computing probabilities over probabilistic models and the corresponding query optimization. Sen and Deshpande [149] gave the method for BN-based representation of correlated tuples to avoid the large amount of probability distributions for query results. Lian and Chen [98, 99] gave the BN-based method for representing correlated uncertain data objects and processing the spatial probabilistic nearest neighbor queries by means of BN's probabilistic inferences and optimization.

Meanwhile, the graphical model has also been applied to the management of lineages of workflow and uncertain data. Acar *et al.* [1] extended the previously-developed dataflow language and produced a workflow-style provenance graph that can be explicitly queried. Chapman *et al.* [26] aimed to formally model and compute trust utilizing provenance information, and described a BN-based model of provenance and belief that supports inference about evidence provided by data. Kanagal *et al.* [88] proposed the method for computing the probabilities of large scale lineage expressions over correlated probabilistic databases based on junction trees, which are actually a simple and special case of BN. Jha *et al.* [82] proposed partial lineage, a mixed symbolic/numeric expression used to combine extensional query evaluation with intensional symbolic processing, and proposed a representation of lineage expressions called AND–OR networks that are also a special case of BN. Furthermore, Rekasinas *et al.* [137] gave the approach to increase the efficiency of intensional methods by representing correlations using factor graphs and introducing annotated arithmetic circuits. However, the probabilistic-model-satisfied BN construction and its corresponding probabilistic semantics were not interpreted, so that the correctness of probabilistic inferences cannot be guaranteed theoretically and generally. Meanwhile, the requited BN cannot be constructed by the learning method from data [109], since the classic probability theory may not always hold with respect to the uncertain dataset and efficiency cannot be guaranteed as well.

We [182] previously explored the PGM-based representation of lineages in uncertain data, where we gave the method to transform the Boolean lineage expressions of safe relational SPJ query plans into a PGM and discussed its probabilistic semantics theoretically. However, the PGM-based representation of unsafe query plans has not been addressed.

For the situation concerning logical and probabilistic knowledge, currently logical knowledge was adopted to improve the capability of BN's probabilistic inferences [81], or BN was adopted to improve the capability of the representation of logical knowledge [95]. For fusing logical and probabilistic knowledge, we gave the method for transforming the first-order predicates into the qualitative probabilistic network [102]. However, the equivalent representation from logical expressions to probabilistic ones was not concerned.

4.3   BN-Based Representation of Lineages

As concluded in [149], tuples in uncertain databases are not always independent, and the correlations may be produced in the SPJ queries even when the original tuples are assumed to be independent. In line with this conclusion, we will not assume the tuples are independent as well and consider the situations for general correlations or dependencies among uncertain tuples.

According to the description of uncertain data in [12, 41, 48], we know x-relation is a specific formalism of uncertain database and a good fit for applications of lineage analysis. An x-relation is a multiset of one or more tuples, called alternatives. An x-tuple may be annotated with a '?', in which case it is called a maybe x-tuple. An x-relation represents the set of possible instances that can be constructed as follows: choose exactly one alternative from each x-tuple in the x-relation that is not a maybe x-tuple, and choose zero or one alternative from each x-tuple in the relation that is a maybe x-tuple. Now we first define the uncertain database with lineages based on the concept of x-relation and the tuple-level uncertainty, as the basis of later discussions.

Definition 4.1. By extending the relational model, an uncertain database with lineages, denoted as D, is a triple $(\overline{S}, I(\overline{S}), \lambda)$, where

(1) $\overline{S} = S_1, S_2, \ldots, S_n$ is the set of input base x-relations (i.e., the x-relations not derived from others), where each S_i is a multiset of tuples.
(2) Each tuple in D has a unique identifier and an associated probability that means the confidence of the tuple appearing in D, and $I(\overline{S})$ is the set of all identifiers.
(3) λ is the lineage function represented as Boolean formulae. Let x-relation R be the set of SPJ query results on $\overline{S}$, and let $I(R)$ be the set of identifiers of the tuples in R. $\lambda(t) : I(\overline{S}) \rightarrow I(R)(t \in I(R))$ is defined as the Boolean formula on $\overline{S}$, and $\lambda(t) \rightarrow t$ is called the lineage expression of t.

Note that $\lambda(t) \rightarrow t$ reflects the process to obtain the query result t, and $\lambda(t)$ is a Boolean formula that includes only the tuple identifiers in $I(\overline{S})$ rather than those of the intermediate results. Looking upon tuple identifiers as atomic formulae, 1 (True) and 0 (False), as the value of an atomic formula, represent whether the tuple is included in $\lambda(t) \rightarrow t$ or not.

Example 4.2. For the SPJ queries in Example 1, *EventRoster* $=$ $\pi_{person,event}$ (*Attends* $\bowtie$ *Events*), *EventAttendees* $= \pi_{person}$(*EventRoster*), the lineage expression of result tuple 41 is $(11 \wedge 21) \vee (12 \wedge 23) \rightarrow 41$, where 11, 21, 12 and 23 are the identifiers of the tuples in base relations *Attends* and *Events*.

To construct a BN as the equivalent representation of the lineage expression, the DAG and CPTs should be constructed.

4.3.1 *Deriving dependency model from lineage expressions*

In this section, by transforming the given lineage expression into Horn clauses equivalently, we first define the concepts of lineage dependency model and conditional independence implied in the Horn clauses. Following, as our main proposal, we give the algorithm to transform Horn clauses of the lineage expression into DAGs as the dependency model for concerned uncertain tuples. Finally, we discuss the probabilistic semantics of the constructed DAG theoretically and prove it is a probabilistic model that can be adopted as the graphical structure of a BN.

A Horn clause is a disjunction of literals with at most one positive literal, and can be transformed into equivalent logical implications conveniently [132, 142]. Accordingly, we look upon the tuple identifiers as atomic formulae, whose negatives are also atomic formulae. Then, by the equivalent transformation between logical implications and Horn clauses, we can transform $\lambda(t) \rightarrow t$ into the conjunction of Horn clauses, where the set of Horn clauses corresponding to $\lambda(t) \rightarrow t$ is denoted as $\sum$.

Example 4.3. The lineage expression $(11 \wedge 21) \vee (12 \wedge 23) \rightarrow 41$ can be transformed equivalently as follows: $(11 \wedge 21) \vee (12 \wedge 23) \rightarrow 41 \Leftrightarrow \overline{(11 \wedge 21) \vee (12 \wedge 23)} \vee 41 \Leftrightarrow (\overline{(11 \wedge 21)} \wedge \overline{(12 \wedge 23)}) \vee 41 \Leftrightarrow (\overline{11} \vee \overline{21} \vee 41) \wedge (\overline{12} \vee \overline{23} \vee 41)$ as the conjunction of Horn clauses $(\overline{11} \vee \overline{21} \vee 41)$ and $(\overline{12} \vee \overline{23} \vee 41)$.

To represent the correlations (or dependencies) among uncertain tuples, we are to derive a dependency model, whose general definition is given as follows:

Definition 4.2 [128]. Let U be a finite set of variables, and let X, Y and Z stand for three disjoint subsets of variables in U. Let M be a dependency model as a rule that expresses X is independent of Y given Z, denoted as $\langle X|Z|Y \rangle_M$.

In this chapter, the dependency model with respect to lineages in an uncertain database is called a lineage dependency model, denoted as M_Σ, where atomic formulae in $\sum$ and their logical combinations are looked upon as variables. To represent the lineage expression by M_Σ that reflects the conditional independencies among corresponding variables from the probabilistic semantics perspective of a PGM, we first give the definition of conditional independency implied in Horn clauses.

Definition 4.3 [102]. Let F be the set of atomic formulae in $\sum$. Let X, Y and Z be three disjoint subsets of atomic formulae in $\sum$. X is independent of Y given Z, denoted as $\langle X|Z|Y \rangle_{M_\Sigma}$, $Z = F\backslash(X \cup Y)$, if

(1) there is a set of Horn clauses $CS \subseteq \Sigma$, such that the set of atomic formulae in CS also includes X and Y

(2) and there is no Horn clause C_i in Σ, such that the set of atomic formulae in C_i includes X and Y.

Example 4.4. Suppose $\Sigma = \{C_1 = \overline{A} \vee \overline{B} \vee C, C_2 = \overline{A} \vee D, C_3 = \overline{B} \vee D\}$, and $S' = \{\overline{A}, \overline{B}, C, D\} \subseteq F$. Then, there is $CS = \{C_1, C_2, C_3\}$, such that $X = \{C\}, Y = \{D\}$, and $\{\overline{A}, \overline{B}, C, D\} \supseteq X \cup Y$. There is no any $C_i (i = 1, 2, 3)$, such that the set of atomic formulae in C_i includes X and Y. Therefore, we have $Z = S'\backslash(X \cup Y) = \overline{A} \cup \overline{B}$ and $\langle X|Z|Y \rangle_{M_\Sigma}$, that is $\langle C|\overline{A} \cup \overline{B}|D \rangle_{M_\Sigma}$.

For the lineage expression $A_1 \wedge A_2 \wedge \cdots \wedge A_n \rightarrow B$, it is straightforward to obtain the equivalent Horn clause $C_i = (\overline{A_1} \vee \overline{A_2} \vee \cdots \vee \overline{A_n} \vee B)$, where B is the tuple identifier of the query result, and $A_1 \wedge A_2 \wedge \cdots \wedge A_n$ are those of input uncertain tuples as the basis of the dependencies in C_i. Intuitively, C_i implies $A_1 \wedge A_2 \wedge \cdots \wedge A_n \rightarrow A_i (i = 1, 2, \ldots, n)$ and $A_1 \wedge A_2 \wedge \cdots \wedge A_n \rightarrow B$. Therefore, $C_i = (\overline{A_1} \vee \overline{A_2} \vee \cdots \vee \overline{A_n} \vee B)$ can be transformed into $C_j = (\overline{A_1} \vee \overline{A_2} \vee \cdots \vee \overline{A_n} \vee \overline{A_1 \wedge A_2 \wedge \cdots \wedge A_n} \vee B)$ equivalently, where $\overline{A_1 \wedge A_2 \wedge \cdots \wedge A_n}$ is called the core of C_j, denoted as $Core_j$. For expression convenience, $A_1 A_2, \ldots, A_n$ is used to represent $A_1 \wedge A_2 \wedge \cdots \wedge A_n$. Now we consider constructing a DAG for the lineage expression, as the dependency model specified in Definition 4.2 to represent the implied conditional independencies specified in Definition 4.3.

DAG $G = (V, E)$ of Horn clause C_j is called a lineage graph, abbreviated as LG, where V is the set of nodes and E is the set of directed edges. Each node in G corresponds to an atomic formula or a conjunction of atomic formulae. For two different variables X and Y in V, if $X \rightarrow Y$ is implied in C_j, then there is a directed edge from X to Y. Therefore, each C_j can be transformed into the logically-equivalent DAGs G_1 and G_2, shown as Figures 4.2 (a) and 4.2(b) respectively. But G_1 is not a PGM, since it does not satisfy the conditional independencies and probabilistic semantics of a PGM [128], which will be discussed later. Thus, we construct the LG for each Horn clause as G_2, and then consider combining all LGs of all the Horn clauses to obtain the global model.

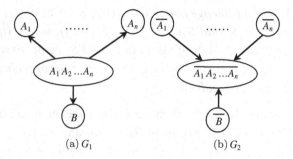

Figure 4.2 Two DAGs corresponding to C_j.

In view of the characteristics of SPJ queries over uncertain databases, safe plans can be evaluated by regular relational plans, and every unsafe query is shown to be #P hard [41, 83]. In unsafe query plans, atomic events are dependent and shared in intermediate results, which will make the LG constructed by the above idea not satisfying the conditional independence in Definition 4.3.

Example 4.5. Considering the lineage expression $(11 \wedge 21) \vee (12 \wedge 23) \rightarrow 41$ including a safe SPJ query $(11 \wedge 21) \vee (12 \wedge 23)$ in Example 2, intermediate results $11 \wedge 21$ and $12 \wedge 23$ include the pairs of tuples in each participating x-relation, and correspond to the two independent cores $\overline{11 \wedge 21}$ and $\overline{12 \wedge 23}$, respectively. Considering the lineage of unsafe query $(12 \wedge 23) \vee (13 \wedge 23) \rightarrow 51$ on the x-relations in Figure 4.1, intermediate results $12 \wedge 23$ and $13 \wedge 23$ that share the common tuple 23, correspond to the two dependent cores $\overline{12 \wedge 23}$ and $\overline{13 \wedge 23}$, respectively.

Currently, the common practice to evaluate unsafe queries is to use intensional techniques [41, 83]. For example, Jha *et al.* [83] proposed partial lineages and introduced symbolic expressions for offending tuples that may lead to unsafety. In this section, we are to achieve a general representation of lineages for both safe and unsafe SPJ queries while preserving the conditional independency as given in Definition 3. Therefore, inspired by the ideas in [83, 182], for each SPJ query we make an equivalent transformation while considering the disjunction of all tuples in the same x-relation as a whole, called composite formula. Theorem 4.1 guarantees the conditional independency of the preprocessed lineage functions.

Theorem 4.1. *For the lineage function* $\vee_{i,j}((t_{i1} \vee \cdots \vee t_{ik}) \wedge (t_{j1} \vee \cdots \vee t_{jl}))$ *of the SPJ query on* S_i *and* $S_j (i \neq j, S_i, S_j \in \overline{S})$, *where* $(t_{i1}, \ldots, t_{ik})$ *and* $(t_{j1}, \ldots, t_{jl})$ *are the sets of tuples in* S_i *and* S_j *respectively, suppose* $x = t_{i1} \vee \cdots \vee t_{ik}$ *and* $y = t_{j1} \vee \cdots \vee t_{jk}$. *Then, any two cores corresponding to* $\vee_{i,j}(x \wedge y)$ *are independent.*

Proof. First, we have $x \cap y = \emptyset$, since x and y are the result of selection from S_i and S_j $(i \neq j)$ respectively. Then, for any $x_1, x_2 \subseteq S_i$ and $y_1, y_2 \subseteq S_j$, we know $x_1 \cap y_1 = \emptyset$, $x_2 \cap y_2 = \emptyset$, since $x_1 \neq x_2$ and $y_1 \neq y_2$. Therefore, any two cores $\overline{x_1 \wedge y_1}$ and $\overline{x_2 \wedge y_2}$ are independent. □

Example 4.6. The lineage of unsafe query $(12 \wedge 23) \vee (13 \wedge 23) \to 51$ in Example 4.5 can be transformed as $(12 \vee 13) \wedge 23 \to 51$, where $12 \vee 13$ is looked upon as an atomic formula. Based on Theorem 1, the lineage expression $(12 \vee 13) \wedge 23 \to 51$ can be further transformed as $\overline{x} \vee \overline{23} \vee 51$ equivalently, where $x = 12 \vee 13$.

It is straightforward that if we always looked upon x as a whole and precomputed its marginal probabilities beforehand based on its Boolean lineage expression, such as $12 \vee 13$, then the lineage processing will still be a problem, since the computation of x's marginal probabilities cannot be made effectively and generally upon a solid theoretical basis. This motivates us to explore the general methodology that can also be applied to composite formulae in unsafe query plans. Actually, composite formulae also imply the general Horn clauses, from which the LGs can also be derived on the atomic formulae of x, given in Theorem 4.2 as follows:

Theorem 4.2. *For any composite formula* $x = x_1 \vee \cdots \vee x_m$, *a directed edge* $x_i \to x$ *for each* x_i $(1 \leq i \leq m)$ *can be derived.*

Proof. It is known that $x = x_1 \vee \cdots \vee x_m$ is equivalent to $\overline{x} = \overline{x_1 \vee \cdots \vee x_m}$. Then, we have $\overline{x_1 \vee \cdots \vee x_m} \to \overline{x_i}$ $(1 \leq i \leq m)$, since

$$\overline{x_i} \vee x_1 \vee \cdots x_i \vee \cdots \vee x_m$$

$$= T \Leftrightarrow x_i \to x_1 \vee \cdots x_i \vee \cdots \vee x_m$$

$$\Leftrightarrow x_i \to \overline{\overline{x_1} \wedge \cdots \wedge \overline{x_i} \wedge \cdots \wedge \overline{x_m}}$$

$$\Leftrightarrow \overline{x_1} \wedge \cdots \wedge \overline{x_i} \wedge \cdots \wedge \overline{x_m} \to \overline{x_i}$$

$$\Leftrightarrow \overline{x_1 \vee \cdots \vee x_m} \to \overline{x_i}$$

Thus, we have $\bar{x} \rightarrow \overline{x_i}$ and $x_i \rightarrow x$ for each x_i, which makes a directed edge from x_i to x exist. □

Actually, x can be looked upon as the tuple identifier of the query result on $x_1, \ldots, x_m$, and the composite formulae can be transformed into DAG structures based on Theorem 4.2. Accordingly, given lineage expressions can be transformed into LG substructures uniformly without regard for the safety of the corresponding SPJ queries. We now give the algorithm for constructing LGs for every Horn clause in $\lambda(t) \rightarrow t$.

Algorithm 4.1 Constructing LGs for each C_i

Input: Lineage expression $\lambda(t) \rightarrow t$
Output: LGs corresponding to C_i
Steps:
1: Initialization:

- $\sum \leftarrow \phi$ // Let Σ denote the set of Horn clauses
- Transform $\lambda(t) \rightarrow t$ into a conjunction of Horn clauses equivalently by satisfying Theorem 4.1
- Transform each $C_i = (\overline{A_1} \vee \overline{A_2} \vee \cdots \vee \overline{A_n} \vee B)$ into $C_j = (\overline{A_1} \vee \overline{A_2} \vee \cdots \vee \overline{A_n} \vee \overline{A_1 \wedge A_2 \wedge \cdots \wedge A_n} \vee B)$ equivalently
- Generate Horn clause $\overline{A_{ij}} \vee A_i$ for each composite formula A_i, and make $\sum \leftarrow \sum \cup \{\overline{A_{ij}} \vee A_i\}$

2: For each Horn clause in $\sum$ Do // Construct LGs

- For each $C_j = (\overline{A_1} \vee \overline{A_2} \vee \cdots \vee \overline{A_n} \vee \overline{A_1 \wedge A_2 \wedge \cdots \wedge A_n} \vee B)$, construct the LG as shown in Figure 4.3(a)
- For each $C_k = (\overline{A_i} \vee B)$, construct the LG as shown in Figure 4.3(b)

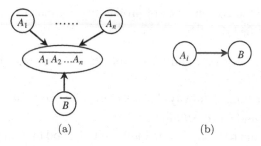

(a)   (b)

Figure 4.3 LGs corresponding to C_j and C_k. (a) LG of C_j, (b) LG of C_k.

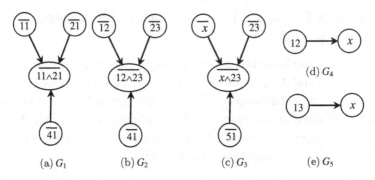

Figure 4.4 LGs corresponding to $\lambda(41) \to 41$ and $\lambda(51) \to 51$.

Example 4.7. For lineage expression $(11 \wedge 21) \vee (12 \wedge 23) \to 41$, the corresponding Horn clauses are $(\overline{11} \vee \overline{21} \vee 41)$ and $(\overline{12} \vee \overline{23} \vee 41)$. By Algorithm 4.1, the LGs can be constructed as Figures 4.4(a) and 4.4(b) (denoted as G_1 and G_2), respectively. Similarly, for lineage expression $(12 \wedge 23) \vee (13 \wedge 23) \to 51$, the corresponding LGs can be constructed as Figures 4.4(c)–4.4(e) (denoted as G_3, G_4 and G_5), respectively.

It is worth noting that the above LGs should be combined, since just the conjunction of all Horn clauses corresponds to the given lineage expression $\lambda(t) \to t$. Note that two kinds of atomic formulae point to the cores of the corresponding LG: the negative of atomic formulae of the input tuple identifier, and that of the query result. As well, all atomic formulae of the input tuple identifiers point to the corresponding composite formula simultaneously. From these two observations, we give the steps for combining LGs by preserving logical equivalence as follows:

(1) Oriented to the convenience of probability computation, for the query result identifier t

 - Replace $\overline{t} \to Core_i$ and $\overline{t} \to Core_j$ by $t \to \overline{Core_i}$ and $t \to \overline{Core_j}$ respectively.
 - Introduce node $\bot$ (always False), $\overline{Core_i}$ and $\overline{Core_j}$, and make $\bot$ point to $\overline{Core_i}$ and $Core_i$ simultaneously.
 - Remove the redundant $\bot$ in multiple LGs, and then make $\bot$ point to all the nodes that are originally pointed by $\bot$.

(2) For the composite formula x

- Remove the redundant x, and make $x_1, \ldots, x_m$ point to x simultaneously.

According to Theorem 4.1, we know that there does not exist $\overline{A_i}$ that points to the cores of C_k and C_l ($k \neq l$) simultaneously. Moreover, both $\perp \rightarrow \overline{Core_i}$ and $\perp \rightarrow Core_i$ are True, since $\perp = \overline{Core_i} \wedge Core_i$ is always False. Therefore, the LGs after combination are logically equivalent to the original ones obtained by Algorithm 1. By the above ideas, we can obtain a global LG ultimately if $\lambda(t)$ includes a safe SPJ query, and obtain several LGs if $\lambda(t)$ includes an unsafe SPJ query, where there is a global LG and one or more LG subgraphs of composite formulae.

Example 4.8. For the LGs in Figure 4.4, the result LG obtained by combining G_1 and G_2 is shown in Figure 4.5(a), and those by combining G_3, G_4 and G_5 are shown in Figure 4.5(b), including a global LG and an LG subgraph for the composite formula.

Now we consider the time complexity of constructing and combining LGs where two x-relations are concerned in the SPJ query. Let $|\sum|$ represent the number of Horn clauses corresponding to the given lineage function $\lambda(t)$, and $|\sum|$ is linear to the number of disjunctions in $\lambda(t) \rightarrow t$. Suppose each Horn clause includes no more than n atomic formulae, and each

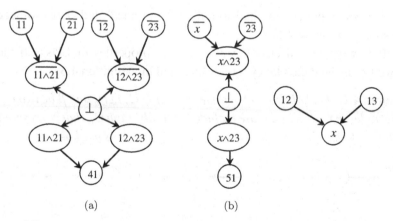

(a)   (b)

Figure 4.5 LGs after combination. (a) Combining G_1 and G_2. (b) Combining G_3, G_4 and G_5.

composite formula includes no more than m atomic formulae. Without regard for the equivalent logical transformation from $\lambda(t) \rightarrow t$ to Horn clauses satisfying Theorem 4.1, the time complexity for LG construction and that for LG combination is $O((m + n)|\sum|)$ and $O(m + |\sum|)$, respectively. In realistic situations, $|\sum|$ is always less than both m and n, and therefore LGs can be constructed and combined almost in linear time with respect to the number of tuples concerned in $\lambda(t) \rightarrow t$.

It is aforementioned that LG can be regarded as a dependency model of the desired PGM, only if it reflects the conditional independencies among the uncertain tuple concerned in $\lambda(t) \rightarrow t$. On the other hand, it is well known that d-separation [128] is the basic concept and criterion for representing conditional independencies among random variables by DAGs, defined as follows:

Definition 4.4. Let X, Y and Z be three disjoint sets of nodes in a DAG G. X and Y are d-separated by Z, denoted as $\langle X|Z|Y \rangle_G$, if and only if every path between X and Y is "blocked", where the term "blocked" means that there is an intermediate variable set V (distinct from X and Y) such that:

(1) the connection through V is "tail-to-tail" or "tail-to-head" and V is instantiated
(2) or the connection through V is "head-to-head" and neither V nor any of V's descendants have received evidence.

The graph patterns of "tail-to-tail", "tail-to-head" and "head-to-head" are shown in Figure 4.6.

Following, we discuss the d-separation properties of LGs and then prove LG is the dependency model specified in Definition 4.3.

Lemma 4.1. *Let U be the set of nodes in an LG G. Let α and β be two non-core nodes in G. If α and β are included in a subgraph G_α that corresponds to some clause $C_i \supseteq \alpha$, then $\langle \alpha|U - \alpha - \beta|\beta \rangle_G$ does not hold.*

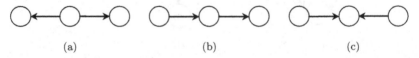

(a)	(b)	(c)

Figure 4.6 Patterns for paths through a node. (a) Tail-to-tail. (b) Tail-to-head. (c) Head-to-head.

Proof. By Algorithm 4.1, we know that there is a path from α to β including the core node $Core_\alpha$ of G_α with converging arrows. By the definition of d-separation, $\langle \alpha | U - \alpha - \beta | \beta \rangle_G$ does not hold, since $Core_\alpha$ is in $U - \alpha - \beta$. $\qquad \square$

Lemma 4.2. *Let U be the set of nodes in an LG G. Let α and β be two non-core nodes in G. If α and β are not included in a subgraph G_α that corresponds to some clause $C_i \supseteq \alpha$, then $\langle \alpha | U - \alpha - \beta | \beta \rangle_G$ holds.*

Proof. By Algorithm 4.1, we can see that every path r_i between α and β has to include $Core_\alpha$ and $Core_\beta$ (or $\perp$), where $Core_\alpha$ and $Core_\beta$ are the core nodes of G_α and G_β respectively.

Case (1): r_i includes $\perp$. Note that $\perp$ is a non-converging node and $\perp \in U - \alpha - \beta$. By Definition 4, r_i is blocked.

Case (2): r_j includes $Core_\alpha$ and $Core_\beta$. There must exist a non-core node θ as a converging node, $\theta \in U - \alpha - \beta$, since $Core_\alpha$ and $Core_\beta$ are not adjacent. By Definition 4, r_i is blocked by $U - \alpha - \beta$. Thus, we have $\langle \alpha | U - \alpha - \beta | \beta \rangle_G$. $\qquad \square$

From Lemmas 4.1 and 4.2, we can conclude that LG is the desired dependency model specified in Definition 3.

Theorem 4.3. *Suppose $\sum$ is the set of Horn clauses for the given lineage expression, F is the set of atomic formulae in $\sum$, and G is an LG corresponding to $\sum$. Let X and Y be two disjoint sets of atomic formulae in $\sum$, and $Z = F \backslash X \cup Y$. Let U be the set of nodes in G. Let $\mathcal{X}, \mathcal{Y}$ and $\mathcal{Z} = U - \mathcal{X} - \mathcal{Y}$ be the disjoint sets of nodes corresponding to X, Y and Z, respectively in Σ. If $\langle \mathcal{X} | \mathcal{Z} | \mathcal{Y} \rangle_G$ holds, then $\langle X | Z | Y \rangle_{M_\sum}$ holds as well. Meanwhile, if $\langle \mathcal{X} | \mathcal{Z} | \mathcal{Y} \rangle_G$ does not hold, then $\langle X | Z | Y \rangle_{M_\sum}$ does not hold as well. That is, $\langle \mathcal{X} | V - \mathcal{X} - \mathcal{Y} | \mathcal{Y} \rangle_G \Leftrightarrow \langle X | F - X - Y | Y \rangle_{M_\sum}$.*

4.3.2 *Probabilistic semantics of the dependency model*

According to the inherence of PGM, a dependency model can be used for probabilistic inferences only if the model is also a probabilistic model. Pearl [128] has proved the necessary conditions that a dependency model should satisfy to be looked upon as a probabilistic model: symmetry, decomposition, weak union, contraction and intersection. Thus, to guarantee the effectiveness of LG-based probabilistic inferences, we now discuss the constraints that LGs satisfy with respect to a probabilistic model.

Theorem 4.4. *Suppose $\sum$ is the set of Horn clauses of the given lineage expression. Let X, Y and Z be three disjoint sets of the atomic formulae in $\sum$. $\langle X|Z|Y \rangle_{M_{\sum}}$ satisfies the following conditions:*

(1) *Symmetry:* $\langle X|Z|Y \rangle_{M_{\sum}} \Leftrightarrow \langle Y|Z|X \rangle_{M_{\sum}}$.
(2) *Decomposition:* $\langle X|Z|Y \cup W \rangle_{M_{\sum}} \Rightarrow \langle X|Z|Y \rangle_{M_{\sum}} \wedge \langle X|Z|W \rangle_{M_{\sum}}$.
(3) *Weak union:* $\langle X|Z|Y \cup W \rangle_{M_{\sum}} \Rightarrow \langle X|Z \cup W|Y \rangle_{M_{\sum}}$.
(4) *Contraction:* $\langle X|Z|Y \rangle_{M_{\sum}} \vee \langle X|Z \cup Y|W \rangle_{M_{\sum}} \Rightarrow \langle X|Z|Y \cup W \rangle_{M_{\sum}}$.
(5) *Intersection:* $\langle X|Z \cup W|Y \rangle_{M_{\sum}} \vee \langle X|Z \cup Y|W \rangle_{M_{\sum}} \Rightarrow \langle X|Z|Y \cup W \rangle_{M_{\sum}}$.

Proof.

(1) Symmetry can be easily proved to be correct from the definition of the independency expression.

(2) Now we suppose $\langle X|Z|Y \cup W \rangle_{M_{\sum}} \in M_{\sum}$. According to Definition 4.3, we know that there are three sets of connected clauses, $F_1 \supseteq X \cup Z$, $F_2 \supseteq Y \cup Z$, $F_3 \supseteq W \cup Z$, but no $C_i \supseteq x, y$ (or $C_i \supseteq x, w$), where x, y and w are the atomic formulas in X, Y and W respectively. Also according to Definition 4.3, if $\langle X|Z|Y \rangle_{M_{\sum}} \in M_{\sum}$ and $\langle X|Z|W \rangle_{M_{\sum}} \in M_{\sum}$, then there are $F_1' \supseteq X \cup Z$, $F_2' \supseteq Y \cup Z$, $F_3' \supseteq W \cup Z$, but no $C_j \supseteq x, y, C_k \supseteq x, w$. Note that there are no such C_i, C_j and C_k in $\sum$, so we know $F_1 = F_1'$, $F_2 = F_2'$ and $F_3 = F_3'$. Therefore, we have $\langle X|Z|Y \cup W \rangle_{M_{\sum}} \Rightarrow \langle X|Z|Y \rangle_{M_{\sum}} \wedge \langle X|Z|W \rangle_{M_{\sum}}$.

(3) From $\langle X|Z|Y \cup W \rangle_{M_{\sum}} \in M_{\sum}$, we know that there are three sets of connected clauses $F_1 \supseteq X \cup Z$, $F_2 \supseteq Z \cup Y$, and $F_3 \supseteq Z \cup W$ in $\sum$, but no $C_i \supseteq x, y$ (or $C_i \supseteq x, w$). According to Definition 4.3, if $\langle X|Z \cup W|Y \rangle_{M_{\sum}} \in M_{\sum}$, then there are two sets of connected clauses $F_1' \supseteq X \cup Z \cup W$ and $F_2' \supseteq Z \cup W \cup Y$ in $\sum$, but no $C_j \supseteq x, y$. Note that if F_1 and F_3 are two sets of connected clauses in $\sum$, then F_1' is a set of connected clauses in $\sum$. If F_2 and F_3 are two sets of connected clauses in $\sum$, then F_2' is a set of connected clauses as well. $\sum$ does not include C_j, since there is no C_i in $\sum$.

Thus, we have $\langle X|Z|Y \cup W \rangle_{M_{\sum}} \Rightarrow \langle X|Z \cup W|Y \rangle_{M_{\sum}}$.

(4) From $\langle X|Z|Y \rangle_{M_{\sum}} \vee \langle X|Z \cup Y|W \rangle \in M_{\sum}$, we know that there are four sets of connected clauses $F_1 \supseteq X \cup Z$, $F_2 \supseteq Y \cup Z$, $F_3 \supseteq X \cup Z \cup Y$

and $F_4 \supseteq Z \cup Y \cup W$ in $\sum$, but no $C_i \supseteq x, y$ and $C_j \supseteq x, w$. According to Definition 4.3, if $\langle X|Z|Y \cup W \rangle_{M_{\sum}} \in M_{\sum}$, then there are two sets of connected clauses $F_1' \supseteq X \cup Z$ and $F_2' \supseteq Z \cup Y \cup W$ in $\sum$, but no $C_k \supseteq x, y$ (or $C_k \supseteq x, w$). Note that $F_1 = F_1'$, $F_4 = F_2'$. $\sum$ does not include C_k, since there are no C_i and C_j in $\sum$. Thus, we have $\langle X|Z|Y \rangle_{M_{\sum}} \vee \langle X|Z \cup Y|W \rangle_{M_{\sum}} \Rightarrow \langle X|Z|Y \cup W \rangle_{M_{\sum}}$.

(5) From $\langle X|Z \cup W|Y \rangle_{M_{\sum}} \vee \langle X|Z \cup Y|W \rangle_{M_{\sum}} \in M_{\sum}$, we know that there are three sets of connected clauses $F_1 \supseteq X \cup Z \cup W$, $F_2 \supseteq Z \cup W \cup Y$ and $F_3 \supseteq X \cup Z \cup Y$ in $\sum$, but no $C_i \supseteq x, y$ and $C_j \supseteq x, w$. Note that $F_1 \supseteq F_1'$, $F_2 = F_2'$. $\sum$ does not include C_k, since there are no C_i and C_j in $\sum$. Thus, we have $\langle X|Z \cup W|Y \rangle_{M_{\sum}} \vee \langle X|Z \cup Y|W \rangle_{M_{\sum}} \Rightarrow \langle X|Z|Y \cup W \rangle_{M_{\sum}}$. $\qquad\square$

We can conclude from Theorem 4.4 that LGs are not only the dependency model but also the probabilistic model of $\sum$, that is, LG can equivalently represent the logical and the probabilistic semantics described by the lineage expression $\lambda(t) \rightarrow t$. Theoretically, this guarantees that LG is the DAG of a BN that can be used for effective probabilistic inferences.

4.3.3 *Computing probability parameters*

To construct the BN ultimately, we now consider computing the CPT for each node in an LG. We note that the nodes in an LG can be classified into two classes: those without parents and those with parents. Actually, the former class of nodes corresponds to the uncertain tuples in the given x-relations, from which we can obtain the CPTs for these nodes directly. For example, $P(\overline{11}) = 0.2$ can be achieved from the uncertain tuples in Figure 4.1. Following, we focus on the CPT computation for the second class of nodes by starting from the properties of an LG in line with the methods for its construction and combination.

Property 1. When combining multiple LG subgraphs of a lineage expression, $\perp$ nodes were introduced to guarantee the logical equivalence. Actually, $\perp$ does not influence the description and probability computation of the SPJ query in $\lambda(t) \rightarrow t$. Thus, we ignore the $\perp$ nodes during CPT computation and probabilistic inferences, and then we look upon the pair

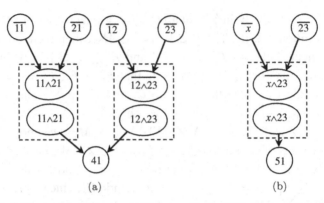

Figure 4.7 LG by ignoring ⊥ nodes. (a) Ignoring ⊥ in the LG in Figure 4.5(a). (b) Ignoring ⊥ in the LG in Figure 4.5(b).

of A and $\overline{A}$ pointed by ⊥ as a whole, since A and $\overline{A}$ describe the same intermediate result from the perspective of query processing.

Example 4.9. The LGs derived from Figures 4.5(a) and 4.5(b) are shown as Figures 4.7(a) and 4.7(b) respectively, where the nodes in the dotted-line rectangle are looked upon as whole.

Property 2. In a global LG, the nodes without parents and that without children correspond to the given uncertain tuples and the SPJ query result respectively. Other nodes in the global LG correspond to the intermediate results and are mutually independent. In an LG's subgraph of a composite formula specified in Theorem 4.2, the node without children corresponds to the result of the disjunctive query. This means that we can compute the CPTs for the intermediate nodes separately, and the idea for CPT computation can work uniformly for the global LG and the LG subgraph(s) of a composite formula.

Property 3. For the SPJ query concerning multiple x-relations, the parent nodes in any LG link their common child node by graphical "head-to-head" manner. The input uncertain data are propagated from the parent nodes to their child node, either as an ultimate or intermediate result, by logical OR constraint on the DAG structure, which is consistent with the Boolean formulae in a lineage expression. This means that any intermediate node will not generate new data or probabilities but only propagate the input uncertain data and corresponding probabilities in the given x-relations.

For example, the LG in Figure 4.7 includes $\overline{11} \vee \overline{21} \rightarrow \overline{11} \wedge \overline{21}$ and $(11 \wedge 21) \vee (12 \wedge 23) \rightarrow 41$. The LG subgraph in Figure 4.5(b) includes $12 \vee 23 \rightarrow x$.

It is known that the probabilistic inferences are conducted based on the probability propagation in line with the BN's DAG and CPT [128]. Furthermore, Sen and Deshpande [149] have discussed the method for computing the parameters of factors in a PGM by considering the logical relations between parents and children. Thus, in view of the principle of belief propagation in PGMs and inspired by the basic idea of factor parameters, the conditional-probability assessments required for the child node are simply the logical OR constraints represented by the Boolean lineage expression. Following, to obtain the CPTs of the nodes with parents, we give the function for propagating the value of parent nodes to their child node.

Definition 4.5. Let A be a node with parent nodes in an LG.

$$P(A = a | \overrightarrow{Pa(A)} = (a_1, a_2, \ldots, a_m)) = f^{OR}_{A,\overrightarrow{Pa(A)}}$$

$$= \begin{cases} 1 & a = a_1 \vee a_2 \vee \cdots \vee a_m \\ 0 & \text{otherwise} \end{cases}$$

is called the probability-parameter function of A, where $\overrightarrow{Pa(A)} = A_1,$ $A_2, \ldots, A_m$ is the set of A's parent nodes, and a and $a_i \in \{0, 1\}(i = 1, 2, \ldots, m)$ is the value of A and A_i respectively.

It should be noted that $P(A | \overrightarrow{Pa(A)})$ is a probability value that equals 1 or 0, which means the probability that the value of A's parent can be propagated to A. Meanwhile, a or a_i is a Boolean value that equals to 1 or 0, which means whether the corresponding uncertain tuple or intermediate result is included. Revisiting the global LG in Figure 4.7 and the LG subgraph in Figure 4.5(b), the CPTs are computed and illustrated as follows.

Example 4.10.

(1) For the global LG in Figure 4.7(a), the CPTs without parents are obtained directly from the given x-relations in Figure 4.1 and shown in Figure 4.8(a). The probability-parameter functions are defined as $f^{OR}_{\overline{11 \wedge 21}, \overline{11}, \overline{21}}(f^{OR}_{11 \wedge 21, \overline{11}, \overline{21}})$, $f^{OR}_{\overline{12 \wedge 23}, \overline{12}, \overline{23}}$ $(f^{OR}_{12 \wedge 23, \overline{12}, \overline{23}})$ and $f^{OR}_{41, 11 \wedge 21, 12 \wedge 23}$ for the intermediate nodes, shown in Figure 4.8(b).

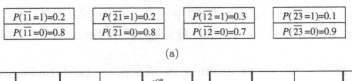

$P(\overline{11}=1)=0.2$	$P(\overline{21}=1)=0.2$	$P(\overline{12}=1)=0.3$	$P(\overline{23}=1)=0.1$
$P(\overline{11}=0)=0.8$	$P(\overline{21}=0)=0.8$	$P(\overline{12}=0)=0.7$	$P(\overline{23}=0)=0.9$

(a)

$\overline{11\wedge21}$ (Boolean)	$11\wedge21$ (Boolean)	$\overline{11}$ (Boolean)	$\overline{21}$ (Boolean)	$f^{OR}_{11\wedge21,\overline{11},\overline{21}}$ (Probability)
0	1	0	0	1
0	1	0	1	0
0	1	1	0	0
0	1	1	1	0
1	0	0	0	0
1	0	0	1	1
1	0	1	0	1
1	0	1	1	1

41 (Boolean)	$11\wedge21$ (Boolean)	$12\wedge23$ (Boolean)	$f^{OR}_{41,11\wedge21,12\wedge23}$ (Probability)
0	0	0	1
0	0	1	0
0	1	0	0
0	1	1	0
1	0	0	0
1	0	1	1
1	1	0	1
1	1	1	1

(b)

$P(12=1)=0.7$	$P(13=1)=0.6$
$P(12=0)=0.3$	$P(13=0)=0.4$

(c)

x (Boolean)	12 (Boolean)	13 (Boolean)	$f^{OR}_{x,12,13}$ (Probability)
0	0	0	1
0	0	1	0
0	1	0	0
0	1	1	0
1	0	0	0
1	0	1	1
1	1	0	1
1	1	1	1

(d)

Figure 4.8 CPTs of the nodes in LGs. (a) CPTs of the nodes without parents in the LG of Figure 4.7(a). (b) CPTs of the nodes with parents in the LG of Figure 4.7(a). (c) CPTs of the nodes without parents in the LG subgraph of Figure 4.5(b). (d) CPTs of the nodes with parents in the LG subgraph of Figure 4.5(b).

(2) For the LG subgraph in Figure 4.5(b) corresponding to a composite formula, the CPTs of the nodes without parents are shown in Figure 4.8(c), and the probability-parameter function of node x, defined as $f^{OR}_{x,12,13}$, is shown in Figure 4.8(d).

To sum up, the CPTs of intermediate nodes in an LG can be computed by Definition 4.5, and thus the desired BN can be constructed ultimately, which we call lineage BN over uncertain data, abbreviated as LBN.

4.4 LBN-Based Lineage Processing

As mentioned in Section 4.1, it is necessary to derive the uncertainty of the result of data production and evolution, and trace the origin of uncertainty during the process of data integration. In this section, pertinent to these two kinds of tasks of lineage processing, we will discuss a general mechanism for probabilistic inferences instead of the Boolean-lineage-expression-based probability computation for the result tuple concentrated by most of the current work [12, 146]. Upon the LBN representation of lineage expressions, we can make full use of the powerful capability of BN's probabilistic inferences to compute the marginal and conditional posterior probability distributions.

4.4.1 *LBN-based query processing*

For the SPJ query over x-relations with lineages, we are to derive the probability of the result tuple by means of marginal probability computation based on the exact probabilistic inferences of LBN. We call this kind of computation as LBN-based query processing to fulfill the same tasks in [12, 149] nevertheless by a general PGM-based probabilistic inference mechanism.

As we know that it is #P complete to compute the probability of the query result directly on the given x-relations. Nevertheless, upon the LBN G of $\lambda(t) \rightarrow t$, the computation of t's marginal probability can be simplified greatly due to the conditional independencies among the concerned uncertain tuples that are described in G. Starting from an example for computing $P(41 = 1)$ and $P(51 = 1)$ with lineage expressions $(11 \wedge 21) \vee (12 \wedge 23) \rightarrow 41$ and $(12 \wedge 23) \vee (13 \wedge 23) \rightarrow 51$, corresponding to a safe and unsafe query plan respectively, we show the basic idea of LBN-based query processing in Example 4.11.

Example 4.11. The x-relations, LBN's DAG and CPTs are given in Figures 4.1, 4.7 and 4.8, respectively. According to the chain rule in probability theory and the conditional independencies in LBN, $P(41 = 1)$ and $P(51 = 1)$ can be computed by the products of conditional probabilities as follows:

(1) $P(41 = 1) = \displaystyle\sum_{\overline{11}} \sum_{\overline{21}} \sum_{\overline{12}} \sum_{\overline{23}} \sum_{\overline{11} \wedge \overline{21}} \sum_{\overline{12} \wedge \overline{23}} P(\overline{11}) \cdot P(\overline{21}) \cdot P(\overline{12})$

$\qquad \cdot P(\overline{23}) \cdot P(\overline{11} \wedge \overline{21} | \overline{11}, \overline{21})$

$\qquad \cdot P(\overline{12} \wedge \overline{23} | \overline{12}, \overline{23}) \cdot P(41 = 1 | 11 \wedge 21, 12 \wedge 23)$

$\qquad = 0.8 \times 0.8 \times 0.7 \times 0.9 \times 1$

$\qquad \times 1 \times 1 + \cdots + 0.8 \times 0.8 \times 0.7 \times 0.1 \times 1 \times 1 \times 1$

$\qquad + \cdots + 0.8 \times 0.8 \times 0.3 \times 0.9 \times 1 \times 1 \times 1 + \cdots + 0.8$

$\qquad \times 0.8 \times 0.3 \times 0.1 \times 1 \times 1 \times 1 + \cdots + 0.8 \times 0.2 \times 0.7$

$\qquad \times 0.9 \times 1 \times 1 \times 1 + \cdots + 0.2 \times 0.8 \times 0.7 \times 0.9 \times 1$

$\qquad \times 1 \times 1 + \cdots + 0.2 \times 0.2 \times 0.7 \times 0.9 \times 1 \times 1 \times 1$

$\qquad = 0.8668,$

where 41 is the observed query variable, $\overline{11}$, $\overline{21}$, $\overline{12}$ and $\overline{23}$ are hidden variables, and we ignore the 0-valued items.

(2) $P(51 = 1) = \displaystyle\sum_{\overline{x}} \sum_{\overline{23}} \sum_{x \wedge 23} P(\overline{x}) \cdot P(\overline{23}) \cdot P(x \wedge 23 | \overline{x}, \overline{23})$

$\qquad \cdot P(51 = 1 | x \wedge 23).$

First, we compute the marginal probabilities of $\overline{x}$ by the probabilistic inferences on the LBN subgraph and CPT of x, shown in Figures 4.5(b) and 4.8(d), respectively.

$\qquad P(\overline{x} = 0) = P(x = 1) = \displaystyle\sum_{12} \sum_{13} P(12) \cdot P(13) \cdot P(x = 1 | 12, 13)$

$\qquad\qquad = 0.7 \times 0.6 \times 1 + 0.3 \times 0.6 \times 1 + 0.7 \times 0.4 \times 1 + 0$

$\qquad\qquad = 0.88 \quad \text{and} \quad P(\overline{x} = 0) = P(x = 1) = 0.12.$

Thus, we have

$$P(51 = 1) = 0.12 \times 0.1 \times 1 \times 0 + 0.12 \times 0.1 \times 0 \times 1 + 0.12$$
$$\times 0.9 \times 1 \times 0 + 0.12 \times 0.9 \times 0 \times 1 + 0.88 \times 0.1$$
$$\times 1 \times 0 + 0.88 \times 0.1 \times 0 \times 0 + 0.88 \times 0.9 \times 0$$
$$\times 0 + 0.88 \times 0.9 \times 1 \times 1 = 0.792.$$

We note that the results of $P(41 = 1)$ and $P(51 = 1)$ in Example 4.11 are exactly the same as those obtained by the method for lineage-based confidence computation [146], which is directly from the Boolean lineage expression under the assumption of tuple independence. This means that the idea of LBN and the corresponding query processing are correct to a great extent. It is worth noting that LBN actually provides a general framework for processing the lineages of both safe and unsafe query plans. For a safe query plan, the marginal probabilities can be computed with the consistent inherence of the method in [146]. More excitedly, for an unsafe query plan, the marginal probabilities of the query result and the intermediate composite formula can also be obtained universally by the mechanism of BN's probabilistic inferences.

Although the computation cost can be reduced due to the conditional independence, the exact-inference-based marginal probability will be still computed in exponential time in general cases. It is known that variable elimination (VE) has been proposed to reduce the computation cost of BN's exact inferences, and it is specifically effective for large scale BNs [142]. As the most common BN's exact inference algorithm, VE eliminates (by integration or summation) the non-observed non-query variables one by one by distributing the sum over the product based on dynamic programming. Therefore, aiming at improving the efficiency of LBN-based query processing, we introduce VE into LBN's exact inferences. Upon the basic idea of general VE, the algorithm for LBN-based query processing is given as follows:

Algorithm 4.2 VE for LBN-based query processing

Input: G: an LBN;

      t: query variable (i.e., result tuple of an SPJ query);

$\overrightarrow{E}$: set of evidence variables (i.e., uncertain tuple identifiers in $\lambda(t)$)

$\overrightarrow{e}$: set of values of $\overrightarrow{E}$

Output: $P(t = 1)$ as the probability of t under $\overrightarrow{E}$

Notations:

Variables (a): returns the variables in a

Parents (x): returns the parents of variable x

Assignments (S): returns all possible value assignments to a set of variables S

$f(v, ftable)$: returns the value in the *ftable* (i.e., the derived CPT by multiplication and summation in computing the joint probability distribution) consistent with the value assignment of v

Steps:

1: Creating f tables as initialization

- *ftables* ← ∅
- For each node y in G Do

  S ← Parents (y)

  Generate a new *ftable*

  For each u in Assignments (S) Do

      $f(u \cup \{y = 1\}, ftable) \leftarrow P(y|u)$

      $f(u \cup \{y = 0\}, ftable) \leftarrow 1 - P(y|u)$

  End For

  Add *ftable* into *ftables*

  End For

2: Eliminating evidence variables

  For each *ftable* in *ftables* Do

  Remove all $f(u, ftable)$ values where u is not consistent with $\overrightarrow{e}$

  Remove Variables ($\overrightarrow{E}$) from *ftable*

  End For

3: Eliminating other variables

  For each y in Variables $(ftables) - \{t\}$ Do

  ytables ← subset of *ftables* that refer to y

  S ← Variables $(ytables) - \{y\}$

  Generating a new *ftable*

  For each u in Assignments (S) Do

      ytrue ← 1; *yfasle* ← 1

      For each *ytable* in *ytables* Do

          ytrue ← *ytrue* * $f(u \cup \{y = 1\}, ytable)$

          yfalse ← *yfalse* * $f(u \cup \{y = 0\}, ytable)$

      End For

$f\ (u, ftable) \leftarrow ytrue + yfalse$
End For
Remove *ytables* from *ftables*
Add *ytable* to *ytables*
End For
4: Computing the result probability

- *ttrue* ← 1; *tfalse* ← 1 // *ttrue* and *tfalse* represent $t = 1$ and $t = 0$ respectively
- For each *ftable* in *ftables* Do
  $ttrue \leftarrow ttrue * f(\{t = 1\}, ftable)$
  $tfalse \leftarrow tfalse * f(\{t = 0\}, ftable)$
  End For
- Return $\frac{ttrue}{ttrue + tfalse}$ // return $P(t = 1)$ after normalization

---

Algorithm 4.2 provides a BN-based method for computing the probability (i.e., confidence) of any SPJ query result over x-relations with lineages, which is more general than the current work directly on the Boolean lineage expressions by *ad hoc* and case-by-case manner [12, 137]. Example 4.12 is given to illustrate the idea of Algorithm 4.2. It is worth noting that Algorithm 4.2 can also be useful for computing the marginal probabilities over any subset of input, intermediate or result tuples, such as $P(11, 12, 23)$ or $P(11, 14)$. In realistic situations, the computation cost of marginal probabilities can be reduced greatly by incorporating VE, which will be tested by experiments in Section 4.5.

Example 4.12. We use Algorithm 4.2 to optimize the exact inference for LBN-based query processing in Example 4.11.

$$P(41 = 1) = \sum_{\overline{11}} \sum_{\overline{21}} \sum_{\overline{12}} \sum_{\overline{23}} \sum_{\overline{11 \wedge 21}} \sum_{\overline{12 \wedge 23}} P(\overline{11}) \cdot P(\overline{21}) \cdot P(\overline{12})$$

$$\cdot P(\overline{23}) \cdot P(\overline{11 \wedge 21} | \overline{11}, \overline{21})$$

$$\cdot P(\overline{12 \wedge 23} | \overline{12}, \overline{23}) \cdot P(41 = 1 | 11 \wedge 21, 12 \wedge 23).$$

Except the observed query variable, all the other variables are hidden and optimized by VE by the order of $\overline{11 \wedge 21}, \overline{12 \wedge 23}, \overline{21}, \overline{23}, \overline{11}$ and $\overline{12}$. Then, we have

$P(41 = 1)$

$\quad = f_{41}(11 \wedge 21, 12 \wedge 23, 41)$

$\qquad \times \sum f_{\overline{11}}(\overline{11}) \sum f_{\overline{21}}(\overline{21}) \underline{\sum f_{\overline{11 \wedge 21}}(\overline{11}, \overline{21}, \overline{11 \wedge 21})}$ (sum)

$\qquad \times \sum f_{\overline{12}}(\overline{12}) \sum f_{\overline{23}}(\overline{23}) \underline{\sum f_{\overline{12 \wedge 23}}(\overline{12}, \overline{23}, \overline{12 \wedge 23})}$

$\quad = f_{41}(11 \wedge 21, 12 \wedge 23, 41)$

$\qquad \times \sum f_{\overline{11}}(\overline{11}) \underline{\sum_{\overline{21}} f_{\overline{21}}(\overline{21}) f_{\overline{11 \wedge 21}}(\overline{11}, \overline{21}, \overline{11 \wedge 21})}$ (product)

$\qquad \times \sum f_{\overline{12}}(\overline{12}) \underline{\sum_{\overline{23}} f_{\overline{23}}(\overline{23}) f_{\overline{12 \wedge 23}}(\overline{12}, \overline{23}, \overline{12 \wedge 23})}$

$\quad = f_{41}(11 \wedge 21, 12 \wedge 23, 41)$

$\qquad \times \sum f_{\overline{11}}(\overline{11}) \underline{f_{\overline{21}, \overline{11 \wedge 21}}(\overline{11}, \overline{21}, \overline{11 \wedge 21})}$ (sum)

$\qquad \times \sum f_{\overline{12}}(\overline{12}) \underline{f_{\overline{23}, \overline{12 \wedge 23}}(\overline{12}, \overline{23}, \overline{12 \wedge 23})}$

$\quad = f_{41}(11 \wedge 21, 12 \wedge 23, 41)$

$\qquad \times \underline{\sum_{\overline{11}} f_{\overline{11}}(\overline{11}) f_{\overline{21}, \overline{11 \wedge 21}}(\overline{11}, \overline{21}, \overline{11 \wedge 21})}$ (product)

$\qquad \times \underline{\sum_{\overline{12}} f_{\overline{12}}(\overline{12}) f_{\overline{23}, \overline{12 \wedge 23}}(\overline{12}, \overline{23}, \overline{12 \wedge 23})}$

$\quad = f_{41}(11 \wedge 21, 12 \wedge 23, 41)$

$\qquad \times \underline{f_{\overline{11}, \overline{21}, \overline{11 \wedge 21}}(\overline{11}, \overline{21}, \overline{11 \wedge 21})}$

$\qquad \times \underline{f_{\overline{12}, \overline{23}, \overline{12 \wedge 23}}(\overline{12}, \overline{23}, \overline{12 \wedge 23})}$ (sum).

By sum and product (underlined) recursively, each factor is computed for once even it will be concerned for multiple times during inferences.

4.4.2 *LBN-based approximate inference query processing*

Inherently, the task of posterior probabilities on a BN is to compute the distribution of a set of random variables conditioned on a set of evidence variables. When it comes to lineage inference query processing, we are to compute the posterior probabilities of input or intermediate tuples under the observation of query results. Specifically in lineage processing over x-relations, it is not trivial to trace the origin of uncertainty during the process of data production, evolution or integration, since the posterior probabilities cannot be computed effectively directly on the Boolean lineage expressions. On the other hand, although VE can also be used for computing conditional and posterior probabilities other than marginal probabilities presented in Algorithm 4.2, it is also not efficient and suitable enough with respect to the LBN-based inference query processing, especially over large scale LBNs. Thus, in view of the high complexity of exact probabilistic inferences and the specialties of lineage processing and posterior probabilities, we will discuss an approximate strategy for LBN inferences in this section.

Gibbs sampling [128, 142] is a Monte Carlo probabilistic algorithm to generate a sequence of samples from a joint probability distribution. By Gibbs sampling, an instance is generated from the distribution of each variable in turn, conditioned on current values of the other variables. The sequence of samples comprises a Markov chain, and the stationary distribution of that Markov chain is just the sought-after joint distribution. Thus, Gibbs sampling is particularly well-adapted to sampling the posterior distribution of a BN, since BN describes the collection of conditional distributions of random variables. This motivates our work for estimating the posterior probabilities approximately for LBN-based inference query processing under the specified conditional distributions among input, intermediate and result uncertain tuples.

In the posterior probability denotation like $P(11|\ 41)$, we call 11 and 41 as query variable and evidence variable, respectively. In each time of making Gibbs sampling, one of the nonevidence variables will be sampled and the random change will be made to the proceeding variables. We look upon an LBN as a particular current state of the joint distribution. The next state will be generated by randomly sampling a value for one of the nonevidence variables, conditioned on the current state. Successive states constitute a series of samples that reflecting the LBN's joint distributions. The main ideas are given as follows:

First, we assign a value to each nonevidence variable randomly and constitute the initial state including those of evidence variables.

Second, we sample one of the nonevidence variables randomly and determine the value of the selected variable from the conditional distribution under the current state. Thus, the new state can be achieved as the basis for next time of sampling. In this process, we adopt Markov blanket [128] to simplify the computation of conditional probabilities. A Markov blanket of a node X, denoted $MB(X)$, in a BN with variable set U is any subset S ($X \neq S$) of nodes for which X is independent of $U - S - X$ given S, that is $MB(X)$ includes the most dependent nodes of X in a BN. Pearl [128, 129] pointed out that in any BN, the union of the following three types of neighbors is sufficient for forming a Markov blanket of X: the direct parents of X, the direct successors of X and all direct parents of X's direct successors. For each sampled variable X, we adopt the conditional probability of X conditioned on the values of $MB(X)$ as that on the current state of the LBN.

We iterate this sampling process until the given threshold number of samples is reached. Then, we can achieve a series of samples, from which the number of each value of the query variable can be counted respectively.

To sum up, Algorithm 4.3 describes the above idea for LBN-based approximate inference query processing.

Example 4.13 is given to illustrate the idea of Algorithm 4.3. It is intuitive that the posterior probability estimation by Algorithm 4.3 is correct only if the sampling results are gradually converged to a certain probabilistic value. Now we discuss the convergence property of Algorithm 4.3.

Algorithm 4.3 LBN-Approximate-Inference

Input:

    G: an LBN with n variables, denoted as $V = (V_1, \ldots, V_n)$, where the value of V_i is 0 or 1, denoted as v_0 and v_1 respectively;

    $\vec{E}$: set of evidence variables (may be input, intermediate or result uncertain tuples);

$\overrightarrow{Z}$: set of nonevidence variables;

t: query variable (may be input or intermediate tuple);

$\overrightarrow{e}$: set of values of $\overrightarrow{E}$, $\overrightarrow{e} = (e_1, \ldots, e_l)$;

m: threshold of total number of samples to be generated

Output: estimate of $P(t|\overrightarrow{e})$

Variables:

  $\overrightarrow{z}$: set of values of $\overrightarrow{Z}$;

  $V_{(-i)} = (V_1, \ldots V_{i-1}, V_{i+1}, \ldots, V_n)$: set of variables except V_i;

  $\overrightarrow{v} = \overrightarrow{e} \cup \overrightarrow{z}$: current state of G;

  $\overrightarrow{N_t(t_i)}(i = 0, 1)$: set of counts of samples where $t = 0$ and $t = 1$

1: Initialization

- $\overrightarrow{z} \leftarrow$ random values of all V_i in $\overrightarrow{Z}$;
  $\overrightarrow{v}^{(0)} \leftarrow \overrightarrow{e} \cup \overrightarrow{z}$; $\overrightarrow{c} \leftarrow \overrightarrow{v}^{(0)}$
  $// \overrightarrow{c}$ is used to denote the current state for expression convenience
- $N_t(t_0) \leftarrow 0$; $N_t(t_1) \leftarrow 0$

2: Generate a sequence of samples

For $k \leftarrow 1$ to m Do

(1) Compute the probabilities of the selected variable over the current state $\overrightarrow{v}^{(k-1)}$

- Select a nonevidence variable V_i from $\overrightarrow{Z}$ randomly
- $B \leftarrow P(V_i = 0|\overrightarrow{c}_{MB(V_i)}) + P(V_i = 1|\overrightarrow{c}_{MB(V_i)})$
  $// \overrightarrow{c}_{MB(V_i)}$ is the set of values of V_i's Markov blanket

(2) Sample V_i from $P(V_i|\overrightarrow{c}_{MB(V_i)})$

- Generate a random value $r_k \in [0, B]$, and then determine the value of V_i:

$$
V_i = v_i = \begin{cases} 0 & r_k \leq P(V_i = 0|\overrightarrow{c}_{MB(V_i)}) \\ 1 & P(V_i = 0|\overrightarrow{c}_{MB(V_i)}) < r_k \leq P(V_i = 0|\overrightarrow{c}_{MB(V_i)}) \\ & \quad + P(V_i = 1|\overrightarrow{c}_{MB(V_i)}) \end{cases}
$$

- $\overrightarrow{v}^{(k)} \leftarrow (\overrightarrow{v}^{(k-1)}_{(-i)}, v_i)$; $\overrightarrow{c} \leftarrow \overrightarrow{v}^{(k)}$

(3) Count $N_t(t_0)$ and $N_t(t_1)$ over the current state

- If $\overrightarrow{c}_t = 0$ Then $// \overrightarrow{c}_t$ is the value of query variable t over the current state $\overrightarrow{c}$

$$
N_t(t_0) \leftarrow N_t(t_0) + 1
$$

Else

$$N_t(t_1) \leftarrow N_t(t_1) + 1$$

End If
End For k

3: Estimate and return $P(t| \overrightarrow{e})$ over the generated series of samples $(\overrightarrow{v}^{(1)}, \ldots, \overrightarrow{v}^{(m)})$

- $P(t = 0| \overrightarrow{e}) = \frac{N_t(t_0)}{m}$; $P(t = 1| \overrightarrow{e}) = \frac{N_t(t_1)}{m}$

Example 4.13. We illustrate the execution of Algorithm 4.3 based on the LBN, whose DAG and CPTs are given in Figures 4.7 and 4.8, respectively. We consider the inference query $P(11|41 = 1)$ (i.e., $P(\overline{11}|41 = 1)$), where the evidence variable 41 is fixed to its observed value, and suppose the initial state $\overrightarrow{v}_{(0)}$ is $(\overline{11} = 1, \overline{21} = 0, \overline{12} = 0, \overline{23} = 0, 11 \wedge 21 = 0, 12 \wedge 23 = 1, 41 = 1)$. The following steps are executed iteratively:

(1) $\overline{21}$ is sampled, given the current value of its Markov blanket, $\text{MB}(\overline{21}) = (\overline{11}, 11 \wedge 21)$. In this case, we can obtain the probabilities when $\overline{21}$ is sampled as 0 and 1 respectively.

$$P(\overline{21} = 0|\overline{11} = 1, 11 \wedge 21 = 0) = P(\overline{11} = 1)P(\overline{21} = 0)$$
$$\times P(11 \wedge 21 = 0|\overline{11} = 1, \overline{21} = 0) = 0.2 \times 0.8 \times 1 = 0.16$$
$$P(\overline{21} = 1|\overline{11} = 1, 11 \wedge 21 = 0) = P(\overline{11} = 1)P(\overline{21} = 1)$$
$$\times P(11 \wedge 21 = 0|\overline{11} = 1, \overline{21} = 1) = 0.2 \times 0.2 \times 1 = 0.04.$$

Suppose $r_1 = 0.18 \in [0, 0.16 + 0.04]$, and then $\overline{21} = 1$, since

$$P(\overline{21} = 0|\overline{11} = 1, 11 \wedge 21 = 0)$$
$$< r_1 < P(\overline{21} = 0|\overline{11} = 1, 11 \wedge 21 = 0)$$
$$+ P(\overline{21} = 1|\overline{11} = 1, 11 \wedge 21 = 0).$$

Therefore, the new state will be

$$\overrightarrow{v}_{(1)} = (\overline{11} = 1, \overline{21} = 1, \overline{12} = 0, \overline{23} = 0,$$
$$11 \wedge 21 = 0, 12 \wedge 23 = 1, 41 = 1).$$

Then, we have $N_{\overline{11}}(\overline{11} = 1) = 1$ and $N_{\overline{11}}(\overline{11} = 0) = 0$.

(2) $\overline{11}$ is sampled, given the current value of its Markov blanket, $MB(\overline{11}) = (\overline{21}, 11 \wedge 21)$. We can obtain

$$P(\overline{11} = 0|\overline{21} = 1, 11 \wedge 21 = 0) = P(\overline{11} = 0)P(\overline{21} = 1)$$
$$\times P(11 \wedge 21 = 0|\overline{11} = 0, \overline{21} = 1) = 0.8 \times 0.2 \times 1 = 0.16$$
$$P(\overline{11} = 1|\overline{21} = 1, 11 \wedge 21 = 0) = P(\overline{11} = 1)P(\overline{21} = 1)$$
$$\times P(11 \wedge 21 = 0|\overline{11} = 1, \overline{21} = 1) = 0.2 \times 0.2 \times 1 = 0.04.$$

Suppose $r_2 = 0.15 \in [0, 0.16 + 0.04]$, and then $\overline{11} = 0$ since $r_1 < P(\overline{11} = 0|\overline{11} = 0, 11 \wedge 21 = 0)$. Therefore, the new state will be $\overrightarrow{v}_{(2)} = (\overline{11} = 0, \overline{21} = 1, \overline{12} = 0, \overline{23} = 0, 11 \wedge 21 = 0, 12 \wedge 23 = 1, 41 = 1)$. Then, we have

$$N_{\overline{11}}(\overline{11} = 1) = 1 \quad \text{and} \quad N_{\overline{11}}(\overline{11} = 0) = 1.$$

The above process will be iterated until the threshold m is reached, and then the series of samples $(\overrightarrow{v}_{(1)}, \ldots, \overrightarrow{v}_{(m)})$ can be achieved. If the process visits 50 samples of $\overline{11} = 1$ and 350 samples of $\overline{11} = 0$, that is

$$N_{\overline{11}}(\overline{11} = 1) = 50 \quad \text{and} \quad N_{\overline{11}}(\overline{11} = 0) = 350.$$

Then,

$$P(11 = 1|41 = 1) = P(\overline{11} = 0|41 = 1) = \frac{350}{400} = 0.875$$
$$\text{and} \quad P(11 = 0|41 = 1) = 0.125$$

which are the answers to the given LBN-based inference query.

Let $P(\overrightarrow{q} \rightarrow \overrightarrow{q'})$ be the probability that the process makes a transition from state $\overrightarrow{q}$ to $\overrightarrow{q'}$. Let $\pi_k(\overrightarrow{q})$ be the probability in state $\overrightarrow{q}$ at time k and $\pi_{k+1}(\overrightarrow{q'})$ be that in state $\overrightarrow{q'}$ at time $k+1$. Given $\pi_k(\overrightarrow{q})$, we can compute $\pi_{k+1}(\overrightarrow{q'})$ by summing:

$$\pi_{k+1}(\overrightarrow{q'}) = \sum_{\overrightarrow{q}} \pi_k(\overrightarrow{q})P(\overrightarrow{q} \rightarrow \overrightarrow{q'}).$$

We say the process has reached its stationary distribution if $\pi_k = \pi_{k+1}$, which means that the sampling process is converged and

$$\pi(\vec{q'}) = \sum_{\vec{q}} \pi(\vec{q}) P(\vec{q} \to \vec{q'})$$

for all $\vec{q'}$.

Fortunately, Russell and Norvig [142] has given the following conclusion to guarantee that the estimate of the posterior probabilities returned by Algorithm 4.3 will converge to the true answer if the total number m of samples is large enough.

Theorem 4.5. *If the following equation holds, then* $\pi(\vec{q'}) = \sum_{\vec{q}} \pi(\vec{q}) P(\vec{q} \to \vec{q'})$:

$$\pi(\vec{q}) P(\vec{q} \to \vec{q'}) = \pi(\vec{q'}) P(\vec{q'} \to \vec{q}) \quad \text{for all } \vec{q} \text{ and } \vec{q'}. \quad \Box$$

Consequently, we know Algorithm 4.3 is consistent with the ordinary Markov Chain Monte Carlo inference, in which the sampling process settles into a dynamic equilibrium. Therefore, the process of executing Algorithm 4.3 can reach the stationary distribution of the variables in an LBN. In view of the generality and inherence of a Monte Carlo probabilistic algorithm, Algorithm 4.3 will obtain more and more exact inference results with the increase of sampling iterations. From Russell's conclusion stated above, we know that the true answers to the LBN-based inference queries will be obtained when convergence is reached. Thus, from the real-world perspective, it is desirable to further consider the efficiency of convergence and the correctness of the inference results to guarantee the effectiveness of Algorithm 4.3, which will be tested by experiments in Section 4.5.

4.5 Experimental Results

4.5.1 *Experiment setup*

To test the methods given in this chapter for BN-based representation and processing of lineages over uncertain data, we implemented the algorithms for LBN construction, LBN-based query processing, and LBN-based inference query processing. The experiment environment is as follows: Intel Pentium (R) Dual-Core 3.00 GHz CPU, 3 GB main memory, running Windows XP Professional operating system. MySQL 5.1 was used to store the uncertain data, LBN and CPTs. All code was written in JAVA.

In the experiments of LBN construction and LBN-based query processing, we adopted the TPCH benchmark [157], where the scale factor was simply set to be 1. We selected two tables, *Orders* and *Lineitems*, abbreviated as O and L respectively, and then we calculated the probability for each different tuple in these two tables. Ultimately, we obtained 30000 and 60000 uncertain tuples respectively in these two tables, denoted $|O| = 30000$ and $|L| = 60000$. Then, by looking upon the join operations as lineages over O and L with tuple-level uncertainties, we obtained the joining result of O and L, denoted OL, including 21000 tuples with uncertainties and lineages. Meanwhile, we adopted the manual Chest-clinic BN [31, 32] in the experiments of LBN's correctness and the effectiveness of LBN-based inference query processing.

In later subsections, we give experimental results and show performance studies from the lineage representation perspective by efficiency of constructing LBNs, space cost of LBNs and correctness of LBN as a PGM, and from the lineage processing perspective by efficiency of LBN-based query processing and effectiveness of LBN-based inference query processing.

4.5.2 *Efficiency of constructing LBNs*

As stated in Section 4.3.1, the efficiency of constructing LBNs is dependent of the number of tuples concerned in the join operation in a lineage expression. To explore the efficiency of constructing LBNs, we first tested the increase of the execution time of LBN construction (including DAG construction and CPT computation) with the increase of total number of concerned tuples both in O and L. By including and excluding the execution time of preprocessing composite formulae (by Theorem 4.2) respectively, two series of the execution times are shown and compared in Figure 4.9, where each execution time was the average of executing five different join operations with the same number of total tuples. It can be seen that the execution time of LBN construction with preprocessing is larger than that

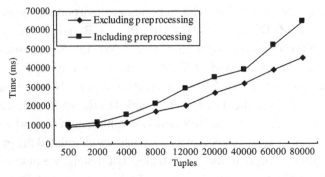

Figure 4.9   Execution time of construction LBNs: including and excluding preprocessing.

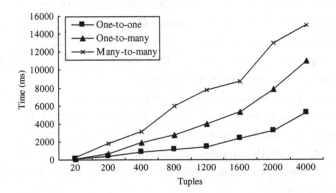

Figure 4.10   Execution time of construction LBNs under different kinds of join operations.

without preprocessing for all cases, but the cost of preprocessing is smaller than that of LBN construction itself after preprocessing. Generally, the execution time of LBN construction is basically linear with the number of concerned tuples, either the preprocessing is included or not. This is consistent with the theoretical conclusion in Section 4.3.1. Thus, LBNs can be constructed efficiently even for unsafe queries corresponding to the lineage function with composite formulae.

We then tested the increase of the execution time of LBN construction including preprocessing with the increase of total number of concerned tuples both in O and L under one-to-one, one-to-many and many-to-many join operations. On 20, 200, 400, . . ., 4000 concerned tuples, three series of execution times are shown and compared in Figure 4.10. It can be seen

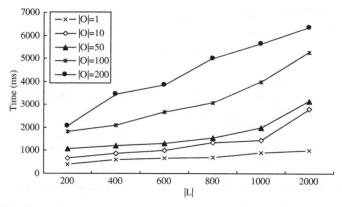

Figure 4.11 Execution time of constructing LBN with different kinds of many-many joins.

that the execution time of LBN construction is increased linearly with the increase of concerned tuples under all these three situations. With the increase of composite formulae corresponding to the cases with sharing tuples in join operations, the execution time is increased accordingly. Specifically for many-to-many join operations, we further tested the execution time of LBN construction including preprocessing when a certain number of tuples in O were joined with different numbers of tuples in L, shown in Figure 4.11. It can be seen that the increase of the execution time of LBN construction is also linear with the increase of the tuples in L under different numbers of the tuples in O. This means that the method for LBN construction is not sensitive to the number of sharing tuples in all possible kinds of join operations. Therefore, we can conclude that LBN can be constructed efficiently and the method is scalable to a great extent.

4.5.3 *Space cost of LBNs*

It is known that the space cost for lineage representation does matter especially for large-scale lineages [132]. For the current work of uncertain data management with lineages [12, 146], we looked upon the total amount of space for storing the Boolean formulae and the probabilities of base tuples as the space cost. For the method given in this chapter, we looked upon the total amount of space for storing the DAG and CPTs of an LBN as the space cost. For the same lineage expression and adopting the text formatted storage, we tested and compared the space costs of these two

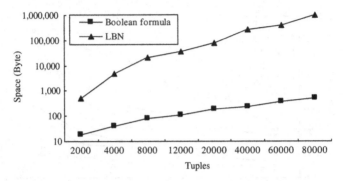

Figure 4.12 Space cost of lineage representation by LBN and Boolean formulae.

kinds of lineage representations with the increase of total tuples, shown in Figure 4.12 (on logarithmic scales). It can be seen that the space cost of LBN is much larger than that of the Boolean formulae with base tuple probabilities by a degree of magnitude, and the more the concerned tuples, the more dramatic the space difference will be. This is reasonable and consistent with the difference of the inherence of these two mechanisms of lineage representation. For LBN, not only the concerned input, intermediate result and ultimate result tuples, but also the DAG and CPTs are included in the storage.

However, LBN establishes a general model or framework in advance for computing probabilities or tracing the origin of uncertainties. Accordingly, it is unnecessary to construct transient and case-by-case underlying models for *ad hoc* queries with respect to a certain process of uncertain data evolution described by the lineage expression. Therefore, LBN construction can be looked upon as the prerequisite of effective lineage processing over uncertain data, and the space cost guarantees the efficiency and scalability.

4.5.4 *Correctness of LBNs*

We start from testing the correctness of the LBN's DAG, as the critical part when constructing a BN. To test the effectiveness of Algorithm 4.1 and the correctness of the obtained DAG, we adopted the Chest-clinic BN (also called Asia network) [31, 32] in the paradigm of uncertainty in artificial intelligence. The Chest-clinic network is a manual and widely-adopted belief network for a fictitious medical domain about whether a patient has tuberculosis, lung cancer or bronchitis, related to their X-ray, dyspnea, visit-to-Asia and smoking status. For expression convenience, we suppose A, B, C, D, E, F and G to represent *Cancer, Tuberculosis, TbOrCa, Smoking, Bronchitis, Dyspnea* and *X-ray*, respectively.

We adopted PowerConstructor [32] to learn the network structure, in which each node has only two possible values (i.e., True or False) described by 1 or 0, respectively. Meanwhile, according to common sense, we derived one of the domain-knowledge fragments of Chest-clinic as follows: $AB \rightarrow C$, $D \rightarrow A$, $D \rightarrow E$, where A means $A = 1$ that we looked upon as the first tuple of the relation of A. Then, the Horn clause was described as $(\overline{A} \vee \overline{B} \vee \overline{AB} \vee C) \wedge (\overline{D} \vee A) \wedge (\overline{D} \vee E)$. By Algorithm 4.1, the lineage graph (LG) can be constructed. Looking upon the Chest-clinic structure learned from sample data by PowerConstructor as the criteria, called criteria graph (CG), which satisfies the probabilistic semantics, we first compared CG and LG on A, B, C, D and E, shown in Figures 4.13(a) and 4.13(b), respectively.

It can be seen that CG and LG are equivalent except those on $\overline{A}$, $\overline{B}$, $\overline{AB}$ and $\overline{C}$, which correspond to the subgraph relevant to the core node $\overline{AB}$ shown in Figure 4.13(b). Theoretically by the concept of d-separation, that $\overline{A}$ and $\overline{B}$ are conditionally independent on $\overline{C}$ holds in both Figures 4.13(a) and 4.13(b). This means that the conditional independencies described in Figures 4.13(a) and 4.13(b) are equivalent, which further means that the constructed LG can represent the conditional independencies and satisfy the probabilistic semantics that are reflected by the CG learned from sample

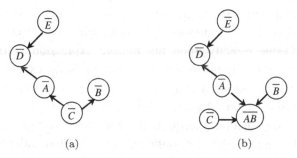

(a)   (b)

Figure 4.13 Comparison of CG and LG. (a) CG learned from sample data. (b) LG constructed by Algorithm 4.1.

data. This verifies that our method for constructing LGs from lineage expressions is feasible to a great extent.

Further, from the practical point of view, we tested the performance of probabilistic inferences on the BN with LG in Figure 4.13(b) by comparing the inference results on that with CG in Figure 4.13(a). We computed their CPTs respectively from sample data in PowerConstructor, and then obtained the inference results based on Netica [121], a widely-used BN inference tool. For the same evidence (including variables and values) and the same query variable, the inference results of some representative cases are shown and compared in Table 4.1, where '×' means that the inference is not concerned.

For each case, we defined the error as the abstract of difference between the two inference results. From Table 4.1, we can easily obtain that the maximal, minimal and average errors of the LG-based inference results are 5.6%, 0 and 2.86%, respectively. This means that the inference results of the BN with LG are basically correct from the practical perspective. Therefore, the correctness of the constructed LBN can be guaranteed both from the DAG that is transformed from the Boolean formulae and from the probabilistic inference that is adopted as the central task for lineage processing over uncertain data.

4.5.5 *Efficiency of LBN-based query processing*

To verify the efficiency of LBN-based query processing by Algorithm 4.2 given in Section 4.4.1, we considered the efficiency for processing the join operations of O and L. For the same join operation that returns one result tuple, we compared the execution time for computing the result probability based on Algorithm 4.2 (denoted LBN-VE) with that for computing the confidence value directly upon the lineage expression [146] (denoted CC). Under different numbers of concerned tuples, the execution time for processing the one-to-many and many-to-many join operations are shown and compared in Figures 4.14(a) and 4.14(b), respectively.

It can be seen that the execution time for LBN-based query processing is almost the same as that for confidence computation under all different numbers of concerned tuples in one-to-one or many-to-many join operations. This means that the LBN-based query processing can be made as

Table 4.1 Inference results of the BNs with LG and CG.

| Evidence | | Inference results of the BN with LG | | | | | Inference results of the BN with CG | | | | |
Variable	Value	$\overline{A}=1$	$\overline{B}=1$	$\overline{C}=1$	$\overline{D}=1$	$\overline{E}=1$	$\overline{A}=1$	$\overline{B}=1$	$\overline{C}=1$	$\overline{D}=1$	$\overline{E}=1$
$\overline{A}$	1	×	0.989	0.935	0.518	×	×	0.998	0.99	0.518	×
$\overline{B}$	1	0.944	×	0.935	0.494	×	0.953	×	0.945	0.498	×
$\overline{C}$	1	0.944	0.989	×	0.494	×	1.0	1.0	×	0.518	×
$\overline{D}$	1	0.989	0.989	0.935	×	0.698	0.989	0.996	0.979	×	0.698
$\overline{E}$	1	×	×	×	0.625	×	×	×	×	0.625	×
$\overline{A}, \overline{B}$	1, 1	×	×	0.935	0.518	×	×	×	0.991	0.518	×
$\overline{A}, \overline{C}$	1, 1	×	0.989	×	0.518	×	×	1.0	×	0.518	×
$\overline{C}, \overline{E}$	1, 1	0.944	0.98	×	0.625	×	1.0	1.0	×	0.654	×
$\overline{B}, \overline{C}, \overline{E}$	1, 1, 1	0.994	×	×	0.625	×	1.0	×	×	0.654	×

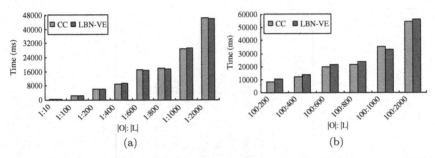

Figure 4.14   Execution time of LBN-based query processing. (a) One-to-many joins of O and L. (b) Many-to-many joins of O and L.

efficiently as the well-accepted lineage-based confidence computation to compute the probability of the result tuple. Thus, the effectiveness and efficiency of Algorithm 4.2 can be guaranteed to some extent, although the exact probabilistic inference algorithm will be fulfilled generally in exponential time.

4.5.6   *Effectiveness of LBN-based inference query processing*

To test the effectiveness of the method for LBN-based approximate inference query processing given in this chapter, we first tested the convergence property of Algorithm 4.3 with the increase of samples from the practical perspective, other than the theoretical analysis in Section 4.4.2.

On one hand, we manually adopted the LBN with 7 nodes, whose DAG and CPTs are shown as Figures 4.7 and 4.8, respectively. The result posterior probabilities of four representative query variables, 11, 21, 12 and 23, are shown and compared in Figure 4.15. It can be seen that the results of LBN's approximate inferences are converged to a relatively fixed probabilistic value for each query variable with the increase of sampling times. All these four posterior probabilities are basically converged when 3200 samples are generated, which means that the convergence can be achieved after finite iterations that can be generally accepted.

On the other hand, we adopted four LBNs with different numbers of nodes, all of which contain 11 (or $\overline{11}$) and 41 (or $\overline{41}$). In Figure 4.16, we give and compare the results of the same inference query $P(11=1|41=1)$ on these LBNs, respectively. It can be seen that each of the four series of LBN-based inference results has converged to a relatively fixed probabilistic value when

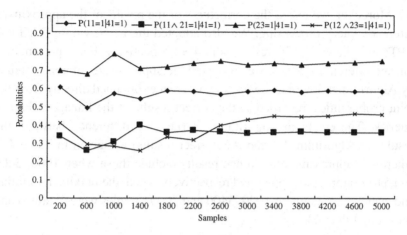

Figure 4.15 Convergence of Algorithm 4.3 in different posterior probabilities.

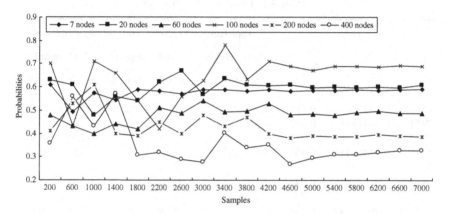

Figure 4.16 Convergence of Algorithm 4.3 on different sized LBNs.

less than 5400 samples are generated. Meanwhile, the more the nodes in an LBN, the slower the convergence of the inference results will be. However, the increase of LBN nodes will not sensitively influence the increase of samples generated for achieving convergence, since only 5400 samples are necessary even for the LBN with 400 nodes.

Therefore, we conclude that Algorithm 4.3 for LBN-based approximate inference query processing is efficient, since the convergence can be obtained efficiently for various posterior probability inference tasks or on various sizes of LBNs.

Moreover, we tested the correctness of the results of the approximate inference query processing. We also adopted the LBN, whose DAG and CPTs are shown in Figures 4.7 and 4.8, respectively. For representative lineage inference queries, we compared the approximate inference results by Algorithm 4.3 with those of exact inferences obtained directly from the joint probabilities, regarded as the correct results of the lineage inference queries. The errors of Algorithm 4.3 (i.e., the difference between the results of Algorithm 4.3 and the correct results) are given in Table 4.2, where the approximate inference results include those when 1000, 3400 and 5400 samples are generated respectively. Then, the maximal, minimal and average errors under 1000, 3400 and 5000 samples were obtained and shown in Table 4.3.

Table 4.2 Errors of Algorithm 4.3.

| Inference query | Exact inference result | Approximate inference result by Algorithm 4.3 | | | | | |
| | | 1000 samples | | 3400 samples | | 5400 samples | |
		Result	Error (%)	Result	Error (%)	Result	Error (%)
$P(11=1 \mid 41=1)$	0.586	0.573	1.3	0.592	0.6	0.585	0.1
$P(11.\wedge 21=1 \mid 41=1)$	0.362	0.34	2.2	0.37	0.8	0.36	0.2
$P(23=1 \mid 41=1)$	0.751	0.72	3.1	0.73	2.1	0.739	1.2
$P(12.\wedge 23=1 \mid 41=1)$	0.45	0.474	2.4	0.429	2.1	0.46	1
$P(11=1, 21=0 \mid 41=1)$	0.209	0.129	8	0.15	5.9	0.163	4.6
$P(11=0, 12=1 \mid 41=1)$	0.276	0.249	2.7	0.262	1.4	0.265	1.1
$P(11=0, 23=1 \mid 41=1)$	0.43	0.424	0.6	0.419	1.1	0.421	0.9
$P(11=1, 23=0 \mid 41=1)$	0.285	0.286	0.1	0.286	0.1	0.285	0
$P(11=1, 21=1, 23=1 \mid 41=1)$	0.349	0.329	2	0.331	1.8	0.332	1.7
$P(11=1, 12=0, 21=1 \mid 41=1)$	0.34	0.37	3	0.334	0.6	0.341	0.1

Table 4.3 Maximal, minimal and average errors.

Samples	Maximal error (%)	Minimal error (%)	Average error (%)
000	8	0.1	2.54
3400	5.9	0.1	1.65
5000	4.6	0	1.09

It can be seen from Tables 4.2 and 4.3 that the more the samples, the smaller the error will be, which is consistent with the inherence of Gibbs sampling. Specifically, the maximal errors of executing Algorithm 4.3 are less than 10% even under the smallest samples. The proportions of the inferences corresponding to more samples and larger errors are 10% and 0% for 3400 and 5000 samples, respectively. This means that Algorithm 4.3 is correct from the perspective of lineage processing.

Therefore, we conclude that the result of LBN-based approximate lineage inference query processing can be converged efficiently to a correct answer, that is, Algorithm 4.3 is effective for approximate LBN-based inference query processing.

4.6 Conclusions

In this chapter, we presented a general and theoretically correct framework for lineage representation and processing over uncertain data. LBN can provide a uniform computational model to obtain the probabilities of lineage-based query results and trace the origin of uncertainties in data evolution. By providing the effective graphical representation and probabilistic inferences, our methods can establish the basis for error detection, experiment reproduction, data integration, etc. Meanwhile, the methods given in this chapter can be used for tracing errors during the data generation or evolution process, and criminal suspect evaluation upon the witness and factual records.

It is worth noting that the method for transforming the Boolean formula lineage expressions into probabilistic graphical models actually provides a valuable idea for fusing logical and probabilistic knowledge, which is important and challenging in the paradigms of knowledge engineering and artificial intelligence.

Consequently, BN-based mechanisms for consistent combination of multiple relative lineage expressions and corresponding probabilistic inferences could be considered upon the algorithms presented in this chapter, since the realistic process of data evolution always includes several subtasks with inherent dependencies. Furthermore, the quality of uncertain data can be explored by incorporating lineages and BNs, including representation and inferences of the influence or coverage of problematic data, which will be discussed in Chapter 5.

Chapter 5

Uncertain Knowledge Representation and Inference for Tracing Errors in Uncertain Data

Data in probabilistic databases may not be absolutely correct, and worse, may be erroneous. Many existing data cleaning methods can be used to detect errors in traditional databases, but they fall short of guiding us to find errors in probabilistic databases, especially for databases with complex correlations among data. In this chapter, we give a method for tracing errors in probabilistic databases by adopting Bayesian Network (BN) as the framework of representing the correlations among data. We first develop the techniques to construct an augmented Bayesian Network (ABN) for an anomalous query to represent correlations among input data, intermediate data and output data in the query execution. Inspired by the notion of blame in causal models, we then define a notion of blame for ranking candidate errors. Next, we provide an efficient method for computing the degree of blame for each candidate error based on the probabilistic inference upon the ABN. Experimental results show the effectiveness and efficiency of our method.

5.1 Motivation and Basic Idea

Many real world applications, such as information extraction, data integration, sensor networks and object recognition etc., are producing large volumes of uncertain data [3, 156]. It is critical for such applications to effectively manage and query the uncertain data, motivating the research on probabilistic databases (PDBs) [20, 45, 83, 86, 137].

In practice, PDBs often contain errors since the data of these databases has been collected by a great deal of human effort through the consultation, verification and aggregation of existing sources. It could be worse when using the Web to extract and integrate data from diverse sources on an unprecedented scale, which the risks of creating and propagating data errors increased [20, 59, 103, 117]. Consequently, a user may detect an anomalous query: (1) some of the probabilities of the result tuples are erroneous; and (2) the tuples contributed to the incorrect output are to be found in the database. To guarantee the data quality, it is necessary to trace the errors in the input data and prevent the errors from propagating to other queries. This can be viewed as a strategy of data cleaning for improving the data quality.

For an anomalous query, it is easy to detect errors in the output by comparing the output values with the given ground truth values. This means that there are errors in the input data, but we do not know which one is not correct, and only know the output is erroneous. In this chapter, we show how to trace errors in PDBs given an anomalous query.

The first step of error tracing is to find out the input data that is related to the output data. Provenance or lineage has been studied recently to describe how individual output data is derived from a certain subset of input data, so it is natural to use lineage to trace all the input data helped to produce the surprising output data [117]. Meliou *et al.* [114, 115] proposed a method to find the causes for surprising queries and the first step is the computation of the query's lineage. However, most of current lineage-based methods make simplistic assumptions about the data (e.g., complete independence among tuples), which makes this kind of methods difficult to be used in real applications that naturally produce correlated data.

It is well known that Bayesian Network (BN) is an effective framework of representing dependencies among random variables [46, 128]. A BN is a directed acyclic graph (DAG), where nodes represent random variables and edges represent dependencies among variables. Each variable in a BN is associated with a conditional probability table (CPT) to give the probability of each state when given the states of its parents. Sen and Deshpande [149] provided a BN based framework that can represent probabilistic tuples and correlations. The query processing problem on this framework is casted as a probabilistic inference problem in an appropriately constructed BN. This means that the correlations among output and input data with respect to a certain query can be represented by a BN. Comparing with the lineage-based methods, this framework can describe not only how the output data is derived from input data, but also the correlations among input data. Therefore, we adopt BN as our underlying framework for probabilistic databases and construct an augmented Bayesian network (ABN) for the anomalous query to trace errors.

A query may involve large volume of input data, which is overwhelming to users. Thus, it is necessary to rank the errors in input data by their degree of contributions to output data. The notion of responsibility is first developed by Chockler and Halpern [35] to measure the degree of contributions of a cause to a result event in causal models when everything relevant about the facts of the world is known (i.e., the context is given). Meliou *et al.* [114, 115] find causes for surprising queries by ranking candidate errors according to their responsibility after examining the lineage of the query. But the method is hampered to be carried on PDBs by two limitations: (1) the context for queries in PDBs is uncertain; and (2) the lineage cannot represent correlations among data in PDBs.

Fortunately, the notion of blame, also developed in [35], can be used when the context of causal models is unknown. Specifically, the blame of a cause is the expectation of responsibility under all of uncertain context. A context of causal models can be viewed as a possible world instance of PDBs. Therefore, inspired by the above research findings, we define the degree of blame of each node in the ABN to measure their contributions to the anomalous output. Then, we rank the candidate errors by their blame degrees for tracing the errors in input data.

Computing the blame has to find out all of the possible world instances related to output data. Since the possible world instances are obtained from probabilistic inferences executed in exponential time upon the ABN, the computation of blame is exponential complexity, which is not efficient and suitable enough with respect to large scale ABNs. Thus, based on the rejection sampling [142], we propose an approximate inference algorithm to obtain the blame of nodes the ABN.

Generally speaking, our main contributions can be summarized as follows:

- We propose a method to construct an augmented Bayesian network for representing complex correlation among input data, intermediate data and output data generated in query processing given an anomalous query.

- We present a definition of blame of nodes in the augmented Bayesian networks to measure the degree of contribution of each node to the anomalous query. Then, we provide an efficient method to compute the degree of the blame and rank the candidate errors by their blame.
- We implement the proposed algorithms and make preliminary experiments to test the feasibility of our method.

5.2 Problem Statement

For a query q on a probabilistic database $D(R, P)$ where R is a set of uncertain relations and P is a BN for representing the correlation among data, the *error tracing problem* is to detect the errors which cause the anomaly that the probability $P(t)$ of result tuple t of q is not equal to the truth value $P'(t)$ [114, 188].

If $P(t) = P'(t)$, then there are no errors, so we will assume that $P(t) \neq P'(t)$ for the rest of this chapter. Clearly, $P(t) \neq P'(t)$ means that $P(t) > P'(t)$ or $P(t) < P'(t)$. We only take the case that $P(t) > P'(t)$ into consideration, since $P(t) < P'(t)$ can be regarded as $P(\bar{t}) > P'(\bar{t})$. Our approach to this problem is to find all candidate errors X (i.e., tuples in D for the anomaly, and rank them by their degrees of blame).

Example 5.1. Figure 5.1(a) shows a probabilistic database D with two uncertain relations: S and T. The positive correlation (i.e., if one variable is increased, the other variable will be also increased and vice versa) among uncertain data is represented by a BN, whose DAG is shown in

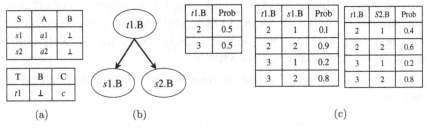

(a)   (b)   (c)

Figure 5.1 (a) A small probabilistic database D with two uncertain relations. (b) DAG of a Bayesian network. (c) CPTs corresponding to the Bayesian network.

Table 5.1 Query result of q in D.

Query result	C	Prob
$r1$	c	0.48

Table 5.2 Errors with degrees of blame.

Error	Blame
$t1.B$	1.0
$s1.B$	0.89
$s2.B$	0.55

Figure 5.1(b) and the corresponding CPTs are shown in Figure 5.1(c). For a query $q = \prod_c S \bowtie_B T$, we can obtain the result shown in Table 5.1. If the truth probability of $r1$ is $P'(r1) = 0$ (for ease of exposition, we assume the truth probability is $P'(r1) = 0$), we are to find the errors that leads to this anomaly. It is clear that $s1.B$, $t1.B$ and $s2.B$ are the candidate errors and their degrees of blame for this anomaly is shown in Table 5.2.

5.3 Related Work

Our work is mainly related to and unifies ideas from work on *probabilistic databases*, *provenance*, *causality* and *data cleaning*.

Probabilistic Database. Several approaches have been proposed for managing uncertainties, such as rule-based systems, Dempster–Shafer theory, fuzzy sets, rough set, but by 1987 the probability model has been dominant [42]. Plenty of probabilistic databases have been designed to manage uncertain data where the uncertainties are quantified as probabilities, and most of those databases are based on possible world semantics. Benjelloum *et al.* [12] introduced a framework, called x-relation, as a representation for databases with uncertainty. X-relations can be extended to represent and query tuple-independent probabilistic data. Tuple-independent probabilistic databases are insufficient for analyzing and extracting information from practical applications that naturally produce correlated data. Wang *et al.* [162] introduced a probabilistic database (BAYESSTORE) that draws results from the Statistical Learning literature to express and reason about correlations among uncertain data. Jha and Dan [83] proposed a Markov views based framework both for representing complex correlations and for efficient query evaluation. Sen and Deshpande [149] provided a framework based on the probabilistic graphical model that can represent not only probabilistic tuples, but also complex correlations among tuples. We adopted Sen's model as our underlying probabilistic databases in this chapter.

Provenance. Different notions of provenance (also called lineage) for database queries have been studied in the past few years [72]. The most common forms of provenance describe correlations between data in the source and in the output, and can be classified into three categories: (1) explaining *where* output data came from in the input; (2) showing inputs to explain *why* an output record was produced; (3) describing in detail *how* an output record was produced [30]. Tracing the lineage of data is important to improve the quality and validity of data [188]. Galhardas *et al.* [66] used a data lineage to improve data cleaning quality by enabling users to express user interactions declaratively and tune data cleaning programs. The first step of finding causes for surprising query result proposed by Meliou *et al.* [114, 115] was the computation of query lineages.

Causality. Causality is typically treated as the concept that either event *A* is a cause of event *B* or it is not. Halpern and Pearl [74] defined a causal model, called actual causes, in terms of structural equations (i.e., a causal network, which can be presented by a directed acyclic graph), and the syntax and semantics of a language for reasoning about causality. Chockler and Halpern [35] extended the causality introduced by Haplern to take into account the degree of responsibility of *A* for *B*. The notion of the blame has been defined as the expected degree of responsibility of *A* for *B* when the context of the causal model is uncertain. For a database query, the responsibility of each input tuple for the query output could be used for error detection [114]. Meliou *et al.* [115] proposed a View-Conditioned Causality to trace errors in output data of a query back to the input data based on responsibility.

Data Cleaning. Data cleaning is one of the critical mechanisms for improving the data quality. Dirty data can be classified into three categories:

incorrect or inconsistent data, missing data and duplicate data [118]. A variety of constraints have been studied for cleaning incorrect data. Beskales *et al.* [13] repaired incorrect or missing data by choosing the values satisfying the given functional dependencies. Fan *et al.* [60] extended functional dependencies to conditional functional dependencies (CFDs) for capturing and correcting the incorrect data which does not satisfy the CFDs. Fan *et al.* [61] proposed a method to clean incorrect data by finding certain fixes based on master data, a notion of certain regions and a class of editing rules. Aggregate and cardinality constraints have been proposed by Chen *et al.* [28] and Cormode *et al.* [38] to clean uncertain databases. Ma *et al.* [108] extended inclusion dependencies to conditional inclusion dependencies (CINDs) to detect inconsistent data.

Statistical inference methods have been studied for cleaning missing data or correcting incorrect data when constraints are not available [111]. We [54] proposed a method for missing data cleaning by adopting BN to represent and infer the probabilities of possible values of missing data. Stoyanovich *et al.* [152] presented a framework, termed meta-rule semi-lattices (MRSL), to infer probability distributions for missing data. Techniques for identifying duplicate data in probabilistic databases have been developed by Panse *et al.* [127]. Geerts *et al.* [68] developed a uniform data cleaning framework for users to plug-in their preference strategies when the cleaning process involves different kinds of constraints, and a commodity data cleaning platform has been developed by Dallachiesa [40].

5.4 Constructing Augmented Bayesian Network

In this section, we will discuss how to construct an ABN for an anomalous query on probabilistic databases.

To trace errors in D, we augment P to represent not only the correlations among input data tuples, but also those among input data, intermediate data and output data of an anomalous query. Two steps are concerned to construct an ABN: constructing the DAG structure of ABN and generating CPTs. Sen and Deshpande [149] proposed a method to construct an ABN for a query q on PDBs, and answers to query q may contain numerous result tuples, but we only concern a special tuple t that is anomalous. The

ABN for tuple t, denoted by $G_t = (V_t, E_t)$, is a subgraph of the ABN $G_a = (V_a, E_a)$ for query q. Thus, we give a method to construct an ABN specific to the anomalous result tuple t according to the process of query execution.

The structure of the ABN is constructed by the following steps:

(1) For each random variable v in PDBs, add a node v to V_q.
(2) Construct E_q by executing the following steps. For each operation $O^{op}(X_S, x_i)$ obtained during operator op's execution on the set of tuples S to generate tuple i:

   - Add a node x_i to V_q and annotate x_i with operator op;
   - For each x in X_S, add an edge $e(x, x_i)$ to E_q.

(3) $V_t = \{v | v \in V_q, v \rightsquigarrow x_t\}$, where x_t denotes the node corresponding to the anomalous result tuple $v \rightsquigarrow x_t$ is true if there is a path from v_i to x_t.
(4) $E_t = \{e = (v_i, v_j) | e \in E_a, v_i, v_j \in V_t\}$.

For the nodes that exist in PDBs (i.e., not generated during query processing), we copy their CPTs from the given PDBs. For other nodes, we generate CPTs according to the logical constraints expressed by the relational operators annotated with them. Without loss of generality, we only take select, project and join operations into consideration.

Select: Let $\sigma_c(R)$ denote the query, where c is the predicate of selection. For each tuple t in R, the probability in the CPT corresponding to $t = 1$ or $t = 0$ for the case that t satisfies c or not respectively.

Project: Let $\Pi_a(R)$ denote the projection, where $a \subseteq attr(R)$ denotes the set of attributes, onto which we want to project. Let r denote the result of the projecting $t \in R$, and the probability of the node corresponding to r is 1 or 0 for the case that $t.a$ equals $r.a$ or not respectively.

Join: Let $R_1 \bowtie_a R_2$ denote the join operation, where R_1 and R_2 are two relations and $a \subseteq attr(R_1) \cap attr(R_2)$. Let r denote the join result of two tuples $t1 \in R_1$ and $t2 \in R_2$, and the probability of the ABN node corresponding to r is 1 or 0 for the case that $t1.a$ equals $t2.a$ or not respectively.

Example 5.2. For the query $\Pi_c(S \bowtie_B T)$ on the PDB presented in Figure 5.1, the ABN for the result tuple is shown in Figure 5.2. We

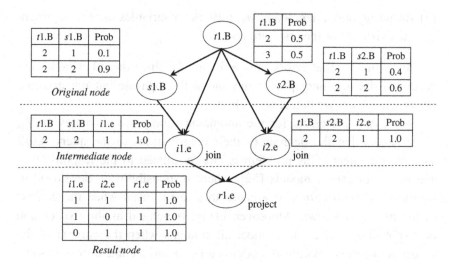

Figure 5.2 ABN for query $\prod_c (S \bowtie_B T)$.

introduce intermediate tuples produced by the join ($i1$ and $i2$) and produce a result tuple ($r1$) from the projection operation. $i1$ exists (i.e., $i1.e = 1$) only when $s1.B$ and $t1.B$ are assigned the value of 2. Similarly, $i2.e$ is 1 only when $s2.B$ and $t1.B$ are assigned the value of 2. Finally, $r1.e$ is 1 when $i1$ or $i2$ or both exist. The query result is the tuple $r1$ with the corresponding probability $P(r1.e = 1)$, which can be computed by many probabilistic inference algorithms, such as enumeration algorithm and rejection sampling [142].

5.5 Detecting Errors

In this section, we will discuss how to detect errors for an anomalous query based on the ABN constructed in Section 5.4.

From Figure 5.2, we can see that there are three kinds of nodes in the ABN:

(1) Original nodes, denoted as N_o, which exist in the PDBs.
(2) Intermediate nodes, denoted as N_i, generated during query processing. These nodes are Boolean variables used to represent the existence of the intermediate tuples.

(3) Resulting node, denoted as n_r, a Boolean variables used to represent the existence of the result tuples.

It is intuitive that errors only exist in N_o, since the other nodes are generated during query processing and will propagate but not generate errors. Therefore, we detect errors in N_o.

The candidate errors for the anomalous query are all nodes in N_o, but it seems that the degrees of their contributions to the query result are not equivalent. This problem is closely related to the responsibility and blame in causal models [52], where responsibility is developed to measure the contribution of a cause to a result event when the context of the model is known. Moreover, blame is defined as the expectation of responsibility of a cause under all contexts when the context of the model is uncertain. A causal model is a DAG and a context of the model is a set of values of each node in the model [52]. A context can be viewed as a possible world instance of PDBs with respect to uncertain databases. It is infeasible to generate all possible world instances, since the number of possible worlds is exponential to that of random variables. Fortunately, only a subset of possible world instances that satisfy the result tuple that needs to be generated, which we call situations. To detect errors, we consider first computing the situations and then defining the blame upon the ABN, followed by ranking the candidate errors by their degrees of blame.

The probability of the result tuple $r1$ in Figure 5.2 is the sum of the probabilities of situations that satisfies $r1.e = 1$. All of these situations can be obtained from the probabilistic inferences with the ABN. For this purpose, we give an efficient method based on rejection sampling, which is particularly well-adapted to sampling the posterior distributions of a BN [142]. The above ideas are described in Algorithm 5.1.

Algorithm 5.1 Situation Computation

Input:
    G : an ABN $G = (V, E)$, where $V = N_o \cup N_i \cup \{n_r\}$
    m : threshold of the total number of samples to be generated
Output:
    I : a vector of counts over samples

Variables:

X : a random variable in V

s : current state of $\{x_1, x_2, \ldots, x_n\}$, where x_i is a value of $X \in V$

Steps:

1: $s \leftarrow$ random values of X in V

2: For $j \leftarrow 1$ to m Do

3:    For each $X_i \in V$ Do

4:      $x_i \leftarrow$ a random sample from $P(X_i | parents(X_i))$ given the values of $parents(X_i)$ in S // $parents(X_i)$ is the set of values of X_i's parent nodes

5:    End For

6:    If s is consistent with $n_r.e = 1$ Then

7:      If I contains s Then

8:        $I[s] \leftarrow I[s] + 1$

9:      Else

10:        insert s into $[s]$

11:        $I[s] \leftarrow 1$

12:      End If

13:    End If

14: End For

15: $I[s] \leftarrow I[s]/m$

16: Return I

For an ABN with n nodes, the complexity of Algorithm 5.1 is $O(mn)$ when generating m samples.

Example 5.3. Three situations $I1$, $I2$ and $I3$ obtained by Algorithm 5.2 for the query $\prod_c (S \bowtie_B T)$ are shown in Table 5.3.

To measure the degree of blame of each node that induces $P(r1.e = 1) = 0.48$, we have to measure all the responsibility degrees under three situations $I1$, $I2$ and $I3$. Intuitively, we say a node has a great responsibility when changing the value of this node would affect

Table 5.3 Situations for the ABN in Figure 5.2.

	$s1.B$	$t1.B$	$s2.B$	$i1.e$	$i2.e$	$r1.e$	Prob
$I1$	2	2	2	1	1	1	0.27
$I2$	2	2	1	1	0	1	0.18
$I3$	1	2	2	0	1	1	0.03

(i.e., decrease or increase) the probability of the new situation. To describe this influence, we give some technical definitions at first.

Definition 5.1. Let X be a node of an ABN with the value domain $\{x_1, x_2, \ldots, x_n\}$, I be a situation and $Z = N_o \cup \{n_r\} - \{X\}$. The value z of Z is assigned from I, the value x_i of X is consistent with I and $\overline{x} \in \{x_1, x_2, \ldots, x_{i-1}, x_{i+1}, \ldots, x_n\}$. Changing $X = x_i$ to $X = \overline{x}$ can generate a new situation $I' = \{X = \overline{x}, Z = z\}$. The absolute value of the difference of the probabilities of I and I' is

$$vd(X) = |P(I) - P(I')|. \tag{5.1}$$

If the degree of responsibility of X is greater than that of Y, then changing the value of X would make the probability $vd(X)$ be greater than that when changing the value of Y. Thus, we define a function $dr(X, I)$ to measure the degree of responsibility of a node X under situation I. The function $dr(X, I)$ ought to satisfy the following properties:

(1) Minimal property: $dr(X, I) = 0$ when changing the value of X cannot influence the probability $P(I')$.
(2) Maximal property: $dr(X, I) = 1$ when changing the value of X can lead to the probability $P(I') = 0$.
(3) For two situations $I = \{X = x_i, Z = z$ and $I' = \{X = \overline{x}, Z = z$, if $P(I) > P(I')$ then $dr(X, I) > dr(X, I')$.

Definition 5.2. The degree of responsibility of X under situation I is defined as

$$dr(X, I) = \lceil \max\{vd(X)\} \rceil \times \frac{P(I)}{P(Z)}. \tag{5.2}$$

Theorem 5.1. *The function $dr(X, I)$ in formula (5.2) satisfies the above-mentioned properties (1)–(3).*

Proof Let the value domain of node X be $\{x_1, x_2, \ldots, x_n\}$. The value x_i is consistent with I and $\overline{x} \in \{x_1, x_2, \ldots, x_{i-1}, x_{i+1}, \ldots, x_n\}$. If changing the value of X to any other values cannot influence $P(I')$ then we can get that

$P(X = x_1, Z) = P(X = x_2, Z) = \cdots = P(X = x_n, Z)$. Therefore, we have $dr(X, I) = |P(X = x_i, Z) - P(X = x_1, Z)| \times P(X = x_i, Z)/P(Z) = 0$.

If changing the value of X can lead to the probability $P(I') = 0$, then we can obtain that all values $\overline{x}$ of X such that $P(X = \overline{x}, Z = z) = 0$. Then, we have $dr(X, I) = |P(X = x_i, Z) - 0| \times P(X = x_i, Z)/P(Z) = 1$.

For two situations $I = \{X = x_i, Z = z\}$ and $I' = \{X = \overline{x}, Z = z\}$, if $P(I) > P(I')$, then we can obtain $P(I)/P(Z) > P(I')/P(Z)$ and $\lceil \max\{vd(X)\} \rceil = 1$. Therefore, we have $dr(X, I) > dr(X, I')$.

Definition 5.3. The degree of blame of node X, denoted as $db(X)$, is the expectation of the degree of responsibility of X for all situations, where

$$db(X) = \frac{\sum_{i=1}^{n} (P(I_i) \times dr(X, I_i))}{\sum_{i=1}^{n} P(I_i)}. \tag{5.3}$$

Algorithm 5.2 shows the steps for computing the blame of each node in ABN and ranking the nodes by their blames for error detection.

Algorithm 5.2 Error Detection

Input:
  I : set of situations
  X : set of candidate errors //original nodes
Output:
  X' : set of errors sorted by the decreasing order of their blame degrees
Variables:
  B : a vector of blame degrees of $x \in X$
Steps:
1: For each x_i in X Do //rejection sampling
2:   $B[x_i] \leftarrow 0$
3:   For each I_j in I Do
4:     $B[x_i] \leftarrow B[x_i] + \lceil \max\{vd(x)\} \rceil] \times P(I_j)/P(Z)$
5:   End For
6:   $B[x_i] \leftarrow B[I_j]/ \sum P(I_j)$
7: End For
8: $X' \leftarrow$ sort X by the decreasing order of $B[x_i]$
9: Return X'

For k situations, the computation of each node's degree of blame is less than $O(k)$ times. Thus, the complexity of computing n nodes' degrees of blame is $O(nk)$.

Example 5.4. Revisiting Example 5.3, $s1.B$, $t1.B$ and $s2.B$ are candidate errors. According to Equations (5.1)–(5.3), we have

$$dr(s1.B, I1) = \lceil |0.27 - 0.03| \rceil \times \frac{0.27}{0.27 + 0.03} = \frac{0.27}{0.3} = 0.9,$$

$$dr(s1.B, I2) = \lceil |0.18 - 0| \rceil \times \frac{0.18}{0.18} = 1,$$

$$dr(s1.B, I2) = \lceil |0.03 - 0.27| \rceil \times \frac{0.03}{0.27 + 0.03} = \frac{0.03}{0.3} = 0.1,$$

$$db(s1.B) = \frac{\sum_{i=1}^{3} P(I_i) \times dr(s1.B, I_i)}{P(I1) + P(I2) + P(I3)}$$

$$= \frac{0.29 \times 0.9 + 0.18 \times 1 + 0.03 \times 0.1}{0.27 + 0.18 + 0.03} \approx 0.89.$$

Similarly, we can obtain $db(s2.B) = 0.55$ and $db(t1.B) = 1$. The degree of blame of $t1.B$ should be 1 since the joint operation $S \bowtie_B T$ requires the value of $t1.B$ to be 2. Moreover, the value of $s1.B$ is more likely to be 2 than that of $s2.B$ when $t1.B = 1$, so $db(s1.B)$ is 0.89 and $db(s2.B)$ is 0.55.

5.6 Experimental Results

To verify the feasibility of the method given in this chapter, we implemented the presented algorithms. We mainly tested the convergence and efficiency of situation computation, as well as the accuracy and efficiency of error detection.

5.6.1 *Experiment setup*

In the experiments, we used MS SQL Server 2008 on a machine with 2.27 GHz Intel Core i3 CPU and 2 GB of RAM, running Window 7 Ultimate 32-bit operating system. We used a probabilistic database with correlations represented by five classical BNs: Cancer Neapolitan, Chest Clinic, Car

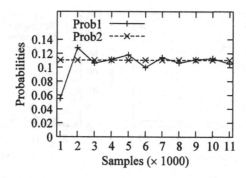

Figure 5.3 Convergence of Algorithm 1.

Diagnosis2, Alarm and HailFinder25. For each BN, we generated an original dataset of 1000 tuples according to their probability distributions from Norsys [121]. To add errors into the original datasets, we randomly modified their probability distributions for one, two and three nodes to generate three kinds of test datasets. Finally, we recorded all the information of those changes as the source of errors.

5.6.2 *Convergence and efficiency of situation computation*

It is pointed out that the posterior probabilities of the situations computed by an approximate algorithm for ABN's inferences are correct only if the sampling results are converged to a certain probability [142]. Thus, we tested the convergence of Algorithm 5.1 by recording the results upon the Chest Clinic ABN under *X-ray result = abnormal*. Prob1 and Prob2 in Figure 5.3 are the probabilities obtained by Algorithm 5.1 and those by the classic enumeration-based algorithm respectively. It can be seen that Prob1 and Prob2 are stable around 0.11 with the increase of generated samples. The result shows that the probabilities returned by Algorithm 5.1 converge to a certain value efficiently with just about 3000 samples.

5.6.3 *Effectiveness and efficiency of error detection*

To test the effectiveness of our method for error detection, we implemented and ran Algorithm 5.2 upon the test datasets and compared the result to the source of errors using the mean average precision (MAP), adopted as the metric of comparison. The MAP is close to 1 when the result of possible

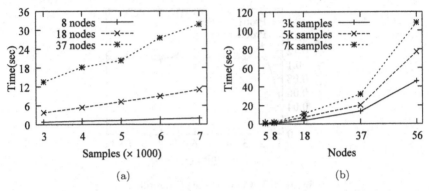

(a)   (b)

Figure 5.4 Execution time of situation computation. (a) Execution time with the increase of samples. (b) Execution time with the increase of nodes.

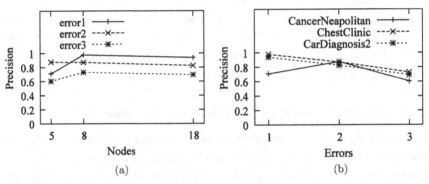

(a)   (b)

Figure 5.5 Precision of error detection. (a) Mean average precision of Algorithm 5.2 with the increase of nodes. (b) Mean average precision of Algorithm 5.2 with the increase of errors.

errors obtained by Algorithm 5.2 is close to that of actual errors, which means that the faulty node ranked first in the result is most likely to be erroneous.

We ran the experiments to detect one, two and three errors in three ABNs that contains 5, 8 and 18 nodes, respectively. Figure 5.5(a) shows that the precision of possible errors obtained by Algorithm 5.2 is stably greater than 60% with the increase of ABN nodes. Figure 5.5(b) shows that the precision is decreased slowly with the increase of the number of errors. This means that the precision of error detection is mainly determined by the number of errors in original databases. From the perspective of real

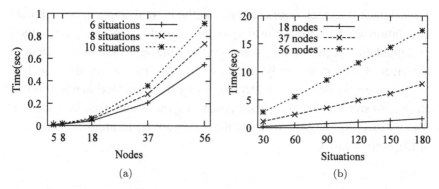

Figure 5.6 Execution time of error detection. (a) Execution time of Algorithm 5.2 with the increase of nodes. (b) Execution time of Algorithm 5.2 with the increase of situations.

applications of error detection on a database with a small number of errors, our method can work effectively.

To verify the efficiency of Algorithm 5.2, upon five ABNs we recorded the execution time of error detection shown in Figure 5.6. It can be seen that the execution time is increased linearly with the increase of nodes and situations of the datasets, which guarantees the efficiency of Algorithm 5.2.

5.7 Conclusions

In this chapter, we presented an ABN-based method for tracing errors in probabilistic databases with respect to the uncertain characteristics of data. Concentrated on the complex correlation among data, we gave a method for constructing an ABN for an anomalous query to represent correlations among input data, intermediate data and output data in terms of the execution process of SPJ queries, analogous to lineages specified in Chapter 4. Then, we defined the blame for each node in the ABN to measure the contributions of each node to the anomalous query result. Finally, we provided an efficient method to compute the blame and rank candidate errors by their degrees of blame.

The method for ABN construction and situation computation establishes the application oriented mechanism for uncertain knowledge representation and that for uncertain knowledge inferences respectively. Starting from the presented method in this chapter, we can further make extensions to correct errors automatically in real applications of data integration and ETL tools. Further, we can consider combining the method presented in Chapter 4 for lineage processing and that in this chapter for error detection to study the strategies for preserving data quality. Simultaneously, we can consider extending the presented method in this chapter to suit the situations with complex queries and massive uncertain data by incorporating the data-intensive computing techniques concerned in Chapters 2 and 3.

Chapter 6

Fusing Uncertain Knowledge in Time-Series Data

In this chapter, we are to achieve the global uncertain knowledge during a period of time for decision making or action selection by fussing or combining the participating uncertain knowledge (represented as Bayesian Networks (BNs)) of multiple time slices consistently while satisfying the demands of high efficiency and instantaneousness. We adopt qualitative probabilistic network (QPN), the qualitative abstraction of BN, as the underlying framework of modeling and fusing time-series uncertain knowledge. BNs in continuous time slices constitute time-series BNs, from which we derive time-series QPNs. Taking as input time-series BNs, we give a QPN-based approach to fuse time-series uncertain knowledge in terms of time-series specialties. First, for each time slice, we enhance the implied QPN by augmenting interval-valued weights derived from the corresponding BN, and then obtain the QPN with weighted influences, denoted enhanced qualitative probabilistic network (EQPN), which provides a quantitative and conflict-free basis for fusing uncertain knowledge. Then, we give the method for fusing the graphical structures of time-series EQPNs based on the concept of Markov equivalence. Following, we give a superposition method for fusing qualitative influences of time-series EQPNs. Experimental results show that our method is not only efficient but also effective. Meanwhile, the simulation results when applying time-series EQPNs and the fusion algorithm to a robotic system show that our method is applicable in realistic intelligent situations.

6.1 Motivation and Basic Idea

By adopting Bayesian Network (BN) as the theoretic model of uncertain knowledge, scene understanding, multi-evidence inferences [79], task execution management [96] and probabilistic intention inference of

135

robotics [56] were studied and the corresponding underlying techniques were developed. Generally, time-series uncertain knowledge exists widely in real applications, such as action selection that a robot will make based on the knowledge inferences in successive time slices [142, 154]. In time-series environments, uncertain knowledge among variables in separate time slices are naturally represented by BNs respectively, which could be learned from time-series databases or established by domain experts [21, 128]. In real-world applications of decision making or action selection, it is desirable to achieve the global knowledge of a historical period of time by aggregating the knowledge and fusing participating uncertainties of multiple time slices consistently.

We can naturally consider reconstructing the desired global BN from the integrated time-series databases, or by combining the time-series BNs directly. However, for the former idea, the original time-series databases may not be available and the efficiency cannot be guaranteed as well due to its dependency on large-scale sample data [21, 76]. For the latter, the combined BN structure can be obtained on the basis of existing methods [54, 112, 124, 147], but the combination of conditional probability tables (CPTs) is not straightforward and inefficient. Both of the above two kinds of ideas adopt BN as the framework for representing ultimate uncertain knowledge. Actually from the practical point of view, the demands of high efficiency and instantaneousness highlighted in time-series applications should be satisfied in the process of global knowledge acquisition. From the knowledge fusion point of view, it is also not realistic to obtain the ultimate BN as exact as those to be combined. Moreover, considering the trade-off among business goals, efficiency and precision, too strict quantitative mechanisms are inappropriately precise for the applications of fusing uncertain knowledge, and excess precision leads to knowledge bases applicable in only narrow domains and not suitable for general time-series applications [163]. For example, a robot can select its actions based on the utility obtained by uncertainty inferences upon the current state, but we concern the utility-based action decision instead of the exact utility values. This means that whether the utility value is exact or not does not matter only if it can be used for action section. Therefore, it is necessary to explore an underlying framework and corresponding mechanisms for efficient modeling and fusion of time-series uncertain knowledge initially described by separate BNs.

Fortunately, a qualitative probabilistic network (QPN) [163, 164] is the qualitative abstraction of a BN by encoding variables and the qualitative influences between them in a directed acyclic graph (DAG). A QPN can be derived from the given BN based on the definition of qualitative influences and has the same DAG of the corresponding BN. The simplified representation and efficient inferences make QPN be applicable for knowledge discovery in temporal situations [101]. These mechanisms of QPN can naturally guarantee the demands of high efficiency when it comes to the representation, discovery and fusion of time-series uncertain knowledge. In this chapter, we adopt QPN as the underlying framework for modeling and fusing time-series uncertain knowledge. Taking as input time-series BNs, we can derive the corresponding time-series QPNs.

To support decision making or action selection in dynamic situations concerning multiple time slices, we are to fuse the time-series QPNs directly instead of obtaining the integrated BN as the intermediate result. For this purpose, we will have to address the following two problems:

• How to fuse DAG structures of the participating time-series QPNs?
• How to fuse qualitative influences of the participating time-series QPNs?

In recent years, various approaches for combining BNs' DAG structures [54, 112, 124, 147] have been proposed from various perspectives or based on various theoretic principles. However, if the DAGs of time-series QPNs were fused by adopting these methods, the time-series specialties and qualitative nature cannot be reflected. Furthermore, when combining multiple DAGs, to obtain the independencies commonly implied in the participating ones is not trivial but the most challenging step [144]. Considering time-series uncertainties in a specific domain, the commonly implied independencies should be semantically equivalent and then included in the ultimate model. However, preserving equivalent independencies has not been well considered in almost all the existing methods for DAG combination.

It is known that the important concept of Markov equivalence, discovered by Verma and Pearl [161], provides a formal method to decide whether two given DAGs are equivalent with respect to independency information. A partially acyclic directed graph (PDAG) is used to represent equivalence classes of DAGs. Completed PDAG (CPDAG) corresponding to an equivalence class is the PDAG consisting of a directed edge for every compelled edge and an undirected edge for every reversible edge in the equivalence class [7, 34, 115]. Andersson [7] pointed out that the equivalence class of a certain DAG can be uniquely represented by the corresponding CPDAG. In this chapter, we focus on obtaining the subgraphs commonly implied in all participating time-series QPNs such that the maximal equivalent-independency information can be preserved. First, for each QPN, we extract the subgraphs including common nodes in all participating QPNs. Then, we derive CPDAGs respectively followed by obtaining the intersection of all these CPDAGs. Accordingly, we recover the DAG based on PDAG's consistent extension [34]. Centered on the DAG commonly implied in participating time-series QPNs, we can easily add all the other edges in line with time-series and qualitative characteristics. According to Markov assumption [128], the edges are added from the latest time slice to earlier ones.

As for the fusion problem of qualitative influences, it is different from that of combining conditional probabilities of BNs. The increment or decrement trend of object values can be represented efficiently based on QPNs [163]. For inferences with a QPN, an efficient algorithm runs in polynomial time, given upon the idea of sign propagation [55, 56]. Due to the high abstraction and coarse level of details, information loss is produced accordingly when QPNs are derived from BNs [163]. Conflicts during inferences will be produced when two contradicting influences (e.g., an increment one and a decrement one) arrive simultaneously at the same target node. Actually, analogous conflicts may be generated probably when fusing time-series QPNs, especially for the sub-graphs with common nodes. Considering the inherence of qualitative influence fusion, we will have to fuse them consistently between the same pair of nodes whether the edges have the same orientations or not (i.e., fusion of the influence on $A \rightarrow B$ and that on $B \rightarrow A$).

To differentiate influence strengths and resolve conflicts during QPN inferences are the subject with great attention [16, 22, 138, 140]. In recent years, various approaches have been proposed to address this problem from various perspectives, but these approaches just concern the composition of parallel influences in a single QPN instead of the combination of multiple influences between the same pair of nodes in multiple QPNs. Therefore, inspired by the idea of conflict resolution of general QPNs, in this chapter we derive the bidirectional interval-value-based weight for each pair of nodes in time-series QPNs taking as input the time-series BNs. That is, the weight of the influence of A on B and that of B on A are derived at the same time. In particular, for a certain directed edge $A \rightarrow B$, we obtain the weight of the opposite orientation (i.e., $B \rightarrow A$) based on the BN's inference algorithms [36, 73, 76]. Consequently, based on the basic principle of evidence combination [100, 150], we propose a superposition method for fusing multiple influences of the same pair of nodes in multiple time-series QPNs.

Generally speaking, the main contributions of this chapter can be summarized as follows:

- We first enhance general QPNs by augmenting interval-valued weights derived from corresponding BNs. Accordingly, we obtained the QPNs with weighted influences, denoted as EQPNs (Enhanced Qualitative Probabilistic Networks), which provide the quantitative and conflict-free basis for time-series uncertain knowledge fusion.
- We give the method for fusing DAG structures of time-series EQPNs based on the concept of Markov equivalence, CPDAG's properties and qualitative characteristics. Thus, the fused network structure can be obtained while preserving the maximal equivalent-independency information commonly implied in participating networks.
- We give a superposition method for fusing qualitative influences of time-series EQPNs. Thus, multiple influences between the same pair of nodes in time-series EQPNs can be fused consistently.
- We make experiments to test the feasibility and performance of our methods, whose efficiency and effectiveness are shown by experimental

results. Meanwhile, by adopting a robotic system [142], we make the simulation for robot's decision making based on our methods, whose applicability is verified.

6.2 Related Work

Time-series analysis, including prediction or decision, has been paid much attention in the paradigm of artificial intelligence oriented to real world applications [130]. BNs have been used in many different perspectives of intelligent and robotic applications, centered on the representation and inferences of uncertainties [73, 96, 128, 139, 154]. The methods for learning BNs from data mainly include the dependency-analysis or scoring & searching methods [21, 31]. BN's inference methods [73] were widely discussed and applied in the real world. PowerConstructor [32] and Netica [121] are effective software tools for BN construction and inference, respectively. Hwang *et al.* [79] gave the BN-based method for scene understanding and uncertainty handling in robotic systems. Lazkano *et al.* [96] used BN learning techniques to manage task execution in mobile robotics. Tahboub [154] modeled the intention-action-state scenario by dynamic BN probabilistic intention inferences. However, the fusion or combination of uncertain knowledge models was not well addressed when incorporating the dynamic characteristics of robotics.

Many researchers proposed various approaches for fusing multiple BNs into one compromising BN. For example, Matzkvich and Abramson [110] proposed the method for topological fusion of BNs by first obtaining a consensus structure and then estimating the model's parameters based on the idea of graph union and edge reversal. Pennock and Wellman [130] derived a series of impossibility returns for the general problem of combining probability distributions. Motivated by aggregating the knowledge provided by multiple specialists under the form of graphical models into a single and more general representation, Sagrado and Moral [144] combined independency graphs based on the union and intersection of independencies regardless of the combination of probability values. Nielsen and Parsons [122] gave the method for fusing BNs based on the formal argumentation in multi-agent systems, in which each agent is equipped with a BN. However, almost all these methods, especially those for fusing BN structures, have not considered the preserving of equivalent independencies commonly implied in all participating networks.

Verma and Pearl [161] showed that any two DAGs imply the same independence constraints if and only if they contain the same skeletons and have the same v-structures. PDAGs, containing both directed and undirected edges, are used to represent the equivalence classes of BN structures. PDAGs are widely studied from various perspectives [7, 34, 113, 161]. For example, Andersson [7] gave the characterization of Markov equivalence classes for DAGs, and presented the necessary and sufficient conditions of CPDAGs, and as well pointed out that the equivalence class of a certain DAG can be uniquely represented by the corresponding CPDAG. Meek [113] gave the rule-based algorithm, DAG-To-CPDAG, to transform a PDAG into a CPDAG, and proved the soundness and completeness of the transformation. Chickering [34] provided an alternative algorithm to implement DAG-To-CPDAG that is computationally efficient. Dor and Tarsi [54] discussed the method to obtain the CPDAG of a given PDAG. Chickering [33] gave the algorithm, PDAG-to-DAG, to obtain the consistent extension of PDAGs. The concept of Markov equivalence and relevant properties of CPDAGs are used in model selection and aggregation [33, 34]. Nevertheless, to our knowledge, the above methods have not discussed the fusion of multiple BN structures with respect to equivalent independencies that are actually important to guarantee the semantic correctness of the fusion result. In this chapter, we are to consider the independency-preserving fusion for common DAG structures of time-series QPNs upon the above theoretic basis.

Wellman [163, 164] gave the concepts, theories, inferences and applications of QPNs. Druzdzel and Henrion [55, 56] proposed the efficient inference algorithm for QPNs. We gave a survey on QPNs including the qualitative representation, inference and application of uncertain knowledge [180]. QPNs have attracted much attention due to their simplified representation and efficient inferences. Adopting QPN as the basis of modeling temporal causalities and knowledge discovery in time-series environments, we extended the general QPN and gave the concepts, learning and inferences of temporal QPNs [130]. Meanwhile, Ibrahim *et al.* [80] adopted QPN to model the time-series and naturally-occurring motifs of gene regulatory networks.

In recent years, trade-off resolution of QPNs has become the subject of intense debate and attracted much attention due to the pervasive demands of QPN inferences in real applications [16, 22, 138, 140]. Renooij and Van [140] proposed the semi-qualitative network by associating an interval influence to each edge in the QPN. By this method, quantification efforts are found on small coherent parts of the network and the QPN can be studied in a stepwise manner. Meanwhile, Campos and Cozman [22] presented the belief updating and learning in semi-qualitative probabilistic networks (SQPNs), where a multilinear programming method was given to generate exact inferences in the SQPN without approximations. Targeting on polytree-shaped networks, Campos and Cozman [24] explored the computational complexity of SQPNs and proposed the polynomial-time inference algorithm. Renooij *et al.* [138] combined QPNs with Kappa values to distinguish several levels of strengths of qualitative influences to resolve more tradeoffs. Renooij and Gaag [139] enhanced the QPN by distinguishing strong and weak influences, in which strong influences dominate over conflicting weak influences. Bolt *et al.* [16] extended the framework of QPNs with the concept of situational signs, and a situational sign is associated with a non-monotonic influence and captures information about the effect of the influence in the current state of the network. These methods augmented strengths or weights to qualitative influences in QPNs and concerned the composition property for resolving trade-offs, which are analogous when fusing multiple influences in time-series QPNs. However, the above methods just concern the composition of parallel influences in a single QPN instead of the combination of multiple influences between the same pair of nodes in multiple QPNs. We gave the weight-augmented enhancement of QPNs based on rough set [180] and interval probability theory [181], respectively, where static QPNs were concerned without regard of time-series specialties. In this chapter, inspired by the idea of quantifying qualitative influences mentioned above, we will give the superposition method for fusing influences of time-series QPNs based on the preliminary principles of evidence combination and the specialties of time-series situations [80, 142].

6.3   Preliminaries and Problem Statement

In this section, we first present preliminaries of this chapter, including the basic concepts of QPN and Markov equivalence, as well as the relevant properties. Then, we give some basic definitions and notations for later discussions and state the problem that will be addressed in this chapter.

6.3.1   *Qualitative probabilistic networks*

As the framework for representing and inferring uncertain knowledge, BN is a directed acyclic graph $G = (V, E)$, in which V is the set of statistical variables, and E is the set of edges that capture probabilistic causal relationships among the variables [128]. Associated with each variable A is a set of conditional probability distributions $P(A|\pi(A))$, where $\pi(A)$ is the set of parents of A in G. We assume all variables to be binary (true or false), writing a for $A =$ True (or $A = 1$) and $\bar{a}$ for $A =$ False (or $A = 0$), in which $a > \bar{a}$ (or $1 > 0$). QPNs [163] are the qualitative abstractions of BNs, and have the same DAG structures of the corresponding BNs. Instead of precise conditional probability distributions, a QPN encodes only qualitative probability distribution over the variables by means of qualitative influences and qualitative synergies. A qualitative influence between two variables describes how the values of one variable influence the probabilities of the values of the other variable. The definition of qualitative influences is given as follows.

Definition 6.1 [163]. A positively influences B, denoted $S^+(A, B)$, if $P(b|ax) - P(b|\bar{a}x) \geq 0$ for all combinations of values x for the set $\pi(B)\backslash\{A\}$ of parents of B other than A.

This definition means observing a higher value of A makes higher value of B more likely, regardless of any other direct influences on B. A *negative* qualitative influence and a *zero* qualitative influence, denoted S^- and S^0, can be defined analogously by substituting $\geq$ by $\leq$ and $=$ respectively. An *unknown* influence of A on B, denoted $S^?(A, B)$, means that the increment or decrement tendency of A on B is not certain.

The set of qualitative influences exhibits various properties [179]. The *symmetry* property states that if the network includes the influence $S^\delta(A, B)$, then it also includes $S^\delta(B, A)$, $\delta \in \{+, -, 0, ?\}$. The *transitivity* property asserts that the signs of qualitative influences along a trail without head-to-head nodes combine into a sign for the net influence with the ⊗-operator. The *composition* property asserts that the signs of multiple influences between nodes along parallel trails combine into a sign for the net influence with the ⊕-operator. The rules of ⊗ and ⊕ operators are given in [163]. For the inference with a QPN, an efficient algorithm is proposed in [55], built on the above three properties. The basic idea is to trace the effect of observing a node's value on the other nodes in the network by message passing between neighbor nodes.

Example 6.1. The QPN shown in Figure 6.1(b) is abstracted from the given BN shown in Figure 6.1(a). Based on the method for QPN inferences with the QPN in Figure 6.1(b), we take C as the target node, and if both of the current signs of node A and B are '+', then the result on C will be '?'.

Actually, influence composition is the special case of fusing qualitative influences in time-series QPNs when it comes to fusing the influences between the same pair of nodes while the orientations are the same in all participating networks. Meanwhile, avoiding ambiguities in the composition result motivates us to explore the superposition method for fusing qualitative influences.

6.3.2 *Markov equivalence and relevant properties*

In this chapter, we take Markov equivalence as the basis for fusing the sub-networks composed of common nodes to preserve the maximal

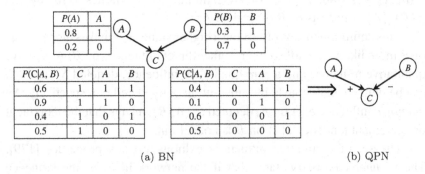

(a) BN   (b) QPN

Figure 6.1 An example of QPN abstracted from BN.

equivalent-independency information. Throughout this chapter, equivalence means Markov equivalence.

The skeleton of any DAG is the undirected graph resulting from ignoring the directionality of every edge. The v-structure in a DAG G is an ordered triple of nodes (x, y, z) such that G contains the directed edges $x \to y$ and $z \to y$, and x and z are not adjacent in G [33]. Two DAGs (BNs' graphical structures) are graphically equivalent if and only if they define the same probability distribution, where the equivalence can be determined by the following theorem.

Theorem 6.1. *Two DAGs are equivalent if and only if they have the same skeletons and the same v-structures.*

A directed edge $A \to B$ is compelled in G if for every DAG G' equivalent to G, $A \to B$ exists in G'. For any edge e in G, if e is not compelled in G, then e is reversible in G. From Theorem 6.1, we know that any edge participating in a v-structure is compelled [33]. An acyclic partially directed graph, or PDAG for short, is a graph that contains both directed and undirected edges. PDAGs are used to represent equivalence classes of BN structures [33, 161].

The completed PDAG, or CPDAG for short, corresponding to an equivalence class is the PDAG consisting of a directed edge for every compelled edge in the equivalence class, and an undirected edge for every reversible edge in the equivalence class [7, 34, 113]. A CPDAG for a given equivalence class of BN structures is unique [33]. We use G^* to denote the CPDAG of DAG G. Andersson [7] gave the following sufficient and necessary condition to decide whether a graph is a CPDAG.

Definition 6.2. Let G be a graph. A directed edge $A \to B$ is strongly protected in G if $A \to B$ occurs in at least one of the following four configurations as an induced subgraph of G:

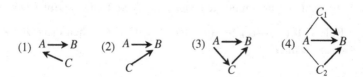

Theorem 6.2. *Let $G = (V, E)$ be a graph that is the CPDAG for some DAG if and only if G satisfies the following four conditions:*

(1) *G is a partially directed graph;*
(2) *Every undirected chain component of G is chordal[a];*
(3) *The configuration $A \rightarrow B - C$ does not occur as an induced subgraph of G;*
(4) *Every directed edge $A \rightarrow B$ is strongly protected in G.*

The concept of consistent extension of a PDAG is used to obtain some certain members of the equivalence class. For a CPDAG G^*, every DAG contained in the equivalence class of G^* is a consistent extension of G^*.

Definition 6.3 [33]. DAG G is a consistent extension of a PDAG P, if G has the same skeleton and the same v-structure as P, and if every directed edge in P has the same orientation in G.

Meek [113] gave the rule-based algorithm, DAG-To-CPDAG, to transform a PDAG into a CPDAG. In this chapter, we adopt this algorithm to obtain the unique representation of independencies implied in a DAG. Chickering [34] gave the algorithm, PDAG-to-DAG, to obtain the consistent extension of PDAGs. We adopt this algorithm to obtain the ultimate result of DAG fusion based on the intermediate result represented by CPDAG. These two algorithms are given as follows.

Algorithm 6.1 DAG-To-CPDAG

Input: DAG G
Output: CPDAG G'
Steps:

1: Transform all directed edges into undirected edges except those in v-structures
2: Let G' be the derived PDAG.
3: While G' contains any undirected edges satisfying following rules Do

> Rule 1: If $(A) \longrightarrow (B) \longrightarrow (C)$ and $A \ldots C \notin G'$ Then make $B \rightarrow C$ be oriented in G'

---
[a]An undirected graph is chordal if every cycle of length $n \geq 4$ possesses a chord [7, 128].

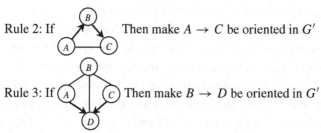

Rule 2: If [diagram] Then make $A \to C$ be oriented in G'

Rule 3: If [diagram] Then make $B \to D$ be oriented in G'

4: End While
5: Return G'

Algorithm 6.2 PDAG-To-DAG

Input: PDAG P
Output: DAG G
Steps:
1: $G \leftarrow P$
2: For each component[b] K in P Do
3:    mark "un-processed" on all nodes in K
4: End For
5: While there are un-processed nodes in K Do
6: select an unprocessed node X with the most parents
7: For each undirected edge $X - Y$ Do
8:    make $X \to Y$ be oriented in G
9: End For
10:    mark "processed" on X
11: End While
12: Return G

6.3.3 Problem statement

Let us illustrate the problems that we will address by an example.

Example 6.2. Suppose A, B, C, D and E represent *investment*, *cost*, *profit*, *price* and *sales*, respectively, and the values of these variables can

---

[b]A component is the connected subgraph generated by removing the orientations in a DAG
[128].

be 1 or 0 that describe the increase or decrease respectively. Figure 6.2 shows three BNs (G_1, G_2 and G_3) corresponding to time slices T_1, T_2 and T_3 of a certain enterprise. We further suppose G_1, G_2 and G_3 are mutually independent. Taking as input G_1, G_2 and G_3, we are desirable to achieve the global knowledge to ultimately reflect the tendency of values' increase or decrease among associated variables for decision-making or prediction. We can derive the QPNs from G_1, G_2 and G_3, respectively for each time slice.

Moreover, we suppose the global knowledge be described by the QPN (denoted as G^*) in Figure 6.3 that will be obtained by fusing the time-series QPNs.

Now, we give the definitions of time-series BNs and times-series QPNs.

Definition 6.4. Let G_1^B, G_2^B, ..., G_n^B be BNs of a specific domain in time slices T_1, T_2, ..., T_n, respectively. For time slice T_i, we suppose the BN is represented by $G_i^B = (V_i, E_i)$, where V_i is the set of variables, E_i is the set of directed edges, and $V_i \cap V_j \neq \phi (1 \le i, j \le n, i \neq j)$. $\{G_1^B, G_2^B, ..., G_n^B\}$ is called time-series BNs, where G_i^B and G_j^B are supposed to be independent.

Definition 6.5. Let G_1, G_2, ..., G_n be QPNs corresponding to G_1^B, G_2^B, ..., G_n^B, respectively, where $G_i = (V_i, Q_i)(1 \le i \le n)$ has the same DAG structure of G_i^B and Q_i is the set of qualitative influences ($Q_i \subseteq \{+, -, 0, ?\}$). $\{G_1, G_2, ..., G_n\}$ is called time-series QPNs.

Taking as input the time-series BNs, the fusion result of time-series qualitative uncertain knowledge is represented by a QPN that will be defined as follows.

Definition 6.6. Let QPN $G^* = (V^*, Q^*)$ be the result of fusing the time-series QPNs, where $V^* = V_1 \cup V_1 \cup \cdots \cup V_n$ be the set of nodes and $Q^* \subseteq \{+, -, 0, ?\}$ be set of qualitative influences in G^*.

To obtain G^* from the given time-series BNs, we will first construct the DAG structure on V^*, by integrating those of G_1, G_2, ..., G_n such that the commonly implied independencies are preserved. Then, with respect to each directed edge in G^*, we will derive the qualitative influence by composing all relevant ones in G_1, G_2, ..., G_n. The above two steps will be discussed in Sections 6.5 and 6.6, respectively.

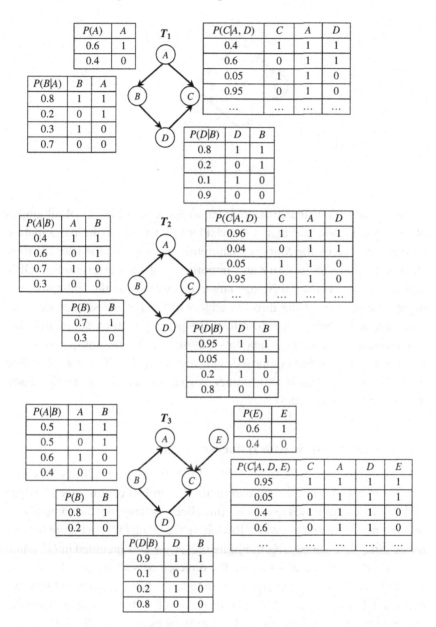

Figure 6.2 Time-series BNs.

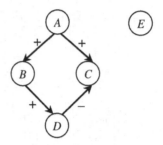

Figure 6.3 Result QPN.

It is worth noting that in the first step we focus on the fusion of subgraphs of common nodes, and then we consider other parts of the participating graphs. Inspired by the Markov assumption, we suppose the later the time slice, the higher the priority and importance of the corresponding QPN will be. In a specific QPN, the larger the weight of the influence, the higher the priority of the directed edge will be. For the second step, we introduce a discount factor to reflect the priority of time slices and also differentiate the strengths of qualitative influences for the same pair of nodes in various QPNs when composed with respect to G^*. These are fulfilled upon the enhanced QPN with influence weights, which will be discussed in Section 6.4 immediately.

6.4   Enhancing QPNs with Influence Weights

For each time slice, we can derive the QPN from the given BN based on Definition 6.1. As for the fusion of qualitative influences on directed edges of the same pair of nodes in various time slices, we consider the composition of influences with respect to G^*. Revisiting the result QPN in Figure 6.3 and the original time-series BNs in Figure 6.2, $A \rightarrow B$ is included in G^* while $A \rightarrow B$, $B \rightarrow A$ and $B \rightarrow A$ are the directed edges between A and B in G_1^B, G_2^B and G_3^B, respectively. According to the basic concept of QPN, we know $S^\delta(A, B) = S^\delta(B, A)$, and thus the result influence can be naturally obtained from the composition of the influences on $A \rightarrow B$, $B \rightarrow A$ and $B \rightarrow A$ in G_1, G_2 and G_3, respectively. However, the ambiguities may be produced when combining conflict influences, such as $+ \oplus + \oplus - =?$. Therefore, to achieve the influence on $A \rightarrow B$ in the result QPN while avoiding ambiguities motivates us to enhance general QPNs by augmenting weights for each directed edge in the time-series QPNs. During the fusion process, we will add the directed edges in time slices $T_1, \ldots, T_{n-1}$ into the QPN of slice T_n. For the same pair of nodes, the edges may have the same or opposite orientations, but have the same qualitative influences. Therefore, the weights not only for the influence of A on B but also for that of B on A are simultaneously necessary for the directed edge $A \to B$, and are denoted as w and w' respectively. Whether the orientation of the edge between A and B is consistent with that in the result QPN decides whether w or w' will be selected.

This means that for each directed edge $A \to B$ in a BN, other than $S^\delta(A, B)$, we are to augment the weight of δ of A on B as well as the weight of δ of B on A at the same time. Taking the time-series BNs as input, we are to obtain the bidirectional weight of the influence on each edge by means of the probability differences corresponding to the qualitative influence derivation.

From the definition of qualitative influences of A on B, $P(b|ax) - P(b|\bar{a}x)$ ($x \in \pi(B) \backslash \{A\}$) describes the probability difference that lies in $[-1, 0]$ or $[0, 1]$. Therefore, starting from a given BN and inspired by the influence strengths in SQPNs [22, 133], for each edge $A \to B$ we can obtain a range of the absolute value of the probability difference, which lies in $[0, 1]$ which we look upon as the strength of the influence of A on B. On the other hand, we can analogously obtain the strength of the same influence of B on A based on $P(a|by) - P(a|\bar{b}y)$ ($y \in \pi(A) \backslash \{B\}$ of parents of A other than B, i.e., $\pi(A)$), which can be calculated by using the method of BN inferences. The bidirectional strengths constitute the bidirectional weight of qualitative influences in a QPN, which will be defined as follows.

Definition 6.7. Suppose δ is the qualitative influence on the edge $A \to B$ ($\delta \in \{+, -, 0, ?\}$). Let $[p, q]$ and $[u, v]([p, q] \subseteq [0, 1], [u, v] \subseteq [0, 1])$ be the strength of δ of A on B and that of B on A respectively, such that

$$p = \min\{|P(b|ax) - P(b|\bar{a}x)|\}, \quad q = \max\{|P(b|ax) - P(b|\bar{a}x)|$$
$$u = \min\{|P(a|by) - P(a|\bar{b}y)|\}, \quad v = \max\{|P(a|by) - P(a|\bar{b}y)|\}$$

for any combination of values x for the set $\pi(B)\backslash\{A\}$ of parents of B other than A, and y for the set $\pi(A)$ of parents of A. $[p, q]$ is called the forward weight of δ and $[u, v]$ is called the backward weight of δ with respect to the edge $A \rightarrow B$. We call $\langle[p, q], [u, v]\rangle$ the bidirectional weight on the edge $A \rightarrow B$. For discussion convenience, we use $\langle w, w'\rangle$ to denote $\langle[p, q], [u, v]\rangle$, where w and w' are two probability interval values.

For the edge $A \rightarrow B$, Definition 6.1 specifies the trend that higher values of A probably make high values of B by means of the differences of conditional probabilities, and Definition 6.7 adopts the absolute values of these probability differences to represent the strength of qualitative influences. This makes qualitative influences represented by a finer manner and the same influence of A on B and that of B on A are differentiated quantitatively.

Definition 6.8. The qualitative influence of A on B associated with the bidirectional weight is called the weighted influence and denoted as $S^{\delta\langle w, w'\rangle}(A, B)$. A QPN in which all qualitative influences are associated with such bidirectional weights is called an enhanced QPN, abbreviated as EQPN. The time-series QPNs with weighted influences are called time-series EQPNs.

It is known that $[p, q] \subseteq [0, 1]$ and $[u, v] \subseteq [0, 1]$. The classical QPN, in which all strengths are exactly in $[0, 1]$, is the special case of the EQPN, which is the intermediate network of the result QPN.

Example 6.3. As for the BN in Figure 6.1(a), we derive the corresponding EQPN to illustrate the basic ideas of Definitions 6.7 and 6.8. First, we consider the bidirectional weight for the influence ('+') of A on C and that of C on A.

(1) The probability differences, denoted $P(c|ax) - P(c|\bar{a}x)$ ($x \in \pi(C)\backslash\{A\}$), can be obtained directly from the conditional probability tables in Figure 1(a):

$$P(C = 1|A = 1, B = 1) - P(C = 1|A = 0, B = 1) = 0.2,$$

$$P(C = 1|A = 1, B = 0) - P(C = 1|A = 0, B = 0) = 0.4.$$

Therefore, the strength of the influence of A on C will be $[0.2, 0.4]$.

(2) The probability difference, denoted as $P(a|cy) - P(a|\bar{c}y)$ ($y \in \pi(A)$), can be obtained based on the algorithm of BN inferences.

$$
\begin{aligned}
P(A = 1|C = 1) &= \frac{P(A = 1, C = 1)}{P(C = 1)} \\
&= \frac{\sum_{B=1,0} P(C = 1|A = 1, B)P(B|A = 1)P(A = 1)}{\sum_{\substack{A=1,0 \\ B=1,0}} P(C = 1|A, B)P(A, B)} \\
&= \frac{0.8 \times 0.3 \times 0.6 + 0.8 \times 0.7 \times 0.9}{\begin{aligned}&0.6 \times 0.8 \times 0.3 + 0.9 \times 0.8 \times 0.7 \\ &+ 0.4 \times 0.2 \times 0.3 + 0.5 \times 0.2 \times 0.7\end{aligned}} = 0.873,
\end{aligned}
$$

$$
\begin{aligned}
P(A = 1|C = 0) &= \frac{P(A = 1, C = 0)}{P(C = 0)} \\
&= \frac{\sum_{B=1,0} P(C = 0|A = 1, B)P(B|A = 1)P(A = 1)}{\sum_{\substack{A=1,0 \\ B=1,0}} P(C = 0|A, B)P(A, B)} \\
&= \frac{0.8 \times 0.3 \times 0.4 + 0.8 \times 0.7 \times 0.1}{\begin{aligned}&0.4 \times 0.8 \times 0.3 + 0.1 \times 0.8 \times 0.7 \\ &+ 0.6 \times 0.2 \times 0.3 + 0.5 \times 0.2 \times 0.7\end{aligned}} = 0.589.
\end{aligned}
$$

Therefore, $P(A = 1|C = 1) - P(A = 1|C = 0) = 0.284$, and the strength of the influence of C on A will be $[0.284, 0.284]$.

(3) Based on (1) and (2), we can conclude that the bidirectional weight on $A \to C$ is $\langle[0.2, 0.4], [0.284, 0.284]\rangle$, and consequently the weighted influence between A and C will be

$$
S^{+\langle[0.2,0.4],[0.284,0.284]\rangle}(A, C).
$$

(4) Analogously, we can obtain the weighted influence between B and C as $S^{+\langle[0.1,0.3],[0.286,0.286]\rangle}(B, C)$, since $P(C = 1|B = 1, A = 1) - P(C = 1|B = 0, A = 1) = -0.3$, $P(C = 1|B = 1, A = 0) - P(C = 1|B = 0, A = 0) = -0.1$ and $P(B = 1|C = 1) - P(B = 1|C = 0) = -0.286$. Consequently, the EQPN corresponding to the BN in Figure 1(a) is shown in Figure 6.4.

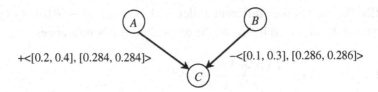

+<[0.2, 0.4], [0.284, 0.284]>   −<[0.1, 0.3], [0.286, 0.286]>

Figure 6.4   An example of EQPN.

As mentioned in Sections 6.1 and 6.3, the larger the weight of the influence, the higher the priority of the directed edge will be when the DAGs of time-series QPNs are combined. It is known that the center of interval $[p, q]$ can be determined by $(p + q)/2$. Based on the interval center, we now give the measure for comparing two forward weights represented as interval values.

Definition 6.9. Let $w_1 = [p_1, q_1]$ and $w_2 = [p_2, q_2]$ be two forward weights on two edges respectively in time-series EQPNs, where $[p_1, q_1]$ and $[p_2, q_2]$ are subsumed in $[0, 1]$. We say w_1 is larger than w_2, written $w_1 \succeq w_2$, if and only if $p_1 + q_1 > p_2 + q_2$.

For the fusion problem, we consider the following two cases when combining two edges: whether the two edges associated w_1 and w_2, respectively, are from the same or different EQPNs. For the former case, this definition will be used to decide the priorities, by which the edges are combined into the result QPN. For the latter case, this definition can be used to decide the composition result of the influences between the same pair of nodes in various EQPNs. Moreover, it is clear that $\succeq$ satisfies reflexivity, anti-symmetry and transitivity properties, and thus $(I, \succeq)$ is a partially ordered set on the space of probability interval values I. For example, we have $[0.3, 0.5] \succeq [0.1, 0.4]$, since $0.3 + 0.5$ is larger than $0.1 + 0.4$.

To sum up, taking as input time-series BNs, we can obtain the time-series EQPNs and provide a quantitative and conflict-free basis for network fusion, which will be discussed in the following sections.

6.5   Fusing DAG Structures of Time-Series EQPNs

In this section, we give the method for fusing DAG structures of time-series QPNs based on the concept of Markov equivalence, CPDAG's properties and qualitative characteristics. For simplification and clear illustration of our idea, we take the fusion of two DAGs as the representative case.

6.5.1 *Fusing equivalent common subgraphs*

As stated in Theorem 6.1, two DAGs are Markov equivalence if they have the same skeletons and v-structures, that is, these two DAGs describe the same probabilistic distribution and the same independency information [7]. Let G_1 and G_2 be two DAGs of two EQPNs respectively. If both G_1 and G_2 are Markov equivalent to some certain subgraphs of G_3, then G_3 is expected to be the fusion result of G_1 and G_2 with respect to graphical equivalence and probabilistic independencies. Meanwhile, the Markov-equivalence-based representation of inclusion relationship between DAGs makes the equivalent independencies of each input DAG be preserved in the result. Therefore, we establish our method based on this idea, such that the original conditional independencies can be preserved as much as possible in the result QPN. First, we give the following definition to describe the inclusion relationship between two DAGs.

Definition 6.10. We say DAG G_1 can be embedded into DAG G_2, if G_1 is Markov equivalent to a subgraph of G_2.

Example 6.4. Figures 6.5(a) and 6.5(b) illustrate two DAGs, denoted as G_1 and G_2, respectively. Figures 6.5(c) and 6.5(d) show the corresponding PDAGs of G_1 and G_2, respectively.

According to Definition 6.10, G_1 can be embedded into G_2, since G_1 is the Markov equivalent to the subgraph of G_2 on $\{A, B, C\}$.

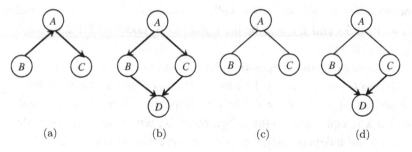

(a)   (b)   (c)   (d)

Figure 6.5 Embedded DAG.

Given two DAGs, $G_1 = (V_1, E_1)$ and $G_2 = (V_2, E_2)$, if there exists a DAG $G_3 = (V_3, E_3)$, such that $V_3 = V_1 \cup V_2$, $E_3 = E_1 \cup E_2$, and both G_1 and G_2 can be embedded into G_3, then G_3 is expected to be the result of fusing G_1 and G_2. Whether the DAG, like G_3, exists for any two given DAGs and how we can obtain the DAG are critical for fusing the DAG structures of time-series EQPNs. Actually, from the independence preservation point of view and people's intuition, the result DAG after fusing two ones ought to satisfy the following two properties:

(1) It should contain all independencies implied in the two participating DAGs.
(2) It should not contain the independencies that are not implied in any of the two participating DAGs.

The first property means that all the v-structures in G_1 and G_2 should be included in G_3. The second property means that there are no new v-structures and cycles generated in G_3 if they are not originally included in G_1 or G_2. These two properties require that the subgraph composed of all common nodes in G_1 and G_2 are Markov equivalent (i.e., free of conflicts), described by Theorem 6.3 as follows.

Theorem 6.3. *Let G_1 and G_2 be two DAGs. There must exist a DAG G_3, into which G_1 and G_2 can be embedded if the subgraphs of all common nodes in G_1 and G_2 are Markov equivalent.*

Proof. To prove this theorem, we will show the existence of G_3, such that both G_1 and G_2 are Markov equivalent to some certain subgraphs of G_3. Without loss of generality, we suppose $G_1 = (V_1, E_1)$, $G_2 = (V_2, E_2)$, and $V_1 \cap V_2 = V^* \neq \phi$. As well, we suppose $G_3 = (V_3, E_3)$ and let $V_3 = V_1 \cup V_2$ and $E_3 = \phi$ be the initial set of nodes and that of edges of G_3 respectively.

According to the supposition, let G_1^* and G_2^* be the subgraphs of V^* in G_1 and G_2, respectively. Due to the Markov equivalence of G_1^* and G_2^*, we add all edges in G_1^* or G_2^* to G_3. Thus, the subgraphs of G_1 and G_2 are Markov equivalent to the subgraph of G_3 with respect to the nodes in V^*, and the independencies on V^* are preserved in G_1, G_2 and G_3 in a conflict-free manner.

Then, for the edges in G_2 and those in G_1 but not in G_1^* and G_2^*, we add them to G_3 one by one if only there are no new v-structures will be generated. Note that all common nodes in G_1 and G_2 are in V^*. For each edge (written e) in G_1 and G_2 but not in G_1^* and G_2^*, e is either in G_1 or in G_2 while it is not possible that e is both in G_1 and in G_2 simultaneously. Thus, G_3 is a DAG on $V_1 \cup V_2$ satisfying $E_1 \subseteq E_3$ and $E_2 \subseteq E_3$.

Following, we prove both G_1 and G_2 can be embedded into G_3 by considering G_1 at first. Based on the above process of generating G_3, the subgraph of G_1 on V^* is Markov equivalent to the corresponding part in G_3 straightforwardly. Then, for the other part of G_1, all nodes and edges are the same with those in G_3. Therefore, we conclude that G_1 has the same skeleton and the same v-structure with the subgraph of G_3, which means the Markov equivalence. This conclusion holds for G_2 as well. $\qquad\square$

6.5.2 *Fusing inequivalent common subgraphs*

Based on Theorem 6.3, we adopt G_3 directly as the result of fusing the subgraphs of common nodes in G_1 and G_2. In the result, all equivalent independency information implied in all participating DAGs can be preserved. However, two properties of the result DAG, given in Section 6.5.1, are too strict for real-world situations, since the DAG in line with Theorem 6.3 frequently does not exist. The reason is that Markov equivalence between the subgraphs of the common nodes of G_1 and that of G_2 does not always hold in real world situations. A typical example is given as follows.

Example 6.5. In Figure 6.6, the subgraphs of common nodes in G_1 and G_2 are not Markov equivalent, since the v-structures in G_1 and G_2 with common nodes $\{B, C, D\}$ are different.

Therefore, it is necessary to discuss the method for fusing the given DAGs under more general cases than that in Theorem 6.3. As for the case that the subgraphs of common nodes are not Markov equivalent, we consider preserving the original independency information as much as possible in the result. That is, we will obtain the DAG as the result of fusing all subgraphs of common nodes by preserving the most equivalent independencies. Now, we first describe the size-based relationship between

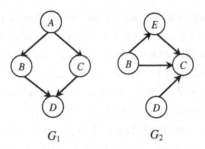

Figure 6.6 DAGs with common nodes $\{B, C, D\}$.

two DAGs, followed by the definition of the maximal equivalent common subgraph.

Definition 6.11 [7]. Let $G_1 = (V_1, E_1)$ and $G_2 = (V_2, E_2)$ be two DAGs. G_1 is larger than G_2, denoted $G_1 \subseteq G_2$, if $V_1 \subseteq V_2$ and $E_1 \subseteq E_2$.

Definition 6.12. The maximal equivalent common subgraph of G_1 and G_2, written G^*, is the subgraph of the common nodes in G_1 and G_2, and

(1) G^* can be embedded into G_1 and G_2 respectively,
(2) there does not exist any other subgraphs that are larger than G^* satisfying (1).

In this definition, (1) means that the independency information commonly implied in G_1 and G_2 can be represented in G^*, while (2) means that the most independency information can be preserved in the combination result. For this purpose, we start from the CPDAGs as the unique equivalent representation and then recover the DAG as the result. To obtain the maximal equivalent common subgraph of G_1 and G_2, our basic ideas and steps are summarized as follows:

(1) Based on Algorithm 6.1, for all the DAGs, we obtain the corresponding CPDAGs as their unique representation in terms of Markov equivalence. Let $CG_1 = (CV_1, CE_1)$ and $CG_2 = (CV_2, CE_2)$ be the CPDAG of G_1 and G_2 respectively.
(2) We obtain the intersection of CPDAGs CG_1 and CG_2, and suppose the PDAG $CG^* = CG_1 \cap CG_2 = (CV_1 \cap CV_2, CE_1 \cap CE_2)$ be the intersection result. We note that CG^* consists of a subset of all common

nodes of G_1 and G_2, corresponding to the subgraphs that are Markov equivalent in G_1 and G_2.

(3) By recovering the consistent extension from the corresponding CPDAG based on Algorithm 6.2, we can obtain the DAG as the fusion result. However, from the conclusion in [34] and the inherence of consistent extension, we know that there does not always exist a consistent extension for any given PDAG, while there may exist consistent extensions for some subgraphs of the given PDAG. Therefore, we obtain the maximal extensible subgraph G_M^* from CG^* such that the consistent extension of G_M^* does exist.

Steps (1) and (2) are straightforward. Following, we mainly discuss the algorithm for addressing Step (3).

It is pointed out that there exists a consistent extension for the PDAG if it has no v-structures and is chordal, or each undirected edge can be oriented as a directed one without generating cycles and influencing the existing v-structures. Accordingly, we preserve the v-structures in CG^* and consider adding other edges as many as possible, if no cycles and new v-structures will be generated.

Example 6.6. Suppose a CG^* is shown as Figure 6.7, where $B \rightarrow D$, $D \rightarrow E$ and $F \rightarrow E$ are not in the v-structures. Starting from the subgraph on $\{A, B, C, F\}$ and $\{A \rightarrow C, B \rightarrow C, F \rightarrow C\}$, if we add $B \rightarrow D$, then we can add $F \rightarrow E$ further, which will lead to a PDAG with five edges. However, if we add $D \rightarrow E$ first, then both $B \rightarrow D$ and $F \rightarrow E$ cannot be added anymore, which will lead to a PDAG with four edges.

Therefore, to add the edges by different orders will lead to different sizes of the result PDAG. To obtain the maximal extensible subgraph, G_M^*,

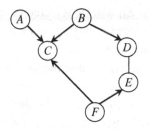

Figure 6.7 A CG^*.

Algorithm 6.3 Max-Subgraph //Obtaining the maximal extensible subgraph of CG^*

Input: $CG^* = (CV_1 \cap CV_2, CE_1 \cap CE_2)$
Output: Maximal extensible subgraph G_M^*
Steps:
1: If CG^* is a DAG Then Return CG^*
2: Initialization:
3:   $V \leftarrow CV_1 \cap CV_2$, $E \leftarrow CE_1 \cap CE_2$, $G = (V, E)$
4:   Initialize a graph $G' = (V', E')$
5:   $V' \leftarrow V$
6:   Add all edges corresponding to the v-structures in G into G', denoted as E'
7:   $E_0 \leftarrow \{e | e \in E, e \notin E'\} = \{e_1, e_2, \ldots e_m\}$, $m = |E_0|$
8: Let $x[1..m]$ be the flags that whether e_i will be added into G', $x_i \in \{0, 1\}$
9: $x[1..m] \leftarrow$ BBG (G', E_0) //Algorithm 6.4 to decide whether the edges in E_0 will be selected and added into G'
10: For $i \leftarrow 1$ To m Do
11:   If $x_i = 1$ Then
12:     $G' \leftarrow G' \cup \{e_i\}$
13:   End If
14: End For
15: Return $G_M^* \leftarrow G'$

---

of CG^*, we consider adding the candidate edges one by one based on the following branch and bound algorithm.

For edge selection, we adopt a max-heap, denoted as T and described as follows:

— *enode*: node in the binary tree T, whose left child and right child are associated with flags 1 and 0 respectively, describing whether the corresponding edge in E_0 will be selected or not;
— *level*: level number corresponding to *enode* as the current node in T;
— *parent*: parent node of *enode*;
— *size*: size of the subgraph including the selected edges from the root to *enode*;
— *nodes*: edges that have been selected currently;
— *upper*: the maximal possible size concerning the nodes that have been selected and those that have not been selected.

Algorithm 6.4 BBG

Input: PDAG G, Candidate edges $E = \{e_1, e_2, \ldots e_m\}$
Output: $\{x_1, x_2, \ldots, x_m\}$, $x_i \in \{0, 1\}$
Steps:

1: Construct an empty max-heap H; initialize a binary tree T
2: *enode* $\leftarrow \phi$, *cSize* $\leftarrow 0$, $i \leftarrow 1$, *maxSize* $\leftarrow 0$, *upper* $\leftarrow 0$, *cNodes* $\leftarrow \phi$, *rNodes* $\leftarrow \phi$
3: While $i \neq m + 1$ Do
4:   If feasible(G, *enode.nodes* $\cup \{e_i\}$) Then //Feasible if no cycles and no new v-structures are generated
5:     *cNodes* $\leftarrow$*enode.nodes* $\cup \{e_i\}$
6:     *cSize* $\leftarrow$*cSize*+1
7:     If *cSize*> *maxSize* Then
8:     *maxSize* $\leftarrow$*cSize*
9:     InsertToHeap(H, i+1, *maxSize*, *cNodes*, 1) //Add e_i and consider the next edge
10:   End If
11:   End If
12:   *rNodes* $\leftarrow \varphi$
13:   For $j \leftarrow i$+1 To m Do
14:     *rNodes* $\leftarrow$*rNodes* $\cup \{e_j\}$//Other edges except e_i
15:     If feasible(G, *rNodes*) Then
16:       *upper* $\leftarrow$*upper*+1
17:     End If
18:   End For
19:   If $|$ *enode.nodes* $\cup$*rNodes*$| \geq 1$ AND *upper* $\geq$*maxSize* Then
20:     InsertToHeap(H, i+1, *upper*, *cNodes*−$\{e_i\}$, 0)
21:   End If
22:   *enode* $\leftarrow$removeMaxHeap(H)
23:   $i \leftarrow$*enode.level*
24:   *enode* $\leftarrow$*enode.parent*
25: End While
26: For $i \leftarrow m$ Downto 1 Do
27:   If *enode.leftchild*=1 Then
28:     $x_i \leftarrow 1$
29:   Else
30:     $x_i \leftarrow 0$

31:      End If
32: End For
33: Return $\{x_1, x_2, \ldots, x_m\}$

The execution time of Algorithm 6.3 mainly depends on that of Algorithm 6.4, which will be $O(2^m)$ at the worst case. Actually, the average execution time of Algorithm 6.4 is much less than that of the worst case to a great extent due to the pruning strategies, which will be tested and verified by experiments in Section 6.7.

6.5.3 *Fusing DAGs of time-series EQPNs*

Considering the temporal specialty and in line with the Markov assumption, for each step when we fuse DAG G_1 and G_2 (whose CPDAGs are denoted as CG_1 and CG_2 respectively), we first derive the maximal equivalent subgraph G^*. Second, we consider adding possible edges in CG_2 into G^*, and then adding those in CG_1. In this process, an edge is feasible if no cycles will be generated and the existing v-structures will not be changed when adding this edge into G^*. For all the participating CPDAGs, CG_1, $CG_2, \ldots, CG_n$, the fusion sequence can be analogously described by the following blanket-based commutation: $CG_1, (CG_2, (\ldots, CG_{n-2}, (CG_{n-1}, CG_n)))$. Third, based on Algorithm 6.2, we can obtain the result DAG by the consistent extension of G^*. The above ideas are summarized and given in Algorithm 6.5, so that the DAGs of the time-series EQPNs can be fused while preserving the most independencies.

In the above steps, Algorithms 6.1 and 6.2 can be executed in polynomial time, where whether two DAGs are Markov equivalent can be checked easily in polynomial time as well. Algorithm 6.3 will be invoked for $O(n)$ times, and the execution time of Algorithm 6.3 is the efficiency bottleneck of Algorithm 6.5, which will be tested by experiments in Section 6.7.

Example 6.7. Considering the DAGs of G_1 and G_2 shown in Figures 6.8(a) and 6.8(b), respectively, the CPDAGs of G_1 and G_2 are shown in Figures 6.9(a) and 6.9(b), respectively. Based on Algorithm 6.3,

---

Algorithm 6.5 Fuse-DAG //Fusing DAGs of time-series EQPNs.

Input: DAGs of the time-series EQPNs $\{G_1, G_2, \ldots, G_n\}$
Output: DAG $G^* = (V^*, E^*)$
Steps:

1: For $i \leftarrow n$ Downto 1 Do //From the latest EQPN to the earliest one
2:    $G_1 = (V_1, E_1) \leftarrow G_{i-1}$; $G_2 = (V_1, E_1) \leftarrow G_i$
3:    $CG_1 \leftarrow$DAG-TO-CPDAG(G_1); $CG_2 \leftarrow$DAG-TO-CPDAG(G_2)
     //Algorithm 6.1
4:    $CG^* = (CV^*, CE^*) \leftarrow CG_1 \cap CG_2 = (CV_1 \cap CV_2, CE_1 \cap CE_2)$ //Intersection
     of G_1 and G_2's CPDAGs
5:    If the subgraphs of G_1 and G_2 on CV^* are not Markov equivalent Then
6:      $G_M^* = (CV_M, CE_M) \leftarrow$ Max-Subgraph(CG^*) //Algorithm 6.3
7:    Else
8:      $G_M^* = (CV_M, CE_M) \leftarrow CG^*$ //Theorem 6.3
9:    End If
10:    If $i = n$ Then
11:      For each edge e in $CE_2 - CE_M$ Do
12:        Let $e = (x, y)$, where x and y are the two nodes of e
13:        If feasible $(CV_M \cup \{x, y\}, CE_M \cup \{e\})$ Then
14:          $V_0 \leftarrow CV_M \cup \{x, y\}$, $E_0 \leftarrow CE_M \cup \{e\}$
15:        End If
16:      End For
17:    End If
18:    For each edge e in $CE_1 - CE_M$ Do
19:      Let $e = (x, y)$, where x and y are the two nodes of e
20:      If feasible $(CV_M \cup \{x, y\}, CE_M \cup \{e\})$ Then
21:        $V_0 \leftarrow CV_M \cup \{x, y\}$; $E_0 \leftarrow CE_M \cup \{e\}$
22:      End If
23:    End For
24:    $G_0 \leftarrow (V_0, E_0)$; $G_{i-1} \leftarrow G_0$
25: End For
26: $G^* \leftarrow$PDAG-TO-DAG(G_0) //Algorithm 6.2
27: Return G^*

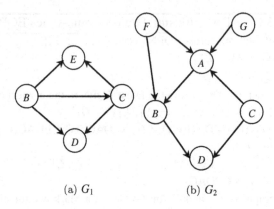

(a) G_1 (b) G_2

Figure 6.8   DAGs.

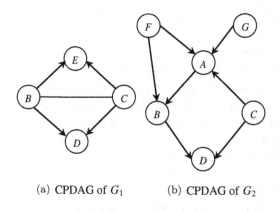

(a) CPDAG of G_1 (b) CPDAG of G_2

Figure 6.9   CPDAGs.

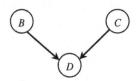

Figure 6.10   Maximal extensible equivalent subgraph by Algorithm 6.3.

the maximal extensible equivalent subgraph upon the common nodes { B, C, D} is shown in Figure 6.10. Based on Algorithm 6.5, the result CPDAG G_M^* by fusing the two CPDAGs in Figure 6.9 is shown in Figure 6.11, and the result DAG G^* is shown in Figure 6.12.

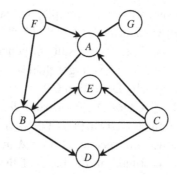

Figure 6.11   Result CPDAG G_M^*.

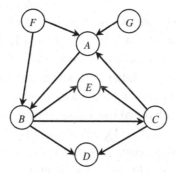

Figure 6.12   Result DAG G^*.

6.6   Fusing Qualitative Influences of Time-Series EQPNs

6.6.1   *Basic idea*

Upon the result DAG, denoted as G^* and obtained by fusing the graphical structures of the time-series EQPNs, in this section we consider fusing all concerned qualitative influences and obtaining the result influence for each edge in G^*. For each edge $A \to B$ in G^*, we are to combine all the concerned qualitative influences between A and B in the time-series EQPNs, denoted as $G_1, G_2, \ldots, G_n$, where we follow the Markov assumption of time-series specialties.

First, based on the weight-based enhancement in EQPN, we can differentiate the qualitative influences when we combine multiple ones between the same pair of nodes. Thus, the opposite influences on $A \to B$

can be combined consistently. For example, we suppose two opposite weighted influences between A and B are $S^{+\langle[0.1,0.3],[0.2,0.25]\rangle}(A, B)$ and $S^{-\langle[0.2,0.5],[0.1,0.2]\rangle}(A, B)$. Then, the result influence between these two nodes will be '$-$', since $0.2 + 0.5$ is larger than $0.1 + 0.3$ and $[0.2, 0.5] \succeq$ $[0.1, 0.3]$ holds accordingly by Definition 6.9.

Second, two kinds of edges $A \rightarrow B$ and $B \rightarrow A$ with opposite directions may exist simultaneously in two EQPNs, although the qualitative influence of A on B is the same as that of B on A in a certain EQPN. The influences can also be combined on the basis of the backward weight of $A \rightarrow B$ or $B \rightarrow A$ according to the direction of the edge between A and B in G^*. For example, we suppose two opposite weighted influences between A and B are $S^{+\langle[0.1,0.3],[0.2,0.25]\rangle}(A, B)$ and $S^{-\langle[0.2,0.5],[0.1,0.2]\rangle}$ (B, A), and further suppose $A \rightarrow B$ exists in G^*. Then, the weighted influences of A on B are '$+[0.1, 0.3]$' and '$-[0.1, 0.2]$' respectively, and $S^{-\langle[0.1,0.2],[0.2,0.5]\rangle}(A, B)$ can be derived from $S^{-\langle[0.2,0.5],[0.1,0.2]\rangle}(B, A)$.

Third, the influences in latter time slices are always more priori and important than those in earlier time slices from the practical time-series point of view. In line with the Markov assumption, we introduce a discount factor, denoted as d ($0 < d < 1$), when combing the influences from the latest EQPN to the earliest one. This means that if the weight on $A \rightarrow B$ in T_n is w_n, then the weight on $A \rightarrow B$ in T_{n-1} will be $d \cdot w_{n-1}$, and the weight on $A \rightarrow B$ in T_{n-2} will be $d \cdot d \cdot w_{n-2}$, and so on. Generally, the discount factor of time slice T_i will be d^{n-i}. For example, we suppose the weighted influences between A and B are $S^{+\langle[0.1,0.3],[0.2,0.25]\rangle}(A, B)$ and $S^{-\langle[0.2,0.5],[0.1,0.2]\rangle}(A, B)$ in T_n and T_{n-1} respectively, and further suppose $d = 0.85$. Then, we can obtain that '$[0.1, 0.3]$' of '$+$' has smaller contribution to the result influence than '$[0.2, 0.5]$' of '$-$', since $0.1 + 0.3 < 0.85 \times (0.2 + 0.5)$. For discussion convenience, following we will not discriminate the original weights or those multiplied by discount factors.

Thus, according to the above ideas, the fusion of weighted qualitative influences can be fulfilled by the composition of the influences and their weights in a pairwise manner while satisfying the following properties:

Property (1): The weight in the fusion result is also subsumed in $[0, 1]$. That is, $w_1, w_2 \subseteq [0, 1]$, and $w \subseteq [0, 1]$, where w_1 and w_2 are the weights of two influences participating in the composition, and w is the weight in the fusion result.

Property (2): Fusing two influences with the same qualitative signs, denoted as δ_1 and δ_2, will result in an influence with greater weight. That is, if $\delta_1 = \delta_2$, then $\delta = \delta_1 = \delta_2$ and $w \geq w_1$, $w \geq w_2$.

Property (3): Fusing two influences with different signs will result in an influence that is dependent on but less than the weightier one. That is, if $\delta_1 \neq \delta_2$ and $w_1 \geq w_2$, then $\delta = \delta_1$ and $w \leq w_1$.

6.6.2 Fusion algorithm

Evidence theory [150] focuses on the methods for combining independent evidences to achieve the desired decision. Uncertainty is introduced in evidence theory and the strict demands in the classical Bayes theory are relaxed, including the complete priori probabilities, conditional probabilities, uniform frame of discernment, etc. By means of evidence theory, the overlapped or conflict evidences can be combined effectively. However, the high time-complexity of general combination rules makes them not be practical for combining two weighted influences to address the composition of the weighted influences during EQPN fusion. A superposition method for combining fuzzy association degrees was proposed in [100], where the combination of multiple association degrees can be fulfilled efficiently. By adopting the evidence superposition idea, we also gave the conflict-free inference methods of QPN with rough-set and interval-probability based weights [181]. Consequently, inspired by the evidence theory, the basic idea of evidence superposition and the conflict-free composition of the weighted influences in general QPNs, in this section we give a superposition method for fusing the weighted qualitative influences for each edge in G^*, reflecting the temporal specialties and conforming to the above properties.

Without loss of generality, we suppose the edge between A and B in G^* is $A \to B$. Thus, we consider the forward weight of the influence of A on B and the backward weight of the influence of B on A, since $S^{\delta\langle w, w' \rangle}(B, A)$ implies that $S^{\delta\langle w \rangle}(B, A)$ and $S^{\delta\langle w \rangle}(A, B)$.

Definition 6.13. Suppose $S^{\delta_1\langle [p,q] \rangle}(A, B)$ and $S^{\delta_2\langle [r,s] \rangle}(A, B)$ are the weighted qualitative influences of A on B in time slice T_1 and

T_2, respectively, and d is the discount factor. $S^{\delta\langle[u,v]\rangle}(A, B) = S^{\delta_1\langle[p,q]\rangle}(A, B) \vee S^{\delta_2\langle[r,s]\rangle}(A, B)$, in which δ, u and v are defined as follows:

(1) If $\delta_1 = \delta_2$, then $\delta = \delta_1 = \delta_2, u = r+d\cdot p-d\cdot r\cdot p, v = s+d\cdot q-d\cdot s\cdot q$.

(2) If $\delta_1 \neq \delta_2$ and $[r, s] \succeq [d\cdot p, d\cdot q]$, then $\delta = \delta_2, u = \min\{|[r, s]-[d\cdot p, d\cdot q]|\} + d\cdot q\cdot r, v = \max\{|[r, s] - [d\cdot p, d\cdot q]|\} + d\cdot p\cdot s$.

(3) If $\delta_1 \neq \delta_2$ and $[d\cdot p, d\cdot q] \succeq [r, s]$, then $\delta = \delta_1, u = \min\{|[d\cdot p, d\cdot q] - [r, s]|\} + d\cdot p\cdot s, v = \max\{|[d\cdot p, d\cdot q] - [r, s]|\} + d\cdot q\cdot r$.

(4) If $\delta_1 \neq \delta_2$ and $[r, s] = [d\cdot p, d\cdot q]$, then $\delta = \delta_1 \oplus \delta_2, u = v = [r, s] = [d\cdot p, d\cdot q]$.

(5) Otherwise, $\delta = \delta_1 \oplus \delta_2, u = 0, v = 1$.

In this definition, $|[r, s] - [d\cdot p, d\cdot q]| = |[d\cdot p, d\cdot q] - [r, s]| = \{|r - d\cdot p|, |r - d\cdot q|, |s - d\cdot p|, |s - d\cdot q|\}|$, and the rule for $\oplus$-operator is given in [163].

Clearly, $[u, v] \subseteq [0, 1]$ holds in the five cases in Definition 6.13, and Property (1) is satisfied. We note that case (1) makes the consistent influences combined by increased weights, and Property (2) is satisfied. The conflicts generated when fusing the opposite influences between the same pair of nodes can be well resolved by case (2) and case (3), and thus Property (3) is satisfied. Case (4) implies the rule of $\oplus$-operator in general QPNs, which will be adopted when the weights of the participating opposite influences are equal. Case (5) gives the fusion method for the case that $[r, s]$ and $[d\cdot p, d\cdot q]$ cannot be compared, which means whether $[r, s]$ is stronger than or equal to $[d\cdot p, d\cdot q]$ cannot be determined.

Therefore, for each edge in G^*, we adopt Definition 6.13 and consider combining the influences that exists in $G_n, G_{n-1}, \ldots, G_1$ one by one. The basic idea for fusing the weighted influences is given in Algorithm 6.6.

Suppose there are $O(m)$ edges in $G_1, G_2, \ldots, G_n$ and G^*. Then, in each iteration for fusing the influences of the current edge in G^*, Step 6 will be executed for $O(n \cdot m)$ times and Step 8 will be executed for $O(n \cdot m \cdot m)$ times. Generally for all edges in G^*, the time complexity of Algorithm 6.6 will be $O(m) \cdot O(n \cdot m \cdot m) = O(m^3 \cdot n)$ at the worst case.

Example 6.8. Suppose the weighted influences of $B \rightarrow D$ in G_1 and G_2 (in Figure 6.8) are '$-[0.2, 0.6]$' and '$+[0.1, 0.8]$' respectively,

Algorithm 6.6 Fuse-Influence

Input: Result DAG G^*, EQPNs $\{G_1, G_2, \ldots, G_n\}$
Output: EQPN of G^*
Steps:

1:   $f \leftarrow d$//Discount factor
2: For each edge e in G^* Do
3:     Let $e = (x, y)$, where x and y are the two nodes of e
4:     For $i \leftarrow n$ Downto 2 Do
5:       $S^{\delta\langle[u,v]\rangle}(x, y) \leftarrow S^{\delta=0\langle[0,1]\rangle}(x, y)$ //Initialization
6:       If (x, y) or (y, x) is in G_i Then
7:         $S^{\delta\langle[u,v]\rangle}(x, y) \leftarrow S^{\delta_i\langle[p,q]\rangle}(x, y)$
8:         If (x, y) or (y, x) is in G_{i-1} Then
9:           $S^{\delta\langle[u,v]\rangle}(x, y) \leftarrow S^{\delta\langle[u,v]\rangle}(x, y) \vee S^{\delta_{i-1}\langle[r,s]\rangle}(x, y)$ //Definition 6.13
10:      End If
11:       $S^{\delta_{i-1}\langle[r,s]\rangle}(x, y) \leftarrow S^{\delta\langle[u,v]\rangle}(x, y)$ // For fusing the previous EQPN
12:      End If
13:     End For
14:     $d \leftarrow f^{n-(i-2)}$// Discount factor for the previous time slice
15: End For

and d is 0.85. From the result DAG in Figure 6.11, $B \rightarrow D$ does exist. By case (2) of Definition 6.13, we can obtain the result of fusing the two participating influences will be '+[0.151, 0.736]', since '$-$' in G_1 is opposite to '+' in G_2 and [0.1, 0.8] $\succeq$ [$d \cdot 0.2, d \cdot 0.6$] according to Definition 6.9.

6.7   Experimental Results and Applied Simulation

In this section, we first show experimental results of our methods for EQPNs' abstraction and their fusion, and further give the simulation when applying our methods to decision making in a robotic system, presented in Subsections 6.7.1 and 6.7.2, respectively.

6.7.1   *Experimental results*

To test the feasibility of our methods, we implemented relevant algorithms and tested the efficiency and correctness of them. The experiments were conducted on the machine running Windows XP Professional, Intel Pentium

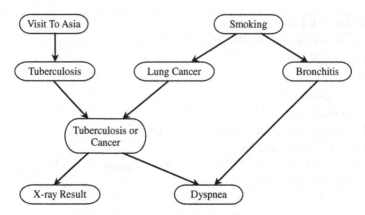

Figure 6.13   Chest-clinic network structure.

processor 2.6 GHz CPU, 1GB memory, and the code was written in JAVA. Our experiments were based on the benchmark chest-clinic network (also called Asia network) [31, 32]. It is well known that the chest-clinic network is a small BN for a fictitious medical domain about whether a patient has *tuberculosis, lung cancer or bronchitis*, related to their *X-ray, dyspnea, visit-to-Asia* and *smoking status*. The general structure of this network is shown in Figure 6.13, which contains 8 nodes and 8 arcs. Each node has only two possible values (i.e., True or False) described by 1 or 0, respectively. For simplification, we use V, T, TOC, X, S, C, B and D to denote *Visit To Asia, Tuberculosis, Tuberculosis or Cancer, X-ray result, Smoking, Lung Cancer, Bronchitis* and *Dyspnea*, respectively.

First, we tested the efficiency of the fusion method given in this chapter. When fusing the time-series EQPNs, Algorithms 6.5 and 6.6 run in polynomial time, which has been analyzed theoretically in Sections 6.5.3 and 6.6.2, respectively. We tested the practical efficiency of Algorithm 6.3, the efficiency bottleneck of the whole fusion method, where we manually generated the DAG pairs with various sizes by referring to the chest-clinic network. The execution time of Algorithm 6.3 on various sized CG^* is shown in Figure 6.14, from which we can see that the execution time is basically linear with the increase of the size of CG^*. This verifies the effectiveness of the pruning strategies that we presented in Algorithm 6.3 and ultimately guarantees the efficiency of the whole fusion method to a great extent.

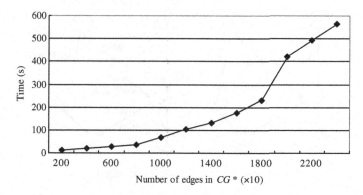

Figure 6.14 Efficiency of Algorithm 6.3.

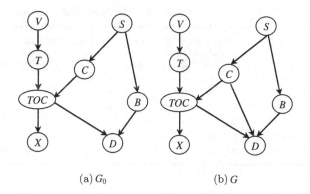

(a) G_0 (b) G

Figure 6.15 G_0 and G.

Second, we tested the correctness of the fusion result by first considering the result of DAG fusion, which is the basis and the most challenging step for fusing the time-series EQPNs. We adopted the DAG learned from the chest-clinic benchmark data [31] as the criteria, denoted as G_0, where we denoted the dataset as D. We then divided D into 10 independent subsets, from which we learned 10 DAGs by PowerConstructor [32] respectively. Following, we fused these 10 DAGs by our fusion method in Section 6.5 and obtained the result DAG, denoted as G. G_0 and G are shown in Figures 6.15(a) and 6.15(b), respectively. By comparing these two DAGs, we can see that the DAG structures of G_0 and G are equivalent basically except that $C \to D$ is in G_0 but not in G. This makes us further consider testing the correctness of our fusion method with respect to the

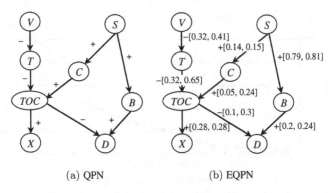

(a) QPN   (b) EQPN

Figure 6.16   QPN and EQPN corresponding to G_0.

Table 6.1   Inference results on the QPN and EQPN of G_0.

Evidence		Inference results on the EQPN to G_0								Inference results on the EQPN to G							
Node	Sign	V	S	T	C	TOC	B	X	D	V	S	T	C	TOC	B	X	D
V	+	+	0	−	0	+	0	+	−	+	0	−	0	+	0	+	−
S	+	0	+	0	+	+	+	+	+	0	+	0	+	+	+	+	+
T	+	−	0	+	0	−	0	−	+	−	0	+	0	−	0	−	+
B	+	0	+	0	+	+	+	+	+	0	+	0	+	+	+	+	+
X	+	0	0	0	0	+	0	+	−	0	0	0	0	+	0	+	−

applicability when incorporating the fusion result into the inferences of uncertain knowledge, which will be shown later in this section.

Meanwhile, we tested the effectiveness of the interval-valued weights and QPN enhancement in resolving the composition conflicts when fusing the qualitative influences. We adopted the chest-clinic QPN (whose DAG is shown in Figure 6.15(a)), derived the corresponding EQPN, and implemented the algorithm for QPN inferences [55]. The QPN and EQPN are shown in Figures 6.16(a) and 6.16(b), respectively. Particularly for the transitivity property when inferring EQPN, in this experiment we simply multiplied the two forward weights as most of the existing methods for conflict-free QPN inferences [29, 30, 39, 40], that is, $S^{\delta \langle [u,v] \rangle}(A, B) = S^{\delta_1 \langle [p,q] \rangle}(A, B) \wedge S^{\delta_2 \langle [r,s] \rangle}(A, B)$, where $\delta = \delta_1 \otimes \delta_2$, $u = p \cdot r$ and $v = q \cdot s$. Then, under the same evidence and target, the inference results of the chest-clinic QPN and EQPN are shown in Table 6.1, from which

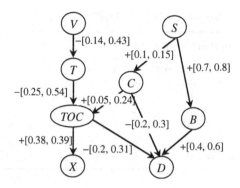

Figure 6.17 EQPN corresponding to *G*.

we can see that the composition conflicts during QPN inferences can be well resolved by EQPN. This verifies that the interval-valued weights and the QPN enhancement proposed in Section 4 are effective for fusing the qualitative influences of time-series QPNs.

Third, based on our method in Section 6.6, we derived the result qualitative influences on *G* (in Figure 6.15(b)) from the 10 participating EQPNs and obtained the result EQPN, shown in Figure 6.17. From the practical application point of view, we compared the inference results on the EQPN (in Figure 6.16(b)) corresponding to G_0 learned from data, and those on the EQPN corresponding to *G* (in Figure 6.17) obtained by our fusion method. Under the same evidence and target, the inference results are shown in Table 6.2, from which we can see that all the inferences on the EQPN of *G* are the same as those on that of G_0. This verifies that the fusion result is correct for uncertainty inferences and also verifies the effectiveness of the fusion method given in this chapter.

The above experimental results show that our algorithm for fusing DAGs by preserving the maximal independencies is efficient to a certain extent, which makes the fusion of time-series EQPNs be able to be fulfilled efficiently. As well, the interval-value-based enhancement of QPN is also effective to resolve the conflict generated when combining several qualitative influences that may appear simultaneously in fusing EQPNs. Moreover, the inference results of uncertainties on the result EQPN are correct with respect to the inference results on the standard EQPN directly learned from data. Generally, the experimental results given in this section

Table 6.2 Inference results on the EQPNs corresponding to G_0 and G.

Evidence		Inference results on QPN								Inference results on EQPN							
Node	Sign	V	S	T	C	TOC	B	X	D	V	S	T	C	TOC	B	X	D
V	+	+	0	−	0	+	0	+	−	+	0	−	0	+	0	+	−
S	+	0	+	0	+	+	+	+	?	0	+	0	+	+	+	+	+
T	+	−	0	+	0	−	0	−	+	−	0	+	0	−	0	−	+
B	+	0	+	0	+	+	+	+	?	0	+	0	+	+	+	+	+
X	+	0	0	0	0	+	0	+	−	0	0	0	0	+	0	+	−

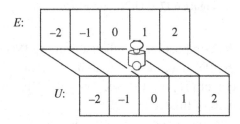

Figure 6.18 A robot in five units.

verify that our method for fusion time-series EQPNs is efficient and effective.

6.7.2 Simulation results

To verify the applicability of our methods in realistic applications, we made simulations by applying our methods to a robotic system as the representative application of time-series decision making upon uncertain knowledge. We adopted a robotic system with a robot (i.e., agent) in five units [142], shown as Figure 6.18. Let $E = \{-2, -1, 0, 1, 2\}$ represent the environment to describe the position of the robot. For each position, there is a utility to select the robot's action, denoted as U. Let A_i represent the action of the robot in time slice i and $A_i = L$ (or R) representing that the robot moves leftward (or rightward) by one unit. We suppose the robot is aware of its position by a sensor signal S_i in time slice i. A dynamic network, i.e., time-series BN, whose structure is shown in Figure 6.19, is used to select the robot's action with the maximal utility based on probabilistic inferences.

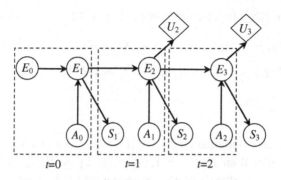

Figure 6.19 Structure of the time-series BN.

Initially, we suppose $E_0 = 0$ and $A_0 = R$ in time slice 0. Part of the CPTs of the variables in time slice 1 is as follows:

$P(E_2 = 1|A_1 = R, E_1 = 0) = 0.5, P(E_2 = 1|A_1 = R, E_1 = 1)$

$= P(E_2 = 1|A_1 = R, E_1 = 2) = 0.25$

$P(E_2 = 1|A_1 = R, E_1 = -1) = P(E_2 = 1|A_1 = R, E_1 = -2) = 0$

$P(S_1 = 1|E_1 = -2) = P(S_1 = 1|E_1 = -1) = P(S_1 = 1|E_1 = 0)$

$= P(S_1 = 1|E_1 = 2) = 0.025, P(S_1 = 1|E_1 = 1) = 0.9$

$P(E_1 = -1|E_0 = 0, A_0 = R) = P(E_1 = 0|E_0 = 0, A_0 = R) = 0.25,$

$P(E_1 = 1|E_0 = 0, A_0 = R) = 0.5$

$P(E_1 = 2|E_0 = 0, A_0 = R) = P(E_1 = -2|E_0 = 0, A_0 = R) = 0.$

U can be computed by probabilistic inferences on the time-series BN shown in Figure 6.19. However, for simplicity, we just focused on underlying probabilistic inferences and ignored the details for obtaining U. Considering the time-series BN in time slices 0 and 1, we tested the effectiveness of the robot's action by comparing those directly on the original time-series BN and the derived EQPN, respectively.

First, we considered the probabilistic inferences to decide the robot's action in time slice 1, that is to decide whether $A_1 = R$ or $A_1 = L$ by computing and comparing $P(E_2 = 1|E_0 = 0, A_0 = R, S_1 = 1, A_1 = R)$ and $P(E_2 = 1|E_0 = 0, A_0 = R, S_1 = 1, A_1 = L)$. Based on the algorithms of BN's precise inferences [121, 128], we obtained

$$P(E_2 = 1 | E_0 = 0, A_0 = R, S_1 = 1, A_1 = R)$$
$$= \sum_{E_1} P(E_2 = 1 | A_1 = R, E_1) P(S_1 = 1 | E_1) P(E_1 | E_0 = 0, A_0 = R)$$
$$= 0.14375.$$

Similarly, we obtained $P(E_2 = 1 | E_0 = 0, A_0 = R, S_1 = 1, A_1 = L)$, which is smaller than $P(E_2 = 1 | E_0 = 0, A_0 = R, S_1 = 1, A_1 = R)$. Thus, the decision of the robot's action should be $A_1 = R$.

From the above results of the precise probabilistic inferences with the time-series BN, we can see that the precise computation of the probability distributions is not efficient, which has been proved to have exponential time complexity [36]. Actually, the precise computation is intuitively unnecessary, since we only need a comparable metric of the probabilities or utilities to decide $A_i = R$ or $A_i = L$. Thus, qualitative representation and inferences of the corresponding time-series BN are well expected to replace the heavy precise probability computation but obtain the same result of the robot's action.

Then, for the time-series BN in Figure 6.19, we used Definition 6.7 to derive the time-series EQPN concerning time slices 0 and 1, shown in Figure 6.20, where the qualitative influences were derived by the following variant of Definition 6.1 especially for the variables with more than two values in the robotic system: $S^+(A, B)$ iff $P(B = b_1 | A, x) > P(B = b_2 | A, x)$ for all $b_1 > b_2$, or $P(B | A = a_1, x) > P(B | A = a_2, x)$ for all $a_1 > a_2$.

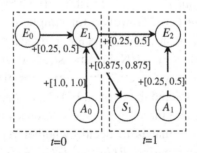

Figure 6.20   Time-series EQPN concerning time slices 0 and 1.

Consequently, qualitative uncertain knowledge can be inferred by the QPN's inference algorithm in polynomial time [55] and Definition 6.13 proposed in Section 6.6. Taking as input '+' on A_0, the ultimate weighted qualitative sign on A_1 will be '+[0.0625, 0.25]', which means that the decision of the robot's action in time slice 1 should be consistent with that in time slice 0, that is $A_1 = R$. This is consistent with the previous action obtained directly by the algorithm of BN's precise inferences, while the computation is more straightforward and the cost has been reduced greatly.

Further, we considered fusing the EQPNs in adjacent time slices in Figure 6.20, and then deciding the action on the fusion result directly. It can be seen that the DAGs in time slices 0 and 1 are equivalent, so we only considered fusing the weighted influences in these two time slices. By Algorithm 6.6, we obtained the result EQPN, shown in Figure 6.21, where the node of the initial action (denoted as A_0) in the first time slice and the node of the unknown action in the last time slice as the target node (denoted as A') will not be combined with those in other time slices. 0.85 is assigned as the discount factor when combining qualitative influences between the same pair of nodes.

Finally, the robot's action in time slice 1 can be selected by the qualitative inferences with the result EQPN. Taking as input the qualitative sign of the initial environment and action ('+' on A and '+' on E), the result weighted qualitative sign on A' will be ('+[0.41, 0.71]'$\oplus$'+[1.0, 1.0]')$\otimes$'+[0.25, 0.5]'='+[0.25, 0.5]'. This means that the robot's action in time slice 1 will be $A_1 = R$, which is consistent with the result obtained on the time-series EQPN shown in Figure 6.20. Therefore, we conclude that equivalent actions of the robot in time slice 1 can be obtained on

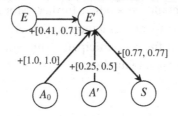

Figure 6.21 EQPN as fusion result.

the time-series BN, the time-series EQPN and the fusion-result EQPN, respectively.

6.8 Conclusions

To achieve the global uncertain knowledge during a period of time for decision making or action selection with respect to the dynamic changing characteristics of data, the method for fusing time-series uncertain knowledge was presented in this chapter by adopting QPN as the framework of uncertainty representation. To fuse the DAGs and the qualitative influences in the time-series QPNs, we enhanced the QPN by interval-valued weights, and then gave the corresponding fusion algorithms, where Markov equivalence and its properties, Markov assumption in temporal situations, and evidence superposition were incorporated.

Theoretic analysis, experimental and simulation results show the efficiency, effectiveness and applicability of the methods presented in this chapter. We conclude that the concept and mechanisms of EQPNs for fusing time-series uncertain knowledge are applicable in realistic intelligent situations. From the perspective of real applications, we note that the computation cost of the inferences on the result EQPN will be less than that on the original time-series EQPN, since the decision is independent of the number of concerned time slices and a certain amount of cost has been spent for fusing time-series EQPNs. In particular, the more the participating time slices, the more efficient the decision will be made on the result EQPN.

The method for fusing time-series uncertain knowledge presented in this chapter establishes basis for further studies on uncertain knowledge fusion. Intuitively, to incorporate the uncertain knowledge in each time slice and that between adjacent time slices will be more general but more challenging. The associations or dependencies between any two QPNs in adjacent time slices could be studied further. Moreover, latent variables could be incorporated into the result model to describe hidden dependencies newly generated when fusing participating uncertain knowledge models while not existing in separate models.

Chapter 7

Summary

Knowledge discovery and knowledge fusion are everlasting and challenging subjects with great interest in several paradigms including data science, artificial intelligence, machine learning, information retrieval, etc. In the background of big data, it is desirable to discover knowledge from massive, distributed, heterogeneous, uncertain and dynamically changing data, such that data understanding, data utilization and information services could be fulfilled pertinently. Meanwhile, it is more and more important to fuse fragmented, heterogeneous, multi-source knowledge from the perspective of big data intelligence and knowledge engineering, such that analysis prediction and decision could be performed appropriately.

Definitely, it is not possible to incorporate all contents of knowledge discovery in one book, and this book is no exception. Thus, by considering the uncertain knowledge represented by probabilistic graphical models (e.g., Bayesian Network) ubiquitous in view of the inherent characteristics of massive, distributed, uncertain and dynamically changing data, we mainly address the discovery and fusion of uncertain knowledge in data. Undoubtedly, it is not feasible and possible to provide universal methodologies for knowledge discovery and fusion, especially for big data analysis driven by applications. Thus, surrounding knowledge acquisition, inference and fusion (highlighted in knowledge engineering) and incorporating the massive, distributed, heterogeneous, uncertain and dynamically changing characteristics (reflected in big data), we are just to systematically illustrate the roadmap of our research findings oriented to specific applications and provide some references for researchers in relevant paradigms.

In this book, we address the discovery of uncertain knowledge represented by Bayesian Network (BN), uncertain knowledge and inferences for lineage analysis/error detection/user similarity discover in social media, uncertain knowledge fusion in dynamic situations. We mainly give the methods for data-intensive learning and inferences of BNs using MapReduce, as well as the semantics-preserving methods for the fusion of logical and probabilistic knowledge and that of time-series probabilistic knowledge. Theoretic analysis or experimental results are given to guarantee the feasibility of these methods.

The contents in this book leave open many challenging problems that are worth following and studying further.

- The efficiency of many recursive and costly operations should be improved for learning and inferences of large-scale BNs. Thus, the mechanisms for both data-intensive and compute-intensive processing should be studied.
- The association and causal relationships implied in massive, distributed, uncertain and dynamic data should be leveraged other than user similarities in social media given in this book. Thus, the mechanisms for representing and inferring customized uncertain knowledge in terms of big data and oriented to specific data-centered applications should be explored.
- The quality of massive, distributed, uncertain and dynamically changing data should be improved for effective knowledge discovery. Thus, the novel algorithms for data cleaning and data quality should be considered by incorporating lineage analysis, entity resolution and knowledge inferences.
- The fusion of uncertain knowledge and that fragmented/heterogeneous/ multi-source knowledge should be generalized to suite practical situations. Thus, the mechanisms should be studied for fusing knowledge frameworks with different theoretic basis or different representations in a specific domain, but without strong assumptions of semantics (e.g., independence between adjacent time slices) in concerned knowledge frameworks.
- A large number of prevalent data analysis applications based on uncertain knowledge representation, inferences and fusion could be studied.

First, latent variables (a.k.a. hidden variables) could be incorporated into BNs to model user behaviors or preferences, and thus the underlying techniques of data-intensive learning and inferences of BNs with latent variables should be studied.

Second, knowledge graphs could be extended by incorporating BNs to make associations among entities described with uncertainties quantitatively. Thus, the novel mechanisms for fusing knowledge graphs in multiple domains and BNs learned from corresponding data should be studied, where the strategies for processing big graphs and massive data should be addressed accordingly.

The above two aspects of data analysis applications are inherent basis for link prediction, association query processing and knowledge completion from the perspective of knowledge graph, and are effective means for combining domain knowledge with probabilistic inferences from the perspective of probabilistic graphical model.

References

1. Acar, U., Buneman, P., Cheney, J., Bussche, J., Kwasnikowska, N., and Vansummeren, S. A graph model of data and workflow provenance. *Proceedings of the 2nd Workshop on the Theory and Practice of Provenance (TaPP)*, 2010.
2. Aggarwal, C. *Managing and Mining Uncertain Data*. Berlin: Springer Publishing Company, Incorporated, 2009.
3. Aggarwal, C. and Yu, P. A survey of uncertain data algorithms and applications. *IEEE Transactions on Knowledge and Data Engineering*. 2009, 21(5): 609–623.
4. Agrawal, P., Sarma, A., Ullman, J., and Widom, J. Foundations of uncertain-data integration. *Proceedings of the VLDB Endowment (PVLDB)*, 2010, 3(1): 1080–1090.
5. Agrawal, D., Abbadi, A., Antony, S., and Das, S. Data management challenges in cloud computing infrastructures. *Proceedings of the 10th International Workshop on Databases in Networked Information Systems (DNIS)*, LNCS 5999, 2010, pp. 1–10.
6. Akcora, C., Carminati, B., and Ferrari, E. User similarities on social networks. *Journal of Social Network Analysis and Mining*, 2013, 3(3): 475–495.
7. Andersson, S. A characterization of Markov equivalence classes for acyclic digraphs. *Annals of Statistics*, 1997, 25(2): 505–541.
8. Anderson, A., Huttenlocher, D., Kleinberg, J., and Leskovec, J. Effects of user similarity in social media. *Proceedings of the 5th International Conference on Web Search and Web Data Mining (WSDM)*, 2012, pp. 703–712.

9. Bahmani, B., Kumar, R., and Vassilvitskii, S. Densest subgraph in streaming and MapReduce. *Proceedings of the VLDB Endowment (PVLDB)*, 2012, 5(5): 454–465.

10. Bao, Z., Koehler, H., Zhou X., and Ling, T. Storage and use provenance information for relational query. *Proceedings of the 16th International Conference on Database Systems for Advanced Applications (DASFAA)*, 2011, pp. 429–433.

11. Basak, A., Brinster, I., Ma, X., and Mengshoel, O. Accelerating Bayesian network parameter learning using Hadoop and MapReduce. *Proceedings of the 1st International Workshop on Big Data, Streams and Heterogeneous Source Mining: Algorithms, Systems, Programming Models and Applications (BigMine)*, 2012, pp. 101–108.

12. Benjelloun, O., Sarma, A., Halevy, A., Theobald, M., and Widom, J. Databases with uncertainty and lineage. *The VLDB Journal*, 2008, 17(2): 243–264.

13. Beskales, G., Ilyas, I., and Golab, L. Sampling the repairs of functional dependency violations under hard constraints. *Proceedings of the VLDB Endowment (PVLDB)*, 2010, 3(1): 197–207.

14. Bhattacharyya, P., Garg, A., and Wu, S. Analysis of user keyword similarity in online social networks. *Social Network Analysis and Mining*, 2011, 1(3): 143–158.

15. Graham-Rowe, D., Goldston, D., and Doctorow, C., *et al.* Big data: Science in the petabyte era. *Nature*, 2008, 455: 8–9.

16. Bolt, J., Gaag, L., and Renooij, S. Introducing situational signs in qualitative probabilistic networks. *International Journal of Approximate Reasoning*, 2005, 38(3): 333–354.

17. Bouhamed, H., Masmoudi, A., Lecroq, T., and Rebaï, A. A new learning structure heuristic of Bayesian networks from data. *Proceedings of the 8th International Conference on Machine Learning and Data Mining in Pattern Recognition (MLDM)*, 2012, pp. 183–197.

18. Brenner, E. and Sontag, D. SparsityBoost: A new scoring function for learning Bayesian network structure. *Proceedings of the 29th Conference on Uncertainty in Artificial Intelligence (UAI)*, 2013, pp. 112–121.

19. Bringmann, B., Berlingerio, M., Bonchi, F., and Gionis, A. Learning and predicting the evolution of social networks. *Journal of Intelligent Systems*, 2010, 25(4): 26–35.

20. Buneman, P., Cheney, J., Tan, W., and Vansummeren, S. Curated databases. *Proceedings of the 27th ACM SIGMOD-SIGACT-SIGART Symposium on Principles of Database Systems (PODS)*, 2008, pp. 1–12.

21. Buntine, W. A guide to the literature on learning probabilistic networks from data. *IEEE Transactions on Knowledge and Data Engineering*, 1996, 8(2): 195–210.

22. Campos, C. and Cozman, F. Belief updating and learning in semi-qualitative probabilistic networks. *Proceedings of the 21st Conference in Uncertainty in Artificial Intelligence (UAI)*, 2005, pp. 153–160.

23. Campos, C. and Ji, Q. Efficient structure learning of Bayesian networks using constraints. *Journal of Machine Learning Research*, 2011, 12(2): 663–689.

24. Campos, C. and Cozman, F. Complexity of inferences in polytree-shaped semi-qualitative probabilistic networks. *Proceedings of the 27th AAAI Conference on Artificial Intelligence (AAAI)*, 2013, pp. 217–223.

25. Cano, A., Masegosa, A., and Moral, S. A method for integrating expert knowledge when learning Bayesian networks from data. *IEEE Transactions on Systems, Man and Cybernetics, Part B*, 2011, 41(5): 1382–1394.

26. Chapman, A., Blaustein, B., and Elsaesser, C. Provenance-based belief. *Proceedings of the 2nd Workshop on the Theory and Practice of Provenance (TaPP)*, 2010, pp. 11–16.

27. Chen, R., Mao, Y., and Kiringa, I. GRN model of probabilistic databases: construction, transition and querying. *Proceedings of the 2010 ACM SIGMOD International Conference on Management of Data (SIGMOD)*, 2010, pp. 291–302.

28. Chen, H., Ku, W. S., and Wang, H. Cleansing uncertain databases leveraging aggregate constraints. *Proceedings of the 26th International Conference on Data Engineering (ICDE) Workshops*, 2010, pp. 128–135.

29. Chen, W., Zong, L., Huang, W., Ou, G., Wang, Y., and Yang, D. An empirical study of massively parallel Bayesian networks learning for sentiment extraction from unstructured text. *Proceedings of the 13th Asia-Pacific Web Conference on Web Technologies and Applications (APWeb)*, LNCS 6612, 2011, pp. 424–435.

30. Cheney, J., Chiticariu, L., and Tan, W. Provenance in databases: Why, how, and where. *Foundations and Trends in Databases*, 2007, 1(4): 379–474.

31. Cheng, J., Bell, D., and Liu, W. Learning belief networks from data: An information theory based approach. *Proceedings of the 6th International Conference on Information and Knowledge Management (CIKM)*, 1997, pp. 325–331.

32. Cheng, J. PowerConstructor System. http://webdocs.cs.ualberta.ca/^jcheng/bnpc.htm, 2011.

33. Chickering, D. Learning equivalence classes of Bayesian-network structures. *Journal of Machine Learning Research*, 2000, 2(3): 445–498.

34. Chickering, D. A transformational characterization of Bayesian network structures. *Proceedings of the 11th Annual Conference on Uncertainty in Artificial Intelligence (UAI)*, 1995, pp. 87–98.

35. Chockler, H. and Halpern, J. Responsibility and blame: A structural-model approach. *Journal of Artificial Intelligence Research*, 2004, 22: 93–115.

36. Cooper, G. The computational complexity of probabilistic inference using Bayesian belief networks. *Artificial Intelligence*, 1990, 42(2–3): 393–405.

37. Cooper, G. and Herskovits, E. A Bayesian method for the induction of probabilistic networks from data. *Machine Learning*, 1992, 9(4): 309–347.

38. Cormode, G., Srivastava, D., Shen, E., and Yu, T. Aggregate query answering on possibilistic data with cardinality constraints. *Proceedings of the 28th IEEE International Conference on Data Engineering (ICDE)*, 2012, pp. 258–269.

39. Crandall, D., Cosley, D., Huttenlocher, D., Kleinberg, J., and Suri, S. Feedback effects between similarity and social influence in online communities. *Proceedings of the 14th ACM SIGKDD International*

Conference on Knowledge Discovery and Data Mining (*KDD*), 2008, pp. 160–168.

40. Dallachiesa, M., Ebaid, A., Eldawy, A., Elmagarmid, A., Ilyas, I. Ouzzani, M., and Tang, N. A commodity data cleaning system. *Proceedings of the 2013 ACM SIGMOD International Conference on Management of Data* (*SIGMOD*), 2013, pp. 541–552.

41. Dalvi, N. and Suciu, D. Efficient query evaluation on probabilistic databases. *Proceedings of the 30th International Conference on Very Large Data Bases* (*VLDB*), 2004, pp. 864–875.

42. Dalvi, N. and Suciu, D. Management of probabilistic data: Foundations and challenges. *Proceedings of the 26th ACM SIGACT-SIGMOD-SIGART Symposium on Principles of Database Systems* (*PODS*), 2007, pp. 1–12.

43. Dalvi, N., Re, C., and Suciu, D. Probabilistic databases: Diamonds in the dirt. *Communications of the ACM*, 2009, 72(7): 86–94.

44. Dan, G. and Heckerman, D. Knowledge representation and inference in similarity networks and Bayesian multinets. *Artificial Intelligence*, 1996, 82(1–2): 45–74.

45. Dan, S. Deriving probabilistic databases with inference ensembles. *Encyclopedia of Database Systems*, 2011, 6493(10): 303–314.

46. Darwiche, A. *Modeling and Reasoning with Bayesian Networks*. Cambridge University Press, 2009.

47. DBLP Datasets. http://dblp.uni-trier.de/xml/, 2015.

48. Dean, J. and Ghemawat, S. MapReduce: Simplified data processing on large clusters. *Communications of the ACM*, 2008, 51(1): 107–113.

49. Dean, J. and Ghemawat, S. MapReduce: A flexible data processing tool. *Communications of the ACM*, 2010, 53(1): 72–77.

50. Deshpande, M., Karypis, G. Item-based top-N recommendation algorithms. *ACM Transactions on Information Systems*, 2004, 22(1): 143–177.

51. Deshpande, A. and Sarawagi, S. Probabilistic graphical models and their role in database. *Proceedings of the 33th International Conference on Very Large Data Bases* (*VLDB*), 2007, pp. 1435–1436.

52. Deshpande, A., Getoor, L., and Sen, P. *Graphical models for uncertain data*. In Aggarwal, C. (ed.), Managing and Mining Uncertain Data. Springer, US, 2009, pp. 1–36.

53. Domingos, P. and Richardson, M. Learning with knowledge from multiple experts. *Proceedings of the 20th International Conference on Machine Learning (ICML)*, 2003, pp. 624–631.

54. Dor, D. and Tarsi, M. A simple algorithm to construct a consistent extension of a partially oriented graph. Technical Report R-185, Cognitive Systems Laboratory, UCLA Computer Science Department, 1992.

55. Druzdzel, M. and Henrion, M. Efficient reasoning in qualitative probabilistic networks. *Proceedings of the 11th National Conference on Artificial Intelligence (AAAI)*, 1993, pp. 548–553.

56. Druzdzel, M. Probabilistic reasoning in decision support systems: From computation to common sense. Ph.D. Thesis, Department of Engineering and Public Policy, Carnegie Mellon University, Pennsylvania, 1993.

57. Duan, L., Yue, K., Qian, W., and Liu, W. Cleaning missing data based on the Bayesian network. *Proceedings of the 14th International conference on Web-Age Information Management (WAIM) Workshops*, LNCS 7901, 2013, pp. 348–359.

58. Duan, L., Yue, K., Jin, C., Xu, W., and Liu, W. Tracing errors in probabilistic databases based on the Bayesian network. *Proceedings of the 20th International Conference on Database Systems for Advanced Applications (DASFAA)*, LNCS 9059, 2015, pp. 104–119.

59. Fan, W. Dependencies revisited for improving data quality. *Proceedings of the 27th ACM SIGMOD-SIGACT-SIGART Symposium on Principles of Database Systems (PODS)*, 2008, pp. 159–170.

60. Fan, W., Geerts, F., Jia, X., and Kementsietsidis, A. Conditional functional dependencies for capturing data inconsistencies. *ACM Transactions on Database Systems*, 2008, 33(2): 2008.

61. Fan, W., Li, J., Ma, S., Tang, N., and Yu, W. Towards certain fixes with editing rules and master data. *Proceedings of the VLDB Endowment (PVLDB)*, 2010, 3(1): 173–184.

62. Fang, Q., Yue, K., Fu, X., Wu, H., and Liu, W. A MapReduce-based method for learning Bayesian network from massive data. *Proceedings of the 15th Asia-Pacific Web Conference (APWeb) Workshops*, LNCS 7808, 2013, pp. 697–708.

63. Friedman, N. and Goldszmidt, M. Sequential update of Bayesian network structure. *Proceedings of the 13th Conference on Uncertainty in Artificial Intelligence (UAI)*, 1997, pp. 165–174.

64. Friedman, N., Getor, L., Koller, D., and Pfeffer, A. Learning probabilistic relational models. *Proceedings of the 16th International Joint Conference on Artificial Intelligence (IJCAI)*, 1999, pp. 1300–1309.

65. Friedman, N., Nachman, I., and Peér, D. Learning Bayesian network structure from massive datasets: the "sparse candidate" algorithm. *Proceedings of the 15th Conference on Uncertainty in Artificial Intelligence (UAI)*, 1999, pp. 206–215.

66. Galhardas, H., Florescu, D., Shasha, D., Simon, E., Saita, C., and Rocquencourt, I. Improving data cleaning quality using a data lineage facility. *Proceedings of the 3rd International Workshop on Design and Management of Data Warehouses (DMDW)*, 2001, Paper ID: 3.

67. Gao, M., Jin, C., Wang, X., Tian, X., and Zhou, A. A survey on data provenance (in Chinese). *Chinese Journal of Computers*, 2010, 33(3): 373–389.

68. Geerts, F., Mecca, G., Papotti, P., and Santoro, D. The LLUNATIC data-cleaning framework. *Proceedings of the VLDB Endowment (PVLDB)*, 2013, 6(9): 625–636.

69. Ghosh, S. and Mitra, S. Clustering large data with uncertainty. *Applied Soft Computing*, 2013, 13(4): 1639–1645.

70. Gomezmarin, A., Paton, J., Kampff, A., Costa, R., and Mainen, Z. Big behavioral data: Psychology, ethology and the foundations of neuroscience. *Nature Neuroscience*, 2014, 17(11): 1455–1462.

71. Gong, N. Z., Xu, W., Huang, L., Mittal, P., Stefanov, E., Sekar, V., Song, D., and Xu, W. Evolution of social-attribute networks: measurements, modeling, and implications using google+. *Proceedings of the 2012 ACM Conference on Internet Measurement (IM)*, 2012, pp. 131–144.

72. Green, T., Karvounarakis, G., and Tannen, V. Provenance semirings. *Proceedings of the 26th ACM SIGACT-SIGMOD-SIGART Symposium on Principles of Database Systems (PODS)*, 2007, pp. 34–40.

73. Guo, H. and Hsu, W. A survey of algorithms for real-time Bayesian network inference. AAAI Technical Report WS-02-15, 2002.

74. Halpern, B. and Pearl, J. Causes and explanations: A structural-model approach: Part 1: Causes. *Proceedings of the 17th Conference in Uncertainty in Artificial Intelligence (UAI)*, 2001, pp. 194–202.

75. He, L., Liu, B., Hu, D., Wen, Y., Wan, M., and Long, J. Motor imagery EEG signals analysis based on Bayesian network with Gaussian distribution. *Neurocomputing*, 2016, 188: 217–224.

76. Heckerman, D., Geiger, D., and Chickering, D. Learning Bayesian networks: The combination of knowledge and statistic data. *Machine Learning*, 1995, 20(3): 197–243.

77. Hrycej, T. Gibbs sampling in Bayesian networks. *Artificial Intelligence*, 1990, 46(3): 351–363.

78. Hu, M., Wang, Y., Zhang, Z., Zhang, D., and Little, J. Incremental learning for video-based gait recognition with LBP flow. *IEEE Transactions on Cybernetics*, 2013, 43(1): 77–89.

79. Hwang, K., Park, H., and Cho, S. Robotic intelligence with behavior selection network for Bayesian network ensemble. *Proceedings of the 2009 IEEE Workshop on Robotic Intelligence in Informationally Structured Space (RiiSS)*, 2009, pp. 151–154.

80. Ibrahim, Z., Ngom, A., and Tawfik, A. Using qualitative probability in reverse-engineering gene regulatory networks. *IEEE/ACM Transactions on Computational Biology and Bioinformatics*, 2010, 8(2): 326–334.

81. Jaeger, M. Relational Bayesian networks. *Proceedings of the 13th Conference on Uncertainty in Artificial Intelligence (UAI)*, 1997, pp. 266–273.

82. Jha, A., Olteanu, D., and Suciu, D. Bridging the gap between intensional and extensional query evaluation in probabilistic database. *Proceedings of the 13th International Conference on Extending Database Technology (EDBT)*, 2010, pp. 323–334.

83. Jha, A. and Dan, S. Probabilistic databases with MarkoViews. *Proceedings of the VLDB Endowment (PVLDB)*, 2012, 5(11): 1160–1171.

84. Jiang, B., Pei, J., Lin, X., and Yuan, Y. Probabilistic skylines on uncertain data: Model and bounding-pruning-refining methods. *Journal of Intelligent Information Systems*, 2012, 38(1): 1–39.

85. Jiang, M., Gui, P., Wang, F., Zhu, W., and Yang, S. Scalable recommendation with social contextual information. *IEEE Transactions on Knowledge and Data Engineering*, 2014, 26(11): 2789–2802.
86. Jin, C., Zhang, R., Kang, Q., Zhang, Z., and Zhou, A. Probabilistic reverse top-k queries. *Proceedings of the 19th International Conference on Database Systems for Advanced Applications (DASFAA)*, 2014, pp. 406–419.
87. Kanagal, B. and Deshpande, A. Lineage processing over correlated probabilistic databases. *Proceedings of the 2010 ACM SIGMOD International Conference on Management of Data (SIGMOD)*, 2010, pp. 675–686.
88. Kanagal, B., Li, J., and Deshpande, A. Sensitivity analysis and explanations for robust query evaluation in probabilistic databases. *Proceedings of the 2011 ACM SIGMOD International Conference on Management of Data (SIGMOD)*, 2011, pp. 841–852.
89. Kleinberg, J. Small-world phenomena and the dynamics of information. *Advances in Neural Information Processing Systems (NIPS)*, 2001, pp. 431–438.
90. Koch, C. and Olteanu, D. Conditioning probabilistic databases. *Proceedings of the VLDB Endowment (PVLDB)*, 2008, 1(1): 313–325.
91. Koller, D. and Friedman, N. *Probabilistic Graphical Models*. Cambridge: The MIT Press, 2009.
92. Kouzes, R., Anderson, G., Elbert, S., Gorton, I., and Gracio, D. The changing paradigm of data-intensive computing. *IEEE Computer*, 2009, 42(1): 26–34.
93. Lam, W. Bayesian network refinement via machine learning approach. *IEEE Transactions on Pattern Analysis and Machine Intelligence*, 1998, 20(3): 240–251.
94. Lam, W. and Segre, A. A distributed learning algorithm for Bayesian inference networks. *IEEE Transactions on Knowledge and Data Engineering*, 2002, 14(1): 93–105.
95. Laskey, K., Costa, P., and Janssen, T. Probabilistic ontologies for knowledge fusion. *Proceedings of the 11th International Conference on Information Fusion (FUSION)*, 2008, pp. 1–8.
96. Lazkano, E., Sierra, B., Astigarraga, A., and Martínez-Otzeta, J. On the use of Bayesian networks to develop behaviours for mobile. *Robotics and Autonomous Systems*, 2007, 55(3): 253–265.

97. Li, B., Mazur, E., Diao, Y., Mcgregor, A., and Shenoy, P. A platform for scalable one-pass analytics using MapReduce. *Proceedings of the 2011 ACM SIGMOD International Conference on Management of Data (SIGMOD)*, 2011, pp. 985–996.

98. Lian, X. and Chen, L. A generic framework for handling uncertain data with local correlations. *Proceedings of the VLDB Endowment (PVLDB)*, 2010, 4(1): 12–21.

99. Lian, X. and Chen, L. Causality and responsibility: Probabilistic queries revisited in uncertain databases. *Proceedings of the 22nd ACM International Conference on Information and Knowledge Management (CIKM)*, 2013, pp. 349–358.

100. Liu, W., Guo. L., and Song, N. Fuzzy association degree with delayed time in temporal data model. *Journal of Computer Science and Technology*, 2001, 16(1): 86–91.

101. Liu, W., Yue, K., Liu, S., and Sun, Y. Qualitative-probabilistic-network-based modeling of temporal causalities and its application to feedback loop identification. *Information Sciences*, 2008, 178(7): 1803–1824.

102. Liu, W., Yue, K., and Gao, M. Constructing probabilistic graphical model from predicate formulas for fusing logical and probabilistic knowledge. *Information Sciences*, 2011, 181(18): 3828–3845.

103. Liu, J., Ye, D., Wei, J., Huang, F., and Zhong, H. Consistent query answering based on repairing inconsistent attributes with nulls. *Proceedings of the 18th International Conference on Database Systems for Advanced Applications (DASFAA)*, 2013, pp. 407–423.

104. Liu, H., Hu, Z., Mian, A., Tian, H., and Zhu, X. A new user similarity model to improve the accuracy of collaborative filtering. *Knowledge-Based Systems*, 2014, 56(3): 156–166.

105. Liu, W., Yue, K., Liu, H., Zhang, P., Luo, Y., Liu, S., and Wang, Q. Associative categorization of frequent patterns based on the probabilistic graphical model. *Frontiers of Computer Science*, 2014, 8(2): 265–278.

106. Low, Y., Bickson, D., Gonzalez, J., Guestrin, C., Kyrola, A., and Hellerstein, J. Distributed graphlab: A framework for machine learning and data mining in the cloud. *Proceedings of the VLDB Endowment (PVLDB)*, 2012, 5(8): 716–727.

107. Ma, N., Xia, Y., and Prasanna, V. Parallel exact inference on multicore using MapReduce. *Proceedings of the IEEE 24th International Symposium on Computer Architecture and High Performance Computing (SBAC-PAD)*, 2012, pp. 187–194.

108. Ma, S., Fan, W., and Bravo, L. Extending inclusion dependencies with conditions. *Theoretical Computer Science*, 2014, 515(1): 64–95.

109. Masegosa, A. and Moral, S. New skeleton-based approaches for Bayesian structure learning of Bayesian networks. *Applied Soft Computing*, 2013, 13(2): 1110–1120.

110. Matzkevich, I. and Abramson, B. The topological fusion of Bayes nets. *Proceedings of the 8th Conference on Uncertainty in Artificial Intelligence (UAI)*, 1992, pp. 191–198.

111. Mayfield, C., Neville, J., and Prabhakar, S. ERACER: A database approach for statistical inference and data cleaning. *Proceedings of the 2010 ACM SIGMOD International Conference on Management of Data (SIGMOD)*, 2010, pp. 75–86.

112. McCallum, A., Corrada-Emmanuel, A., and Wang, X. Topic and role discovery in social networks. *Proceedings of the 19th International Joint Conference on Artificial Intelligence (IJCAI)*, 2005, pp. 786–791.

113. Meek, C. Causal inference and causal explanation with background knowledge. *Proceedings of the 11th Annual Conference on Uncertainty in Artificial Intelligence (UAI)*, 1995, pp. 403–410.

114. Meliou, A., Gatterbauer, W., Moore, K. F., and Suciu, D. The complexity of causality and responsibility for query answers and non-answers. *Proceedings of the VLDB Endowment (PVLDB)*, 2010, 4(1): 34–45.

115. Meliou, A., Gatterbauer, W., Nath, S., and Suciu, D. Tracing data errors with view-conditioned causality. *Proceedings of the 2011 ACM SIGMOD International Conference on Management of Data (SIGMOD)*, 2011, pp. 505–516.

116. Metwally, A. and Faloutsos, C. V-smart-join: A scalable MapReduce framework for all-pair similarity joins of multisets and vectors. *Proceedings of the VLDB Endowment (PVLDB)*, 2012, 5(8): 704–715.

117. Miao, X., Gao, Y., Chen, L., Chen, G., Li, Q., and Jiang, T. On efficient k-skyband query processing over incomplete data. *Proceedings of the*

18th International Conference on Database Systems for Advanced Applications (*DASFAA*), 2013, pp. 424–439.

118. Müller, H. and Freytag, J. *Problems, methods, and challenges in comprehensive data cleansing*. Professoren des Inst., Fur Informatik, 2005.

119. Nakatsuji, M., Fujiwara, Y., Uchiyama, T., and Fujimura, K. User similarity from linked taxonomies: Subjective assessments of items. *Proceedings of the 22nd International Joint Conference on Artificial Intelligence* (*IJCAI*), 2011, pp. 2305–2311.

120. Nandi, A., Yu, C., Bohannon, P., and Ramakrishnan, R. Data cube materialization and mining over mapreduce. *IEEE Transactions on Knowledge and Data Engineering*, 2012, 24(10): 1747–1759.

121. Netica, Norsys Software Corp. http://www.norsys.com, 2015.

122. Nielsen, S. and Parsons, S. An application of formal argumentation: Fusing Bayesian networks in multi-agent systems. *Artificial Intelligence*, 2007, 171(10–15): 754–775.

123. Nillius, P., Sullivan, J., and Carlsson, S. Multi-target tracking-linking identities using Bayesian network inference. *Proceedings of 2006 IEEE Computer Society Conference on Computer Vision and Pattern Recognition* (*CVPR*), 2006, pp. 2187–2194.

124. Nisgav, A. and Patt-Shamir, B. Finding similar users in social networks. *Proceedings of the 21st Annual ACM Symposium on Parallelism in Algorithms and Architectures* (*SPAA*), 2009, pp. 169–177.

125. Onisko, A. Probabilistic causal models in medicine: Application to diagnosis of liver disorders, Ph.D. Dissertation, Institute of Biocybernetics and Biomedical Engineering, Polish Academy of Science, Warsaw, 2003.

126. Pande, B., Herbach, J., Basu, S., and Bayardo, R. Planet: Massively parallel learning of tree ensembles with MapReduce. *Proceedings of the VLDB Endowment* (*PVLDB*), 2009, 2(2): 1426–1437.

127. Panse, F., Van Keulen, M., De Keijzer, A., and Ritter, N. Duplicate detection in probabilistic data. *Proceedings of the 26th International Conference on Data Engineering* (*ICDE*) *Workshops*, 2010, pp. 179–182.

128. Pearl, J. *Probabilistic Reasoning in Intelligent Systems: Networks of Plausible Inference*. San Francisco: Morgan Kaufmann Publishers, 1988.

129. Pearl, J. Evidential reasoning using stochastic simulation of causal models. *Artificial Intelligence*, 2012, 32(2): 245–257.

130. Pennock, D. and Wellman, M. Graphical representations of consensus belief. *Proceedings of the 15th Conference on Uncertainty in Artificial Intelligence (UAI)*, 1999, pp. 531–540.

131. Piwowarski, B., Dupret, G., and Jones, R. Mining user web search activities with layered Bayesian networks or how to capture a click in its context. *Proceedings of the 2nd ACM International Conference on Web Search and Data Mining (WSDM)*, 2009, pp. 162–171.

132. Poole, D. Probabilistic horn abduction and Bayesian networks. *Artificial Intelligence*, 1993, 64(1): 81–129.

133. Purwanto, Eswaran, C., and Logeswaran, R. An enhanced hybrid method for time series prediction using linear and neural network models. *Applied Intelligence*, 2012, 37(4): 511–519.

134. Qian, J., Lv, P., Yue, X., Liu, C., and Jing, Z. Hierarchical attribute reduction algorithms for big data using MapReduce. *Knowledge-Based Systems*, 2015, 73: 18–31.

135. Rafter, M. *10 Companies to Watch: Epinions.Com*. The Industry Standard Magazine, 2000.

136. Ré, C. and Suciu, D. Approximate lineage for probabilistic databases. *Proceedings of the VLDB Endowment (PVLDB)*, 2008, 1(1): 797–808.

137. Rekatsinas, T., Deshpande, A., and Getoor, L. Local structure and determinism in probabilistic databases. *Proceedings of the 2012 ACM SIGMOD International Conference on Management of Data (SIGMOD)*, 2012, pp. 373–384.

138. Renooij, S., Parsons, S., and Pardieck, P. Using kappas as indicators of strength in qualitative probabilistic networks. *Proceedings of the 7th European Conference on Symbolic and Quantitative Approaches to Reasoning with Uncertainty (ECSQARU)*, 2003, pp. 87–99.

139. Renooij, S. and Gaag, L. Enhanced qualitative probabilistic networks for resolving trade-offs. *Artificial Intelligence*, 2006, 172(12–13): 1470–1494.

140. Renooij, S. and Van, C. From qualitative to quantitative probabilistic networks. *Proceedings of the 18th Conference in Uncertainty in Artificial Intelligence (UAI)*, 2002, pp. 422–429.

141. Rissanen, J. Stochastic complexity. *Journal of Royal Statistical Society, Series B*, 1987, 49(3): 223–239.

142. Russell, S. and Norvig, P. *Artificial Intelligence: A Modern Approach.* Boston: Pearson Education, Publishing as Prentice-Hall, 2002.

143. Rvelin, K. and Kekalainen, J. IR evaluation methods for retrieving highly relevant documents. *Proceedings of the 23rd Annual International ACM SIGIR Conference on Research and Development in Information Retrieval (SIGIR)*, 2000, pp. 41–48.

144. Sagrado, J. and Moral, S. Qualitative combination of Bayesian networks. *International Journal of Intelligent Systems*, 2003, 18(2): 237–249.

145. Samet, S., Miri, A., and Granger, E. Incremental learning of privacy-preserving Bayesian networks. *Applied Soft Computing*, 2013, 13(8): 3657–3667.

146. Sarma, A., Theobald, M., and Widom, J. Exploiting lineage for confidence computation in uncertain and probabilistic databases. *Proceedings of the 24th International Conference on Data Engineering (ICDE)*, 2008, pp. 1023–1032.

147. Schall, D. Link prediction in directed social networks. *Social Network Analysis and Mining*, 2014, 4(1): 157.

148. Schelter, S., Boden, C., and Markl, V. Scalable similarity-based neighborhood methods with MapReduce. *Proceedings of the 6th ACM Conference on Recommender Systems (RecSys)*, 2012, pp. 163–170.

149. Sen, P. and Deshpande, A. Representing and querying correlated tuples in probabilistic databases. *Proceedings of the 23rd International Conference on Data Engineering (ICDE)*, 2007, pp. 596–605.

150. Shafer, G. The combination of evidence. *International Journal of Intelligent Systems*, 1986, 1(3): 155–179.

151. Shi, D. and Tan, S. Incremental learning Bayesian network structures efficiently. *Proceedings of 11th International Conference on Control, Automation, Robotics and Vision (ICARCV)*, 2010, pp. 1719–1724.

152. Stoyanovich, J., Davidson, S., Milo, T., and Tannen, V. Deriving probabilistic databases with inference ensembles. *Proceedings of the 27th International Conference on Data Engineering (ICDE)*, 2011, pp. 303–314.

153. Suzuki, J. Learning Bayesian belief networks based on the MDL principle: An efficient algorithm using the branch and bound technique. *IEICE Transactions on Information and Systems*, 1997, E82D(2): 356–367.

154. Tahboub, K. Intelligent human-machine interaction based on dynamic Bayesian networks probabilistic intention recognition. *Journal of Intelligent and Robotic Systems*, 2006, 45(1): 31–52.

155. Tian, F., Zhong, H., Lu, Y., and Shi, C. Incremental learning of Bayesian networks with hidden variables. *Proceedings of the 2001 IEEE International Conference on Data Mining (ICDM)*, 2001, pp. 651–652.

156. Tong, Y., Chen, L., Cheng, Y., and Yu, P. Mining frequent itemsets over uncertain databases. *Proceedings of the VLDB Endowment (PVLDB)*, 2012, 5(11): 1650–1661.

157. Transaction Processing Council (TPC). http://www.tpc.org/tpch, 2007.

158. Tsamardinos, I., Brown, L., and Aliferis, C. The max-min hill-climbing Bayesian network structure learning algorithm. *Machine Learning*, 2006, 65(1): 31–78.

159. Vasilakopoulos, A. and Kantere, V. Efficient query computing for uncertain possibilistic databases with provenance. *Proceedings of the 3rd Workshop on the Theory and Practice of Provenance (TaPP)*, 2011.

160. Velardi, P., Navigli, R., Cucchiarelli, A., and D'Antonio, F. A new content-based model for social network analysis. *Proceedings of the 2nd IEEE International Conference on Semantic Computing (SC)*, 2008, pp. 18–25.

161. Verma, T. and Pearl, J. Equivalence and synthesis of causal models. *Proceedings of the 6th Annual Conference on Uncertainty in Artificial Intelligence (UAI)*, 1990, pp. 255–270.

162. Wang, D., Michelakis, E., Garofalakis, M., and Hellerstein, J. BayesStore: Managing large, uncertain data repositories with probabilistic graphical models. *Proceedings of the VLDB Endowment (PVLDB)*, 2008, 1(1): 340–351.

163. Wellman, M. Fundamental concepts of qualitative probabilistic networks. *Artificial Intelligence*, 1990, 44(3): 257–303.

164. Wellman, M. Graphical inference in qualitative probabilistic networks. *Networks*, 1990, 20(5): 687–701.

165. White, T. *Hadoop: The Definitive Guide*. Sebastopol, CA: O'Reilly Media, Inc., 2009.

166. Wolfe, J., Haghighi, A., and Klein, D. Fully distributed EM for very large datasets. *Proceedings of the 25th International Conference on Machine Learning (ICML)*, 2008, pp. 1184–1191.

167. Wu, X., He, J., Lu, R., and Zheng, N. From big data to big knowledge: HACE+BigKE (in Chinese). *Acta Automatica Sinica*, 2016, 42(7): 965–982.

168. Xiang, Y. and Chu, T. Parallel learning of belief networks in large and difficult domains. *Data Mining and Knowledge Discovery*, 1999, 3(3): 315–339.

169. Xu, C., Gu, Y., Chen, L., Qiao, J., and Yu, G. Interval reverse nearest neighbor queries on uncertain data with Markov correlations. *Proceedings of the 29th IEEE International Conference on Data Engineering (ICDE)*, 2013, pp. 170–181.

170. Xu, J., Yue, K., Li, J., Wang, F., and Liu, W. An approach for discovering user similarity in social networks based on the Bayesian network and MapReduce. *Proceedings of the 2014 International Conference on Behavioral, Economic, and Socio-Cultural Computing (BESC)*, 2014, pp. 1–7.

171. Xu, K., Zou, K., Huang, Y., Yu, X., and Zhang, X. Mining community and inferring friendship in mobile social networks. *Neurocomputing*, 2016, 174: 650–616.

172. Yang, X., Guo, Y., and Liu, Y. Bayesian-inference based recommendation in online social networks. *IEEE Transactions on Parallel and Distributed Systems*, 2013, 24(4): 642–651.

173. Yang, X. and Truong, M. Acquisition of causal models for local distributions in Bayesian networks. *IEEE Transactions on Cybernetics*, 2014, 44(9): 1591–1604.

174. Yasin, A. and Leray, P. Local skeleton discovery for incremental Bayesian network structure learning. *Proceedings of the 2011 IEEE International Conference on Computer Networks and Information Technology (ICCNIT)*, 2011, pp. 309–314.

175. Ying, J., Lu, E., Lee, W., Weng, T., and Tsang, V. Mining user similarity from semantic trajectories. *Proceedings of the 2010 International Workshop on Location Based Social Networks* (*LBSN*), 2010, pp. 19–26.

176. Yu, K., Wang, H., and Wu, X. A parallel algorithm for learning Bayesian networks. *Proceedings of the 11th Pacific-Asia Conference on Advances in Knowledge Discovery and Data Mining* (*PAKDD*), 2007, pp. 1055–1063.

177. Yue, K. *Data Engineering: Processing, Analysis and Services (in Chinese)*. Beijing: Tsinghua University Press, 2013.

178. Yue, K., Wu, H., Fu, X., Xu, J., Yin, Z., and Liu, W. A data-intensive approach for discovering user similarities in social behavioral interactions based on the bayesian network. *Neurocomputing*, 2016, http://dx.doi.org/10.1016/j.neucom.2016.09.042.

179. Yue, K. and Liu, W. Qualitative representation, inference and their application of uncertain knowledge: A survey on qualitative probabilistic networks (in Chinese). *Journal of Yunnan University* (*Natural Science Edition*), 2009, 31(6): 560–570.

180. Yue, K., Yao, Y., Li, J., and Liu, W. Qualitative probabilistic network with reduced ambiguities. *Applied Intelligence*, 2010, 33(2): 159–178.

181. Yue, K., Liu, W., and Yue, M. Quantifying influences in the qualitative probabilistic network with interval probability parameters. *Applied Soft Computing*, 2011, 11(1): 1135–1143.

182. Yue, K., Liu, W., Zhu, Y., and Zhang, W. A probabilistic-graphical-model based approach for representing lineages in uncertain data (in Chinese). *Chinese Journal of Computers*, 2011, 14(10): 1897–1960.

183. Yue, K., Zhu, Y., Tian, K., and Liu, W. Semantics-preserving fusion of structures of probabilistic graphical models. *Proceedings of 2011 International Conference on Intelligent Systems and Knowledge Engineering* (*ISKE*), AISC 122, 2011, pp. 63–68.

184. Yue, K., Zhou, M., Zhang, J., Zhang, P., Fang, Q., and Liu, W. Graph-Based hierarchical categorization of microblog users. *Proceedings of the 2013 IEEE International Congress on Big Data* (*BigData*), 2013, pp. 156–163.

185. Yue, K., Fang, Q., Wang, X., Li, J., and Liu, W. A parallel and incremental approach for data-intensive learning of Bayesian networks. *IEEE Transactions on Cybernetics*, 2015, 45(12): 2890–2904.

186. Yue, K., Qian, W., Fu, X., Li, J., and Liu, W. Qualitative-probabilistic-network-based fusion of time-series uncertain knowledge. *Soft Computing*, 2015, 19(7): 1953–1972.

187. Yue, K., Wu, H., Zhu, Y., and Liu, W. Representing and processing lineages over uncertain data based on the Bayesian network. *Applied Soft Computing*, 2015, 37: 345–362.

188. Zhang, M., Zhang, X., Zhang, X., and Prabhakar, S. Tracing lineage beyond relational operators. *Proceedings of the 33rd International Conference on Very Large Data Bases (VLDB)*, 2007, pp. 1116–1127.

189. Zhang, K., Downey, D., Chen, Z., Xie, Y., Cheng, Y., Agrawal, A., Liao, W., and Choudhary, A. A probabilistic graphical model for brand reputation assessment in social networks. *Proceedings of the 2013 IEEE/ACM International Conference on Advances in Social Networks Analysis and Mining (ASONAM)*, 2013, pp. 223–230.

190. Zhou, A., Jin, C., Wang, G., and Li, J. A survey on the management of uncertain data (in Chinese). *Chinese Journal of Computers*, 2009, 32(1): 1–16.

Index

East China Normal University Scientific Reports
Subseries on Data Science and Engineering

Published (continued from page ii)

Printed in the United States
By Bookmasters